Raymond, The very best thing
I can do for you is give you this
BOOK, that tells the TRUTH,
Pure and clear. You belong to
God. You are His Wisdom for
Many People. Love
Grandma!

Destined To Reign

The secret to effortless success,
wholeness and victorious living

JOSEPH PRINCE

Harrison House
Tulsa, Oklahoma

D0052310

18 17 16 15 14 13 12   14 13 12 11

Destined To Reign
The secret to effortless success, wholeness, and victorious living

ISBN 13: 978-1-60683-009-3
ISBN 10: 1-60683-009-0
Copyright © 2007 by Joseph Prince

Published by Harrison House Publishers
P.O. Box 35035
Tulsa, Oklahoma 74153
www.harrisonhouse.com

Published in association with:
Joseph Prince Teaching Resources
www.josephprinceonline.com

Dedication

This book is lovingly dedicated to:

The glory of my Lord Jesus Christ
Who has blessed me beyond anything I could ever have imagined and who has loved me beyond my comprehension.

Wendy
My darling wife, whose support and love for me never fails to lift me above the clouds of defeat and mediocrity. "Who can find a virtuous woman?" I did!

Jessica
My precious beloved daughter whose life, though still young, has yielded wonderful portrayals of grace that have impacted multitudes. When she is in Daddy's arms, he is the richest man in the whole world.

And the loving community of New Creation Church, whose unfailing support for and loyalty to their pastor are definitely written in the annals of heaven's book of remembrance. They are a blessed joy to their pastor!

Contents

Foreword

It all began in 1997, when I was on vacation with my wife Wendy. She was asleep in the passenger seat, breathing softly next to me as I drove through the dramatic landscapes of the Swiss Alps. Then, I distinctly heard the voice of the Lord on the inside. It wasn't a witness of the Spirit. It was a voice, and I heard God say this clearly to me: "Son, you are not preaching grace."

I said, "What do you mean, Lord? That's a low blow. That's a real low blow!" I added, "I'm a preacher of grace. I have been a grace preacher for years, and like most preachers, I preach that we are saved by grace!" He said, "No. Every time you preach grace, you preach it with a mixture of law. You attempt to balance grace with the law like many other preachers, and the moment you balance grace, you neutralize it. You cannot put new wine into old wineskins. You cannot put grace and law together." He went on to say, "Son, a lot of preachers are not preaching grace the way Apostle Paul preached grace." He then ended emphatically with this statement that revolutionized my ministry: "If you don't preach grace radically, people's lives will never be radically blessed and radically transformed."

That powerful word from the Lord jolted me, and I realized for the first time that I had indeed been preaching a grace message that was tempered with the law. I returned to my church with a strong mandate from the Lord and I began to preach grace radically.

At that time, our congregation had reached a plateau of about 2,000 people. However, soon after my encounter with the Lord in the Swiss Alps, we began to experience explosive growth in the church year after year, and by the grace of our Lord, more than 15,000 people attended our services on the first Sunday of 2007. The Lord has validated His word not only in our growing congregation, but also in the awesome transformation of thousands of precious lives exposed to the radical preaching of grace. Over the years, I have had the privilege of witnessing the restoration of marriages, the supernatural cancellation of debts, miraculous healings, and of feeling the joy of seeing God's children liberated from destructive addictions.

In recent years, the Lord has also opened doors for me to preach the gospel of grace in Norway, Holland, London, Canada, Australia, Thailand and Indonesia. We have also begun broadcasting in America, Canada, Australia and Uganda. The response to what I call the Gospel Revolution has been tremendous. I have received testimony after testimony of how individuals have been set free from the bondage of the law, and are today living and enjoying the new covenant truths and promises that Jesus purchased with His own blood.

You can imagine how this book has been brewing in my heart for many years now. If there is one book that I want to write on this side of heaven, this would be it, and I am so glad that you are now holding it in your hands. I believe that this book will touch you and transform you. What the Lord said to me some 10 years ago about how lives will never be radically blessed and radically transformed without the radical preaching of grace is still reverberating strongly in my heart. This book is therefore about being radically transformed by His grace and His grace alone.

In this book, you will discover the secret of God's way to reigning effortlessly in life! Man has developed many strategies, methodologies, techniques and tactics for achieving personal success. Just look in the bookstores today. In fact, you may be standing in one right now. If you are, take some time to look around. What do you see? You will probably find a large selection of self-help books. Let me declare to you that there is a higher way than relying on your own efforts to achieve success in life. The Bible says in the very first verse of Psalm 1, "Blessed is the man who walks **not** in the counsel of the ungodly." Hence, while there is some "counsel" in "ungodly" resources, there is a higher way for the believer! Why rely on self-help when you can have direct access to God's help? The name of Jesus in Hebrew, *Yeshua,* simply means Savior. Let's call upon Him to save us, rather than depend on our own abilities to save ourselves.

Unfortunately, there are believers today who do not call upon their Savior because they believe the **lie** that they have no right to do so. There are believers who think that their mistakes have disqualified them from calling out to God. Some may even believe that they are undeserving of the Lord's help because they have not attended church regularly, read the Bible sufficiently or prayed enough. My friend, when you are drowning, you don't need a teacher to teach you the right steps to take in order to swim and save yourself. You don't need a list of do's and don'ts. You need a Savior who is willing to plunge fearlessly into the water to save you regardless of what you know or do not know, what you have done or not done! You cannot earn by your own works His desire to save you. It is by His grace!

Let's begin to acknowledge that in and of ourselves, we cannot and do not have the ability and resources to save ourselves. In essence, we owed a debt that we could not pay, but Jesus on the cross paid with His own life, a debt that He did not owe. It is entirely His effort and His doing. Our part is to believe on Him and receive all that He has accomplished on our behalf. Sounds ridiculously simple, one-sided and unfair? Well, my friend, that is exactly what makes grace, grace! Grace is only grace when it is undeserved, unearned and unmerited.

Are you ready to be tremendously blessed and transformed by His grace, and to give up on your own efforts to have success, wholeness and a victorious life? I believe that once you begin to take this journey of discovering His radical grace, your life will never be the same again. My friend, you are destined to reign!

Chapter 1

Destined To Reign

You are destined to reign in life.

You are called by the Lord to be a success, to enjoy wealth, to enjoy health and to enjoy a life of victory.

It is not the Lord's desire that you live a life of defeat, poverty and failure.

He has called you to be the head and not the tail.

If you are a businessman, God wants you to have a prosperous business. If you are a homemaker, you are anointed to bring up wonderful children in the Lord. If you are a student, God wants you to excel in all your examinations. And if you are trusting the Lord for a new career, He doesn't just want you to have a job, He wants you to have a position of influence, so that you can be a blessing and an asset to your organization!

Whatever your vocation is, you are destined to reign in life because Jesus is Lord of your life. When you reign in life, you reign over sin, you reign over the powers of darkness, and you reign over depression, over poverty, over every curse, and over every sickness and disease. You REIGN over the devil and all his devices!

The power to reign does not depend on your family background, your educational qualifications, how you look or how much savings you have in your bank account. The power to reign is based entirely on Jesus and Him alone. My friend, this is not a cliché from some self-help book on positive thinking. The declaration that you will reign is based on a promise that has been recorded for all eternity in the Word of God:

> Romans 5:17
> [17]For if by the one man's offense death reigned through the one, much more those who **receive abundance of grace** and of the **gift of righteousness** will **reign in life** through the One, Jesus Christ.

The word "reign" used in Romans 5:17 is the Greek word *basileuo*[1] where you get the English word "basilica". In ancient Rome, basilicas were used as law courts[2]. So it refers to a kingly, judicial rule. In other words, to reign here is to **reign in life as a king**, to have kingly rule and to possess kingly dominion.

The secret of reigning in life lies with receiving everything that Jesus has accomplished for us on the cross.

If you are living a life of defeat, of being defeated by sin, by perpetual guilt and condemnation, by sicknesses, by anxiety attacks, by financial lack and by broken relationships, you are not living the life that God intended for you. Based on the authority of God's Word, you are destined to "reign in life" as a king, to have kingly dominion over all your challenges and circumstances. You are called to be **above** them all and not be trampled by them. The time has come for you to stop abdicating your right to reign in life!

Today, instead of seeing ourselves reigning in life, we see more evidence of death reigning in the world. The Bible tells us that it was because of "one man's offense" — Adam's sin in the garden of Eden — that death began to reign. It is important that you realize that our lives are wrapped up in those of our ancestors. You wouldn't exist if there hadn't been your grandpa. So we are sinners not because we sin, but because of Adam's sin. Many believers still think that they became sinners by committing sin, but that is not what the Word of God says. What it says is that we are sinners because of Adam's sin. By the same token, we are made righteous in the new covenant not because we do righteous deeds, but because of one Man's (Jesus) obedience on the cross. The secret of reigning in life lies therefore with receiving everything that Jesus has accomplished for us on the cross.

Receiving Versus Achieving

The Bible states very clearly that we are to reign in life through Jesus Christ just by **receiving** two things from Him: The abundance of grace and the gift of righteousness. God's ways are contrary to man's ways. Man thinks that for God to bless him, he needs to deserve, earn and merit God's favor and blessings by his own efforts. Man thinks that God's blessings are based on his performance and good works.

However, this is not God's way. His way is not about achieving, but about receiving. He promised that when we **receive** the abundance of grace and the gift of righteousness, we will reign in life. He did not say that when we **achieve** grace and our own righteousness, we will reign in life. But for some reason, many Christians continue to live based on a system of achievement!

"Pastor Prince, if it's really that easy, why aren't more Christians reigning in life?"

I'm glad that you asked that question. In answer, let me first pose you a question of my own: Do you realize that most people believe that one needs to work hard to **achieve** success in life? The world's system of success is built on the twin pillars of self-effort and diligence. There are always some "laws" that you have to abide by, and some "methods and techniques" that you have to keep on practicing before there can be any results. Most of the time, any result that you may get will start to fade once you cease to follow through with the prescribed methods and steps.

We have been taught to focus on achieving, on doing and on relying on our self-efforts. We are driven to "do, do, do", forgetting that Christianity is actually "done, done, done". The world tells you that the more you do, the harder you work, and the more hours you put in, the more success you will achieve. The world's way is to nag you to work harder, to forget about attending church on Sundays, to spend less time with your wife and kids, and to spend more time in the office working through the nights, weekends and holidays. I'm sure that you've heard that you need to "pay the price", after all, "no pain, no gain", right?

What believers do is that they take the system of the world and apply it to their Christian life. Instead of depending on God's grace for His favor and blessings to flow, they depend on their self-efforts to try to deserve God's favor and blessings.

Yet, God's way is not for us to be blessed by our own efforts. You cannot earn God's blessings by your performance. God's blessings are based entirely on His grace. His blessings over your life have to be undeserved, unearned and unmerited. In other words, there is nothing that you can do to deserve His blessings, for they are based entirely on **receiving Jesus**, and through His finished work, the abundance of grace and the gift of righteousness.

God wants us to stop trying to achieve, and to begin receiving the favor, blessings and healing that Jesus accomplished on the cross. When He hung on the cross some 2,000 years ago, He cried out with a loud voice, "**It is finished!**"[3] Everything that you and I require to reign in life was accomplished at Calvary on our behalf. That's why we call what Jesus did on the cross His "**finished work**"! He finished it. He completed it. It is DONE! The only thing that works is the finished work! Stop doing what's already DONE! Stop doing and start receiving what Jesus has DONE!

The Work Is Finished, Sit Down

I was fellowshipping recently with my dear friend, Brian Houston, and he shared with me that his pet peeve when it comes to worship songs are songs which try to plead for what Jesus has already accomplished for us on the cross. I agree with Brian completely, and I think we all agree that Brian is someone who knows what he's talking about when it comes to worship songs. Brian is the senior pastor of Hillsong Church, and God has truly anointed his church to write beautiful praise and worship songs that have impacted a whole new generation of worshippers in these last days. In fact, some of my favorite worship songs are from Hillsong. In my own quiet moments before the Lord, as I give thanks to Him for paying the full price on the cross for all my sins, sicknesses and poverty, my heart overflows with gratitude and I worship Him:

> You are magnificent, eternally
> Wonderful, glorious
> Jesus
> No one ever will compare to You
> Jesus[4]

Oh, how I love it when the Lord responds by filling my whole study with His tangible presence, and my heart begins to burn in the presence of my lover! I remind my church that we don't always have to feel His tangible presence, for that's not what we live by today. But when you **do** feel His presence, especially during times of deep intimate worship, enjoy Him, savor His love and allow His embrace to wash over you! Relish the times in His presence when He refreshes, restores and heals you. You don't have to wait till Sunday to worship the Lord. You don't need a five-piece band and a worship leader to worship your Savior. Right where you are, without instruments, you can lift up your hands, your voice and your heart, and worship Him and give thanks for His finished work and His grace in your life.

Hallelujah! He is so beautiful!

I love worship songs that are full of the person of Jesus and His finished work. In my church, I have commissioned my music director to ensure that the songs we use in our church services are songs that testify of the finished work of Jesus. For example, under the new covenant, we don't have to keep on asking the Lord in our songs for forgiveness because **He has already forgiven us**[5]. I want you to say this out loud with me:

"I am already forgiven!"

Jesus' blood has cleansed us once and for all!

The Word of God declares this about the finished work of Jesus on the cross:

> Hebrews 10:12–14
> [12]But this Man, after He had offered **one sacrifice** for sins **forever, sat down** at the right hand of God…
> [14]For by one offering He has **perfected forever** those who are being sanctified.

His finished work on the cross was offered as one sacrifice FOREVER, and when you received Jesus Christ into your life, you were PERFECTED FOREVER! And how long is forever? I checked the original Greek word for "forever" in this verse and guess what? "Forever" means forever! You have been perfected forever by Jesus' cleansing blood, not by the blood of animal sacrifices which can **never** take away sins!

You may be surprised to find out that there are many believers today who do not believe that they have been perfected forever by the finished work of Jesus Christ. They are still depending on their self-efforts to qualify themselves. Perhaps you yourself are wondering, "How can I be fully assured that all my sins have already been forgiven?" Good question! Notice that after Jesus offered His life as a sacrifice and payment for all our sins, He "sat down"!

He sat down at the Father's right hand. Do you realize that under the old covenant, "every priest **stands ministering daily** and offering repeatedly the same sacrifices, which can **never take away sins**"[6]? But the Bible goes on to say that Jesus, "after He had offered one sacrifice for sins forever, **sat down**".

Jesus sat down to demonstrate to us that the work is indeed finished. Under the old covenant, the priest who served in the tabernacle of Moses never sat down, but "stands ministering daily" because his work could never be finished. The blood of bulls and goats could "never take away sins". In fact, have you noticed that in the holy place of the tabernacle of Moses, there is not a single piece of furniture prepared for the priest to sit on? You will not find a single chair in the holy place. You will find the altar of incense, the menorah and even a table of showbread, but interestingly, there are no chairs. This is because the work of the priest was **never finished**. Only Jesus' work is a **finished work**. And not only did He sit down at the Father's right hand, He made us SIT WITH HIM!

> Ephesians 2:4–6
> [4]But God, who is rich in mercy, because of His great love with which He loved us, [5]even when we were dead in trespasses, made us alive together with Christ... and made us **sit together** in the heavenly places in Christ Jesus.

Maybe you are wondering, "What is all this business about

'chairs' and 'sitting down'?" Well, my friend, "sitting down" in the Bible is a picture of the believer resting in the finished and completed work of Jesus. He has finished all the work on the cross on your behalf and is now seated at the right hand of God. As it has all been accomplished on your behalf, this means that you can stop depending on your self-efforts to earn and qualify for God's blessings in your life. You can sit down with Jesus at the Father's right hand!

Stop depending on your self-efforts to earn and qualify for God's blessings in your life.

Now, listen carefully to what I am saying. I am not advocating a life of passiveness and laziness. You can take up courses, read books, do your work diligently and so on, but your trust must not be in these things. It must be in what Jesus has done for you. So if you are a student, for example, by all means, study hard. Score straight As for the glory of God! But don't trust in your intelligence or qualifications to bring you the blessings of God.

God's grace does not make you lazy and unproductive. On the contrary, it makes you labor more abundantly for His glory. Apostle Paul, a preacher of God's grace and the finished work of Jesus, said that he "labored more abundantly than they all"[7]. In the new covenant, God's way is to bless you first, and the knowledge of His blessing gives you the power to labor more abundantly. In other words, we do not labor to be blessed, but rather we have the power to labor because **we are already blessed**. Can you see the different premise for laboring in the new covenant?

Many believers are defeated today because they are struggling to qualify themselves for God's blessings by their own works.

Self-effort will rob you of reigning in life by His grace. You cannot earn your salvation, your healing or your financial breakthrough by your own efforts. If the greatest miracle — being saved from hell — comes by grace through faith, and not by your works, how much more the lesser miracles, such as healing, prosperity and restored marriages.

My friend, Jesus has accomplished everything on the cross. Our part is to trust in His perfect work, receive with open arms the abundance of grace and the gift of righteousness, and begin to reign in life through the one, Jesus Christ. Today, let it be your prayer that you will stop trying to earn God's grace and righteousness. Let the Holy Spirit teach you to start depending on Jesus' finished work and to start receiving by His grace. This is God's effortless way to success, wholeness and victorious living!

Chapter 2

The Law Has Been Fulfilled

I remember being invited to speak at a convention some years back and when one of the speakers got up to the podium to preach, he said with great conviction in his voice, "The greatest call in your life is to your family!" The crowd loved it, and the entire auditorium clapped and cheered in agreement. At the next session, another speaker stood up and declared with fiery passion in his eyes that "the greatest call in your life is to missions". This time, the crowd went wild and the entire auditorium reverberated with shouts of "Amen!"

Then, it was my turn to preach, and I prayed, "God, they have used up all the 'greatest calls'. Give me something." And when I stood up, the Lord put this in my heart and I shared, "The greatest call in your life is to be a worshipper!" You see, long after all the missions have been accomplished on earth, and long after families are united in heaven, we will continue worshipping our beautiful Savior Jesus Christ for all that He has done for you and me, for all eternity.

It is all about Jesus! It is all about His finished work!

The more you appreciate the finished work of Jesus and all that He has done for you to reign in life, the more you will worship and glorify Him! Let's look at the Word of God to see more of His finished work.

John 1:17, KJV

[17]For the law was given by Moses, but grace and truth came by Jesus Christ.

Have you noticed that truth is on the side of grace, not the law? Notice also that the law was **given**. This implies a sense of distance. In contrast, grace **came**! Grace is personal and came as a person — the person of Jesus Christ. The law is hard, cold and impersonal. You cannot have a relationship with two pieces of stone. But grace is gentle and warm. Grace is not a teaching or doctrine. Grace is a person and you can have a relationship with a person. God is not interested in mere obedience and submission. He is a God of love and He longs to have an intimate relationship with you. This is what makes Christianity unique. Many of the world's belief systems are governed by moral codes, rules and laws. But Christianity is not about these things. It is about having a relationship with Almighty God.

Our God came, died a cruel death on the cross and paid the full debt of sin with His own life so that you and I can reign in life today. His sacrifice on the cross speaks of relationship. Jesus came to reconcile sinful man with a holy God. When you receive Jesus Christ as your Lord and Savior, you are made holy and righteous by His blood once and for all. And you can enter boldly into the presence of Almighty God without any guilt, condemnation or expectation of punishment. Because of the cross, the price for sin has been paid, the judgment executed, the anger toward sin exhausted, the veil torn and the way to intimacy with God opened. Sin no longer hinders you from entering His presence. His blood has removed all vestiges of your sins!

Our God came, died a cruel death on the cross and paid the full debt of sin with His own life so that you and I can reign in life today.

Jesus Fulfilled The Law

The moment you place the law of Moses between you and God again, you are negating the finished work of Jesus, for if righteousness could come through the law, then Christ died in vain[1]. Christianity cannot be reduced to an impersonal list of do's and don'ts. Jesus' death has fulfilled the righteous requirements of the law of the old covenant. The Word of God tells us that the "handwriting of requirements" has been nailed to the cross[2]. Jesus came to fulfill all the requirements of the law on our behalf, so that the way to God is now opened. Hallelujah!

"Pastor Prince, you are saying that we are no longer under the law. But Jesus Himself said that He did not come to abolish the law."

That is exactly right my friend, but you have to quote what Jesus said completely. He said, "I have not come to abolish the law, **but to fulfill it**."[3] Jesus did not sweep the law under the carpet. He came and fulfilled every requirement of the law perfectly on our behalf. All that we were unable to do, He did on our behalf. So by Jesus, the law has been fulfilled!

When you have fulfilled your debt to the bank for the mortgage on your house, my advice to you is to stop sending in your monthly payments because the debt has already been fulfilled. If the bank sends you a letter demanding more payment from you, all you have to do is produce the title deed to your home. In the same sense, the debt that you and I owed to the law has already been fulfilled by our Savior Jesus Christ! Hallelujah! When the devil comes to accuse you with the law, and shows you how you have fallen short and failed, all you have to do is point to the payment that Jesus made on the cross. Christ is your title deed, which is why you are called a **Christ**ian today. You are not your own. You have been purchased with the precious blood of Jesus Christ. The law has no hold over you anymore!

The Devil Has Been Disarmed

You probably know that the issue of "nuclear disarmament" is big news in the world today. But are you aware that there is someone more sinister who has already been disarmed? The Bible says that God has "disarmed principalities and powers". We know from the book of Ephesians that "principalities and powers" refer to Satan and his cohorts[4]. So the devil has already been disarmed! But do you know what weapon he was wielding before his forced disarmament? Let's see what the Word of God says about this:

> Colossians 2:14–15
> [14]having wiped out the **handwriting of requirements** that was against us, which was contrary to us. And He has taken it out of the way, having nailed it to the cross. [15]Having disarmed principalities and powers, He made a public spectacle of them, triumphing over them in it.

Based on the context of the verse, the devil was armed with the "handwriting of requirements that was against us". What "handwriting of requirements" was so powerful that it required the death of Jesus to wipe it out? On Mount Sinai, God wrote the Ten Commandments on two tablets of stone. The "handwriting of requirements" was thus a reference to the law that was written by the finger of God. The devil then armed himself with the **law** to accuse and condemn man! Now listen carefully to this: God didn't give the law to arm the devil, but the devil, knowing that the law was against man, took advantage of it and has been using it against man.

You have been redeemed from the curse of the law.

The law always condemns and keeps man away from God. Hence, the devil uses it as his weapon to further alienate man from God. That's why when God nailed the law to the cross, He made a public spectacle of the devil and all the powers of darkness! Once the law was nailed to the cross of Jesus, God knew that the law no longer had the power to condemn man as long as he believed on Jesus. Therefore, when you know and believe that **Jesus has fulfilled completely the righteous requirements of the law, the devil cannot use the law to condemn you every time you fail.** Even if he uses the law and points to your sins today, you can point to the cross of Jesus and reject the condemnation. You may say, "No one can blot out God's handwriting." Yes, you are right. No man can, but God can! And God did it righteously. My friend, you have been redeemed from the curse of the law. The devil and his crew have been disarmed. Hallelujah!

However, if you insist on being under the law, you are actually arming the devil again! God has nailed the law. He has blotted out its requirements, taken it out of the way and disarmed the devil. But when you subject yourself to the old covenant system of the law, you are putting that weapon back into the devil's hands. Every teaching that says, "We have to keep the law to be blessed by God," is putting the weapon of the law back into the devil's hands. Instead of resting in God's disarmament, people are rearming and remilitarizing the powers of darkness!

Let me stress that the law is holy, just and good. Please don't misconstrue that I am saying otherwise. But even though the law is holy, just and good, it has no power to make you holy, just and good. You see, the law was designed to expose your weaknesses, your sins, and your inability to be holy, just and good. It is like a mirror that exposes your flaws — your blemishes and pimples. But you cannot take the mirror, and begin to rub your face with it to clean off your blemishes and pimples, because that is not the mirror's purpose! You need to understand that no amount of keeping the law can make you holy. Only the blood of Jesus can do that. Nevertheless, the law **is** holy. It is not from the devil. It is from God Himself.

The Purpose For The Law

God gave the law for one purpose, and that is by the law, the world would have the knowledge of sin[5], and recognize their need for a Savior. Without the law, there would be no sin[6]. For example, if there were no law on how fast you can drive on a particular road, that is, there were no speed limit, the state trooper cannot stop you and give you a ticket for speeding. In simple terms, no law equals no sin. No recognition of sin equals no need for a Savior! The law was given to bring man to the end of himself so that in his despair, he would see his need for Jesus. Because of the law, no man can say that he is not a sinner and no man can say that he doesn't need Jesus. That is the purpose of the law. It was not designed to make you godly, but to expose your ungodliness.

What the devil has done is to keep the law over people's heads all the time, so that they will constantly feel condemned and guilty. The devil is the master legalist who constantly reminds you of how unworthy you are. He is known as the accuser of the brethren[7]. Here are some of his common attacks:

"You call yourself a Christian?"

"You are a hypocrite!"

"Forget about praying. God will never listen to your prayers."

"Look at your life. You dare step into church?"

My friend, these are lies, ALL lies! The devil is using the law to make you conscious of all your shortcomings. But through Jesus Christ, you are no longer under the condemnation of the law. The devil has been disarmed by the power of the cross! Jesus, who knew no sin, has been condemned on your behalf on the cross. Through Jesus Christ, you are now made righteous apart from the works of the law. So when you hear the voice of the accuser condemning you, remind yourself that you are the righteousness of God through Jesus Christ. Declare it out loud! Come on, say it with me three times, each time louder than the first:

"I am the righteousness of God through Jesus Christ!"

"I am the righteousness of God through Jesus Christ!"

"I am the righteousness of God through Jesus Christ!"

Righteousness is a gift. It is not a reward for perfect obedience to the law. You are clothed today not in your own righteousness, which is self-righteousness, but with the righteousness of Jesus Christ. God sees you as righteous as Jesus Himself.

Only Grace Brings Hope

Only the radical preaching of grace brings hope to believers. Only the finished work of Jesus can bring us wholeness, completeness and shalom-peace. Some people say that the Christian life is very hard. My friend, it is not hard, it is impossible! The only one who can live it is Jesus Himself, and He wants to do it in us today. That is why it is not up to our own efforts to fulfill the law of Moses. It was fulfilled on our behalf and the price for our sins has been paid on the cross. Our part today is to believe in our Savior, and receive from Him the abundance of grace and the gift of righteousness. The Christian life is a life of rest in Christ Jesus and His finished work. It is time to rest from your own efforts and to enjoy Jesus! The devil hates the gospel of grace because it causes the believer to reign in life. And when you reign, the devil does not!

Only the finished work of Jesus can bring us
wholeness, completeness and peace.

Chapter 3

Controversies Surrounding The Gospel Of Grace

Have you ever wondered why the moment you say the word "grace", (let's not even talk about the abundance of grace yet), people's defenses go up?

You will hear people saying, "Oh… be careful of that grace preacher. I hear that he's coming to town," or "You have to be careful now, too much grace is not good for you. It must be balanced with the law." Have you wondered where all these fears and apprehensions come from?

Think of all the Indiana Jones movies that you have watched. Before the hero Indy can lay hold of any priceless relic, he must overcome the obstacles and traps surrounding the prized artifact. Fiery darts whiz by on his left. Poison arrows fly toward him from the right. Hidden pits filled with jagged spears lie in front of him and giant boulders hurtle down from above. So many obstacles have been erected simply because there is a treasure at the end.

For the same reason, the devil has erected so many obstacles and fences around the gospel of grace. He is well aware that the

---

The moment you learn to receive grace, you will start to reign in life!

---

moment you learn to receive grace, you will start to reign in life! The devil comes to steal, kill and destroy[1]. He wants to see you broke and broken. He does not want to see you reigning in life. So he has been working hard to prevent believers from receiving the abundance of grace and the gift of righteousness.

Controversies — The Devil's Strategy

The devil's strategy is to surround the truths of God with controversies. To prevent God's people from benefiting from the fullness of God's promises, he erects controversies as fences around these truths. **You can always tell how powerful a truth is by the number of controversies the devil surrounds it with!** The Word of God reminds us not to be ignorant of the devil's devices. When Jesus died on the cross, the serpent's head was crushed. God gave the devil a PHD — **p**ermanent **h**ead **d**amage! So you will find that the devil's strategies are always lacking in creativity — what he has done in the past, he is still doing now.

For example, when God was restoring the truth of healing to the body of Christ, the devil put up a signpost that said, "Heresy!" For many years, the church looked at this signpost and backed off, saying, "Oh, that's heresy. That's dangerous and controversial. Let's forget about talking about healing in the church."

Instead of studying the Word of God to see what God Himself says about healing, the church backed off! It didn't matter that when Jesus walked on the earth, more than two-thirds of His ministry involved healing the sick. He went about healing the sick and all who touched Him were healed. The

Bible records that "the whole multitude sought to touch Him, for power went out from Him and **healed them all**"[2].

I wish that somebody in Hollywood would produce the scene that took place in Luke 6:19. (Mel Gibson, are you reading this?) All who were sick, lame and blind came to Jesus, and bam! The healing virtue of Jesus was powerfully released as all who touched Him were healed! That's a powerful image to have in your mind whenever you are believing God for healing!

The world doesn't have the truth. They package fiction and present it as truth. They present creatures from outer space and make you believe that aliens are real! On the flip side, we believers have the truth, but we present and package the truth as if it was fiction. Come on! Believers, we have the truth. Let's proclaim the truth of the gospel of Jesus with boldness! Only the truth of Jesus' grace and power has the anointing to liberate and set people free. I believe with all my heart that God is raising up a new generation of directors, producers and scriptwriters worldwide who will present the truth of the gospel of Jesus in all its purity and power.

Now, when God was restoring the truth of prosperity to the church, signposts were again put up, calling it heresy. For many years, the church backed away from the teaching of prosperity because it was controversial. Again, it didn't matter that the Bible declared that Jesus Christ became poor on the cross, that we through His poverty might be prosperous.[3] The church backed off, saying, "Let's forget about it. It's too controversial."

I don't understand why some believers would fight for the right to be sick and poor.

Would you as a parent want your children to be diseased and living in abject poverty?

Why do you take your children to the doctor when they are unwell?

Why do you give them the best education you can afford?

Isn't it because you want your children to be blessed, healthy and to have a prosperous future? Do you think that your heavenly Father would want anything less for you? Do you seriously think that your heavenly Father will bless you with a meager hand when the streets of heaven are made of pure gold? Listen carefully: The streets of heaven are not plated with gold. They are made of solid gold! Think about this for a moment. If you on earth know how to give good gifts to your children, **how much more your Father in heaven[4]**!

Recognize that the devil has been using controversy as a device down through church history to prevent believers from having access to the most powerful truths of God. He built fences of controversy around healing, prosperity and grace to keep believers from reigning over sickness, poverty and sin. The more controversies you find around a truth of God, the more powerful that truth must be.

Pay close attention to what I am saying. Not all controversies are based on the truth of God's Word. We have to test everything against what the Bible says. Nevertheless, controversy is a tool that the devil uses to prevent God's people from accessing His truths. He is a crafty liar and deceitful thief, so we have to base what we believe on the Word of God and test everything against the Scriptures. Don't back down from grace just because you have heard that it is controversial. Study the Word of God yourself and see what it has to say about grace!

Deserved Versus Undeserved Favor

"Oh, so you are one of those 'prosperity gospel' preachers!"

My friend, there is no such thing as a "prosperity gospel". There is only one gospel in the Bible and that is the gospel of Jesus Christ. However, when you believe the gospel of Jesus, which is based entirely on His grace, it will result in health and prosperity. In fact, the gospel of Jesus Christ leads to blessings, success, healing, restoration, protection, financial breakthroughs, security, peace, wholeness and MUCH MORE!

God blesses you not because you are good,
but because He is good.

God blesses you not because you are good, but because He is good. Grace is based on His faithfulness and goodness toward you. It is not contingent on your performance, but is based on His **undeserved** favor. If it were contingent on how good you are, then it would no longer be based on grace, and would instead be based on the system of the law. It would be **deserved** favor. This is the difference between the old covenant of law and the new covenant of grace:

Law is deserved favor — When you obey the commandments perfectly, you will be blessed.

Grace is undeserved favor — Jesus obeyed God perfectly, and you will be blessed by believing in Him.

My friend, which covenant are you under today? The old covenant of law or the new covenant of grace? Deserved favor or undeserved favor? If being blessed by God today is dependent on your doing, your ability to keep the law and your ability to make yourself righteous, then there would be no difference between being under the old covenant of law and being under the new covenant of grace. The good news would not be that good after all, since there is no real difference between the old and the new. Come on, my friend, God found fault with the old covenant[5], and for a good reason!

Fences Around The Abundance Of Grace

A good friend of mine who's a fellow minister once suggested to the dean of a reputable Bible school that "grace" be incorporated into the school's curriculum. The dean replied, "You have to be careful when it comes to grace." This apprehension toward grace is prevalent in many Christian circles. The moment they hear "grace", they go on high alert!

I told my minister friend that I actually do not agree that grace should be a topic in a Bible school's curriculum. Grace is not a topic — grace **is** the gospel. It is the good news! The word "gospel" simply means "good news". Grace is not a theology. It is not a subject matter. It is not a doctrine. It is a person, and His name is Jesus. That's the reason the Lord wants you to receive the abundance of grace, for **to have the abundance of grace is to have the abundance of Jesus!**

"How can you say that grace is a person and that person is Jesus Himself?"

Excellent question! Let's look at what the Word of God says about this:

> John 1:17, KJV
> 17For **the law was given** by Moses, but **grace and truth came** by Jesus Christ.

Notice that the law was **given**, but grace and truth **came** by **Jesus Christ**. The law was given, implying a sense of distance, but grace came! Grace came as a person and His name is Jesus Christ. Jesus is the personification of grace. Jesus **is** grace! It is important that you begin to realize that truth is on the side of grace, and not on the side of the law. The Word of God declares that if you know the truth, the truth will set you free. Well, my friend, grace is **the** (definite article) truth that will set you free, not the law of Moses. The law is on the side of Moses, but grace and truth are on the same side as our Savior. Yet, there are people today holding on to the law of Moses and preaching it as if it is the "truth" that liberates. My friend, the grace of God is the only truth that liberates. Truth is on the side of grace!

If the devil can keep you under the law, he can keep you defeated.

You never hear, "Oh, be careful of the Ten Commandments," or "Be careful of that law preacher. I hear that he is coming to town." Why is there no controversy about the Ten Commandments? This is because the devil wants you to be subject to the law. He doesn't want you to know that Jesus has liberated you from the law. If he can keep you under the law, he can keep you defeated.

Interestingly, people are afraid that when you tell a believer that he is completely forgiven by grace, and no longer has to earn his right standing before the Lord via the law of Moses, it would cause him to go out and live a life of sin and debauchery. However, the Bible is very clear that the "strength of sin is the law"[6]. It is not grace that gives people the strength to sin. It is the law! The more you are under the law, the more sin is strengthened! Conversely, the more you are under grace, the more sin will be depleted of its strength.

In fact, the Bible declares that "sin shall not have dominion over you, for you are not under law but under grace". Now, don't just gloss over this powerful revelation. Read the verse again. It is from Romans 6:14 — "For **sin shall not have dominion over you,** for you are **not under law** but **under grace.**" This means that the more grace you receive, the more power you have to overcome sin. In other words, sin shall not have dominion over you when you receive the abundance of grace!

Unfortunately, there are well-meaning people today who are preaching a completely different message. They preach that sin shall not have dominion over you when you are under the law. So when they see sin, they preach more of the law! That, my friend, is like adding wood to fire because the strength of sin is the law. Sin is strengthened when more law is preached! But the power to have dominion over sin is imparted when more grace is preached! So who is the one who switched the roles? Will the real gospel please stand up? The devil has pulled the wool over the eyes of God's sheep! It is time to preach the truth. It is time to remove the wool from our eyes and break down the fences surrounding the gospel of grace!

Fences Around The Gift Of Righteousness

The devil has also succeeded in erecting fences around the gift of righteousness. Today, conventional theology teaches you that not only is there such a thing as "positional righteousness", there is also something known as "practical righteousness". They are saying that even though you were made righteous by grace, you now have to do right and keep the law to continue being righteous. They call this having "practical righteousness".

My friend, this is something that Apostle Paul never taught! There is only one righteousness in Christ Jesus. Let's see what Paul says about those who are ignorant of this righteousness. He said, "For they being ignorant of God's righteousness [that's what some people term 'positional righteousness'], and seeking to establish their own righteousness [now that would be what they call 'practical righteousness'], have not submitted to the righteousness of God."[7] So it is clear that Paul is against any teaching that says that you have to earn and merit your own righteousness. You are either righteous or you are not. There is no such thing as first having "positional righteousness" and then having to maintain that through "practical righteousness". You are the righteousness of God in Christ, period!

Notice that the strategy here is to deceive the believer into believing that righteousness is something that you need to achieve by keeping the law perfectly. It all sounds very good to the flesh, but if that is so, then the promise of the **gift** of righteousness is completely thrown out of the window. The devil is very crafty. He has no problem with righteousness, but he wants to deceive you into pursuing your own righteousness through the law. He wants you to depend on your own self-righteousness, so he throws out the little word "gift" from the phrase "gift of righteousness". Then, he gives you a false impression that you are responsible for earning your own righteousness through your own works and self-efforts, instead of depending on the finished work of Jesus.

You are the righteousness of God in Christ, period!

There are many believers who are very sincere about keeping the law and earning their own righteousness, but I'm sorry to say this: They are sincerely wrong. God's way is by grace. Righteousness cannot be earned by good works. It can only come as a gift. A gift is no longer a gift if you have to work for it.

For example, if I gave you a brand new dazzling red Ferrari on the condition that you pay me US$20,000 every month for the rest of your life, is the Ferrari really a gift? Of course not! How can it be a gift if you have to pay or work for it? That is double-talk! But that is what some people are preaching today. They say that God gives you the gift of righteousness, on the condition that you keep the Ten Commandments for the rest of your life to remain righteous. Now, is this a real gift? Come on, when God gave you the gift of righteousness, it was a real gift. Stop trying to earn it with your own works. God's gifts to us are unconditional!

Start believing that righteousness is a gift in the new covenant! Many believers are defeated today because they are trying to earn their own righteousness by their law-keeping and good works. My friend, righteousness is a gift because of what Jesus has accomplished on the cross for you. All your sins — past, present and future — have been washed clean by His precious blood. You are completely forgiven and from the moment you received Jesus into your life, you will never be held liable for your sins ever again. You have been made as righteous as Jesus not through your behavior, but by faith in Him and His finished work on the cross[8].

There is nothing that you can do that will make God love you more and there is nothing that you can do that will make Him love you less.

Perhaps you are saying, "But… but… I didn't do anything to become righteous!" That is exactly right. You did nothing to become righteous. And Jesus did nothing to become sin. You are clothed not with your own righteousness, but with Jesus' perfect righteousness. It is a gift that He purchased for you with His own blood! Therefore, righteousness before the Lord cannot be earned. Your righteous standing or right standing before Him can only be received as a gift. Today, your right to be righteous is a blood-bought right! There is nothing that you can do that will make God love you more and there is nothing that you can do that will make Him love you less. He loves you perfectly and He sees you clothed with Jesus' righteousness. So begin to see yourself clothed in Jesus' righteousness.

License To Sin?

"But, Pastor Prince, if you preach that one is forever righteous before the Lord apart from his works and law-keeping, won't people go out and live a licentious life? Won't it give people a license to sin?"

Another fantastic question! Let me begin by asking you this: Have you noticed that people are already sinning without a "license"? We all have the same goal of wanting people to live a life of victory over sin. Allow me to make this explicitly clear in black and white, so that there is no doubt:

I, Joseph Prince, am vehemently, completely, aggressively and irrevocably AGAINST SIN!

Sin is evil. I do not condone sin. A lifestyle of sin leads only to defeat and destruction. So while our goal is the same, where we differ is the "how" of getting to the victorious life. Some think that it is by preaching more law. I am convicted that it is by preaching the grace of God.

When you visit our church, you won't find a congregation that, having received the good news of the abundance of grace and the gift of righteousness, wants to run off and start living in sin. Of course not! In fact, some of the top business people, management executives, entrepreneurs, lawyers, accountants and consultants in my country attend our church, and you will find a congregation that is deeply in love with the person of Jesus. You will hear wonderful and amazing testimonies of how marriages have been restored, how huge debts that had run into the millions have been supernaturally cancelled, how terminal diseases have been miraculously healed and other awesome testimonies that the good news of Jesus brings!

Sin loses its appeal when you encounter the Person of grace, Jesus Christ, and realize all that He has blessed you with and done for you on the cross. You begin to realize that you have been given this great gift of righteousness and that you did nothing to deserve it. You did nothing to earn it and you did nothing to merit it.

Now, what happens? Does this encounter with Jesus cause you to want to go out and sin? Of course not! On the contrary, it will cause you to fall in love with Jesus all over again. It will make you a better husband, a better father, a better housewife, a better student. It will make you someone who desires with all your heart to guard the glory of our Lord Jesus by living a life that is victorious over sin, by His grace and strength! The preoccupation with Christ instead of with self, will cause you to start reigning in life through the one, Jesus Christ — that is the Gospel Revolution! The Word of God says, "Awake to righteousness, and sin not."[9] The more you realize that you are righteous, the more victory you will experience over sin! Wake up every morning and give thanks that you are the righteousness of God through Jesus Christ.

The Final Restoration

Down through the centuries, God has been restoring His truths to the church, and I believe that the last and final truth is the person of Jesus Christ and all that He has accomplished on the cross. The revelation of the **finished work** of Jesus will get stronger and stronger in the end times, and man will begin to enjoy the full benefits of the new covenant of grace.

Jesus did not die on the cross for us because any one of us deserved it. We all deserved hell's fire, but we have been redeemed by Jesus Christ. The word "redeem" literally means to buy with a price. The price here is Jesus Himself. He gave Himself up as a ransom for you and me. He gave Himself up, so that you and I can receive the abundance of grace and the gift of righteousness to reign in life. It is all about Jesus!

It is time for the church to stop backing away from grace and to stop worrying that it might be too controversial. Study the Scriptures and begin to see for yourself that this is the power of God to salvation. Stop backing away from grace!

Discerning The Gospel Of Grace

Let me teach you how to discern if the grace teaching that you are hearing is doctrinally sound. When you hear the new covenant of grace preached, it is always Christ-exalting. It always reveals more and more of Jesus. It always unveils the beauty of Jesus and the perfection of His finished work on the cross. Jesus is always glorified when grace is taught. There is no grace without Jesus!

So don't be too easily impressed just because somebody tells you that he preaches grace. The Word of God tells us to test everything. God wants us to be wise as serpents and innocent as doves[10]. Even as you read this book, I don't want you to take my word for it. I want you to crack open your Bible and study the Word of God for yourself, and see the grace of our Lord Jesus in the new covenant coming alive. Grace is not a doctrine. Grace is a person and His name is Jesus. Therefore, there is no grace teaching without Jesus Christ. You cannot separate Jesus and grace! If someone keeps dropping the word "grace" in his sermons, but there is no exaltation of Jesus and His finished work, it is **not** the gospel of grace.

Similarly, to further discern if what you are hearing is the gospel of grace, note that grace does not point to your efforts, your performance or your doing. It makes nothing of man's self-efforts and points completely to Jesus' efforts and what He has done. The law makes one self-conscious. It is always asking, "What must I do?" But grace makes one Christ-conscious. It is always asking, "What has Jesus done?"

Your part is to only believe on Jesus Christ, and when you believe, you are blessed and made righteous!

Under law, the burden is on you to perform. Under grace, the burden is on what Christ has performed on the cross. That is why Jesus said, "Come to Me, all you who are weary and heavy laden, and I will give you rest, for My yoke is easy and light."[11] Jesus was not speaking to people who were tired and weary from their secular jobs. He was talking to people who were weary and heavy laden by the requirements of the law of Moses. The yoke of the law is hard and heavy. Jesus came to reveal grace, and the yoke of grace is easy and light because it involves none of you and all of Christ. He has borne the burden of sin on your behalf. Under grace, your part is to only believe on Jesus Christ, and when you believe, you are blessed and made righteous! Isn't this amazing grace?

The new covenant of grace is so powerful that there have been attempts to pervert the teaching on God's grace. There are so-called preachers who are preaching a "grace" that is not of God! They believe in "universal salvation" and claim that because of God's grace, all will be saved, even without believing in Jesus. **This is a lie from the pit of hell**! No man can be saved except through our Savior Jesus Christ. Jesus is the way, the truth and the life[12]. No man comes to the Father and receives eternal life except through Jesus! There is no grace without the person of

Jesus. The teaching of "universal salvation" is a LIE that dishonors Jesus and negates His work on the cross! True grace always makes Jesus the center of everything. It is all about Jesus!

It is time for the church to tear down these fences of controversy around grace and start unveiling more and more of Jesus. This is the heartbeat of my ministry — the unveiling of Jesus and seeing more of Jesus, His loveliness, His perfection and His grace. It is all about bringing the "amazing" back to grace!

When believers don't understand that God's grace is His undeserved, unearned and unmerited favor, they will depend on their own efforts to keep the law of Moses to deserve, earn and merit His favor. Similarly, when believers don't understand that righteousness is a gift, and that it is about "right standing" and not "right doing", they will depend on their own efforts to earn this gift.

Pulling Down The Fences Of Controversy

My friend, you are destined to reign in this life. It is our Lord's good pleasure to see your marriage blessed, family blessed, storehouses overflowing with more than enough and your body full of the resurrection life of Jesus!

Begin to see that the devil has entrenched fences and built strongholds that are so fortified that today, they are like thick walls. These thick walls surround the abundance of grace and the gift of righteousness. By the grace of God, we are going to pull down these thick walls, for the weapons of our warfare are not carnal but mighty in God for pulling down strongholds. Let's pull down these strongholds that have robbed believers of their destiny to reign in life. Start receiving the treasures that were purchased for you by the blood of Jesus, and begin reigning in every area of your life!

It is our Lord's good pleasure to see your family blessed, storehouses overflowing and your body full of the resurrection life of Jesus!

Chapter 4

We Have Been Robbed!

"*Sometimes God is angry with me, sometimes He is happy with me.*"

"*Sometimes He blesses me, sometimes He curses me.*"

"*Sometimes God cares for me, sometimes He leaves me.*"

"*Today, He prospers me, but tomorrow, He may give me poverty to humble me.*"

"*Today, He heals me, but tomorrow, He may give me a disease to teach me a lesson.*"

"*Today, He forgives all my sins. Tomorrow, I am responsible for my sins.*"

Welcome to schizophrenic Christianity! This is what many believers are hearing and believing today: Sometimes God is good, sometimes He is not! Sometimes He is happy, sometimes He is not! They are tossed to and fro, never anchored on the rock of Jesus Christ. Such believers are living between two covenants — the old covenant of law and the new covenant of grace. They believe in a mixed message that tells them that there are times when God is angry with them and times when He is happy with them.

When you ask them, "When is God happy with you?" they will say, "When I do right."

When you ask them again, "Does that mean that when you do wrong, God is angry with you?" they will say, "Yes! God is angry with me when I do wrong."

My friend, those who believe that God is sometimes angry with them are still living under the old covenant of the law and not under the new covenant of grace. Under law, God demanded righteousness from man. Under grace, God provided righteousness for man. Under law, everything depended on man and his obedience. But under grace, everything depends on Jesus and what He did on the cross. The law demands, but will not lift a finger to help, while grace imparts and has accomplished everything on your behalf.

Have you noticed that in the old covenant based on the law of Moses, it was all based on what YOU had to **do** and **not do**? Just count the number of times the phrase "**you** shall not…" appears in Exodus 20 where the Ten Commandments were given. Compare this with the new covenant of grace where the Lord says:

> Hebrews 8:8–12
> [8]"… I **will** make a new covenant with the house of Israel… [9]not according to the covenant that I made with their fathers… I **will** put My laws in their mind and write them on their hearts; and I **will** be their God, and they shall be My people… [12]For I **will** be merciful to their unrighteousness, and their sins and their lawless deeds I **will** remember no more."

The old covenant of law is based on "you shall not… you shall not… you shall not…" while the new covenant of grace is the Lord saying, "I will… I will… I will…" It is clear that the emphasis and demand of the covenant of law is on **you** performing, while the emphasis and demand of the covenant of grace is on **God Himself** performing! He will do everything on our behalf. In fact, because Jesus has already died on the cross for us, He has already **done** everything on our behalf. Remember, Christianity is "done, done, done", not "do, do, do". Jesus came to establish the new covenant of grace and under this new covenant, God is no longer angry with you because His anger and wrath have already been exhausted on the body of Jesus on the cross.

Grace imparts righteousness and has accomplished everything on your behalf.

Pay close attention to this, for it will radically transform your life: The only reason Jesus could cry out "It is finished!" on the cross was that the full anger of God against sin had been totally exhausted on His body. Jesus cannot lie! And if the anger of God has already been completely exhausted, how can God be angry with you today? How can God be angry with you when He has already declared, "Your sins and your lawless deeds I will remember no more"?

How Do You See God Today?

The reason many believers are living a life of defeat is that they believe the LIE that God is angry with them. The reason many are not able to reign in life and experience a life of victory is that they carry around with them this guilt and condemnation that God is angry with them because of something that they have done in the past. My friend, be careful when you hear sermons that make God look like an old man with a big stick, waiting to unleash His wrath on you when you fail to live up to His standards!

When I was growing up in the Lord, that was exactly how I pictured God. In my mind, He was an elderly, unsmiling man with white hair, white eyebrows and a white beard. I used to see Him holding a big club, waiting to bash me on the head as soon as I sinned. Of course, when I grew in the understanding of God, I started to see Him without that big menacing club, but He was still not smiling and He was still very old.

One day, when I was a teenager, I was on a bus and praying to the Lord, and I heard God's voice saying to me, "Son, why do you picture Me like that, as an old man?" I replied confidently, "Well, you are a Father and that's how fathers look like, right?" He replied, "Son, do you know that growing old is part of the curse that came upon the earth because of Adam's sin? In heaven, there is no curse. We are forever young."

When I heard Him say that, all of a sudden, I began to see God as the same God who spoke with Abraham as a friend under the terebinth trees and showed him the stars, the same God who parted the Red Sea and delivered the children of Israel from slavery, the same God whose hand of favor made a young shepherd boy king over all of Israel. That's how I see my God today. **He is forever young, strong and loving!** He is not wielding a club and ready to punish me. His arms are spread wide, ready to embrace me.

My friend, do you see an angry God today, or a God who is

smiling and ready to embrace you? Because of Jesus' finished work, we are no longer under the covenant of law where God is happy with you sometimes and angry with you at other times. **Today, He is always well-pleased with you because of Jesus Christ**.

Let that truth sink in and fall in love with Him all over again.

What About God's Wrath?

Several years ago, I was walking to my car after a preaching engagement when a guy came running after me from the auditorium. Just as I was about to open my car door, he stopped right in front of me, wheezed and said, "Wait, pastor…" He was panting very hard and trying to recover from his sprint. "Wait… I have a question for you."

He looked very disturbed and said, "You talked about God's love, but the Bible also says that God is wrath!"

Right there in the parking lot, I began my next sermon. I explained that while God **has** wrath, the Bible never defines God **as** wrath. Instead, according to the Bible's definition, God is **love**.

He then exclaimed, "But Pastor Prince, sometimes I see God being angry!"

I explained, "We do see God being angry in the Old Testament, and in the book of Revelation, where His anger is toward those who have rejected Jesus. But for you and me, believers in the new covenant, we are not part of the Old Testament and we will never be punished because we have already received Jesus. As believers, God is no longer angry with us because all His anger for our sins fell upon Jesus at the cross. Jesus became the Lamb of God who takes away all our sins. On the cross, Jesus cried out, 'My God, My God, why have You forsaken Me?' Why do you think He cried that? He cried that so that we would all know specifically that at that point in time, God's wrath fell upon Him. He became our sin offering and the fire of God's wrath devoured Him completely as He who knew no sin became our sin, so that you and I will never experience God's wrath again."

God is no longer angry with us because all His anger for our sins fell upon Jesus at the cross.

After I had explained this, he thanked me. The disturbed look that had creased his face had given way to a smile. I believe that as he walked away, there was a peace and assurance in his heart that God was no longer angry with him because his sins had already been judged completely on the cross at Calvary. Hallelujah!

There are many sincere believers today who are like this man. They believe that God is a God of love, but at the same time, they also believe that He can be a God of great wrath. When they read the Bible, they get confused because they see an often-angry God in the Old Testament, but a loving God in the New Testament. Is God schizophrenic? Is He really angry sometimes and loving at other times? Let's find out in the next segment.

Rightly Dividing The Covenants

It is important that we understand that God works through covenants because that explains how God blesses people. Under the old covenant of Moses, if the children of Israel obeyed the "big ten" — the Ten Commandments — they would be blessed, otherwise, they would be cursed and punished. Think about this for a moment: Were they cursed because God is a God of wrath? No, they were cursed because they had failed to keep the terms of their covenant. It was a covenant that depended on their ability to keep the law and they could not.

The good news is that you and I are no longer under the requirements of the old covenant. Through Jesus' finished work, we are now under the new covenant, and in this covenant, we are blessed not because we are good or because we do good. To put it simply, we are blessed because **Jesus** is good, and **He** made us good and accepted by washing away all our sins with His own blood! We have to rightly divide the covenants.

"Pastor Prince, are you saying that God has gone 'soft' on sin?"

No way, my friend! Listen carefully to what I am saying: God is holy and righteous, and He hates sin. There is no question about that. But the full anger and judgment of God against sin fell upon Jesus on the cross. Have you ever wondered how it was possible for Jesus to be punished for sin since He committed no sin? The Bible says that He who knew no sin became sin[1]. Jesus committed no sin, but the past, present and future sins of humanity were all collectively punished on His body! He knew no sin, but was punished for our sins. So God has not gone soft on sin. Sin has been judged at the cross of Jesus!

All Your Sins Have Been Forgiven

"Pastor Prince, how can you say that even our future sins have been forgiven?"

My friend, when Christ died on the cross, you weren't even born yet. You weren't even an idea to your parents! All your sins were thus "future" sins. So **all** your sins have been forgiven, and it was accomplished through one sacrifice, by one Man. His name is Jesus. Jesus' finished work is outside of time. His blood that was shed forgives **all** your sins — past, present and even future sins.

Many Christians have the erroneous belief that only their past sins have been forgiven. They believe that when they received Christ, only their past sins were forgiven. So they believe that they have to be very careful from that point onwards. That was the impression that I was given by preachers and teachers when I was growing up.

Then, I read the Bible for myself and saw that it said that God, "having forgiven you **all trespasses**..."[2] My friend, "all" means **all**. It refers to **all** the sins of our lifetime! God didn't just take away one segment of our trespasses. He forgave all — past, present and future — of our trespasses! God's definition of "all" is not limited by time and space the way man's definition of "all" is. When God said "all", He really meant all! Understand that Jesus does not have to be crucified again for your future sins. They were all forgiven at the cross as well!

Let me illustrate it this way. Imagine that you and your family have managed to wriggle your way to the front of a jostling crowd in Disneyland, where the street parade is about to start. You and your children can't wait to see Mickey Mouse and his friends riding past on their beautiful floats. Donald Duck sails past and your children wave in excitement. Next comes Goofy, and then Pluto, and wow... is that Mickey coming up next? That's how we see life. We have a linear perspective and we see events unfold day by day. However, God's perspective is different. He has a "helicopter's view". He is up there, high above the parade, and He sees all the floats from the beginning to the end. He is "the Alpha and the Omega, the Beginning and the End"[3].

In the same way, when God forgave your sins at the cross, He saw the sins of your entire life from beginning to the end. God has taken all your sins, even the sins that you have not yet committed, and put them all on Jesus. All your "future" sins have been fully judged on the cross!

Does knowing this make you go, "Whoopee! I can do anything and commit any sin I want since I'm already forgiven"? Or does it make you want to live a life of honor that glorifies your God, who loves you so perfectly and completely?

When you are under God's grace and His perfect forgiveness, you will experience victory over sin.

I don't believe for one moment that a believer who has truly encountered the complete forgiveness of Jesus and the perfection of His finished work would desire to live a life of sin. It is His grace and forgiveness that gives you the power to overcome sin. Apostle Paul said, "Sin shall not have dominion over you, for you are not under law but under grace."[4] When you are under God's grace and His perfect forgiveness, you will experience victory over sin.

Testimony Of His Grace

I received this written testimony from a precious brother in my church:

Pastor Prince, I just want to share with you what the grace of God has done for me in my life. I was born into a Christian family. When I was growing up, I was forced to attend church. All I learnt was that Jesus hung on the cross, but why He was there, I did not know. I hated going to church. My parents would force me to go and reprimand me, but it didn't help.

In high school, I got involved with gangs, and started to smoke and drink heavily. I started to live a life of crime, stealing, vandalizing and getting into fights. I became rude, hot-tempered and extremely vulgar. My parents, teachers and school counselors tried to help me, but nothing worked. It wasn't long before I was expelled from school and became a full-time gangster. I frequented the pubs every day, and became a heavy drinker and smoker. Most of my friends were drug addicts. I got involved in armed robberies and I saw my life going into a downward spiral. It went from bad to worse and there was a cry within me for things to change.

This whole bondage by the devil came to an end just a few years ago when I got to know this girl called Faith. Even though Faith was a new believer, she would tell me about the grace, mercy and love of God, and why Jesus died for me. I was amazed at her knowledge of Jesus. I was born into a Christian family, but this new convert knew more about Jesus than I did. She then brought me to her church, called New Creation Church, and as you began to minister, I felt a warmth all over me and I started to cry. I felt like I was falling in love, but I did not know with whom. It was a love beyond the love of man, and I raised my hands up high and said the sinner's prayer at the end of the service.

From that point on, my life was no longer the same. Jesus began to deliver me from so many bondages. I heard you share a testimony about how another church member was delivered from a smoking addiction by confessing the righteousness of God and I started to do the same. I would smoke and confess that Jesus had taken my smoking addiction on the cross and that He still loves me even though I was still smoking.

Amazingly, two weeks later, nine years of heavy smoking and six years of alcoholism were gone! And as time went by, Jesus delivered me from the gang that I was in. I was even delivered from many other bad habits, like my addiction to pornography. I truly became a new creation in Christ Jesus! Everyone who knew me was shocked at my transformation. I was even healed of a 10-year urinary problem. I used to have to go to the toilet many times in the night, but now I am able to sleep through the night in peace.

*Pastor Prince, what man could not do, Jesus did. It was the grace of God that changed me. I did not deserve it, but I thank God for the blood of Jesus. He took me just as I was and now I am a child of God. When I heard you preach the grace of God, I did not go out to start a new gang, smoke, drink or sleep around. **It is a lie that when God's grace is preached, people will go out and sin more.** In fact, it was His grace that changed a wretch like me. I believe that God has blessed me to be a blessing. I want to spread this good news that only Jesus can make a difference in our lives.*

Pastor Prince, your ministry has blessed me. I have been attending New Creation Church for five years now and I am proud to say that this is my church.

Victor King
Singapore

Hallelujah! Isn't it amazing to see what the grace of God can do in a person's life? You see, the more revelation you have of the grace of God and His forgiveness, the more you will have the power to reign over all your challenges and addictions.

We Have Been Robbed

Many Christians have been robbed of fellowship and intimacy with God because they believe the **lie** that God is still angry with them because of their sins. They avoid having contact with God, thinking that He gets angry with them whenever they fail. So instead of going to God when they fail, they run in the opposite direction. Instead of running to the solution, they run away from it.

The truth is this: God is no longer angry with you. His wrath toward all your sins has already been exhausted completely on the body of your Savior Jesus Christ. All your sins have been judged and punished in the body of another.

Schizophrenic teaching that tells you that God is sometimes angry and sometimes happy with you based on your performance is unscriptural and will make you a schizophrenic believer. It's time to get out of confusion and to start seeing your God for who He really is.

God is (present tense) love. Stop being robbed of true intimacy and a relationship with your gracious and forgiving Savior Jesus Christ. Instead of avoiding Him when you fail, know that He is the answer to all your problems. You can go to Him and receive grace for your failures. His grace is greater than all your failures. He loves you perfectly, so go to Him with all your imperfections. In the same way that He restored that precious brother from our church, He will love you into wholeness!

The more revelation you have of the grace of God and His forgiveness, the more you will have the power to reign over all your challenges and addictions.

Chapter 5

Is God Judging America?

Soon after the tragedy of September 11 had taken place, some believers publicly declared that God was judging America because of its sins. When I heard that, I could just imagine Osama bin Laden in a cave somewhere in Afghanistan agreeing with them and thinking that "god" was indeed using him to judge America. Come on, when Christians attribute such events to God's judgment, terrorists would be the first to say, "Amen! Preach it!" Can you see that something is amiss when both believers and terrorists agree on the same thing? Thousands of people died, and many families, friends and loved ones were thrown into grief. How can that be the work of our loving Father? Read the Bible for yourself. It says that God is "not willing that any should perish"[1]. Terrorism is the work of the devil. It is not the work of our loving Father.

I have also heard some believers pronouncing, "If God does not judge America for all its sins, God has to apologize to Sodom and Gomorrah." Well, let me say this with honor and respect: If God judges America today, He has to apologize to Jesus for what He has accomplished on the cross! My friend, God is not judging America (or any country in the world today). America and its sins have already been judged! Where? At the cross of Jesus! Sin has been judged at the cross!

What About Evidence Of God's Fiery Judgment?

"But Pastor Prince, didn't God use Elijah to call down the fire of judgment on those who opposed him? And didn't God rain fire and brimstone on Sodom and Gomorrah?"

Let's look at Elijah's story. It happened during the reign of King Ahaziah of Israel, whom the Bible describes as someone who "did evil in the sight of the Lord"[2]. Ahaziah deployed a captain with 50 soldiers to confront Elijah, who was sitting on top of a hill. The captain shouted at Elijah, "Man of God, the king has said 'Come down!'" So Elijah answered and said to the captain of 50, "If I am a man of God, then let fire come down from heaven and consume you and your 50 men." And fire came down from heaven and consumed the captain and his men. So Ahaziah sent another captain with 50 men, and again, fire came down from heaven and consumed them. Ahaziah then sent a third captain with 50 of his soldiers, but this time, the captain pleaded with Elijah, and his life and the lives of his men were spared[3].

As for Sodom and Gomorrah, the Bible records that the Lord rained brimstone and fire on the two cities. He "overthrew those cities, all the plain, all the inhabitants of the cities, and what grew on the ground"[4].

Rightly Dividing The Word

"There, Pastor Prince... clear biblical evidence that God rains down judgment to punish His people!"

You need to understand how to **rightly divide the Word of God**. When we read the Bible, we need to follow the advice that Apostle Paul gave to his young apprentice, Timothy. Timothy was a young pastor of the church of Ephesus, and Paul told him to be "diligent to present yourself approved to God, a worker **who does not need to be ashamed, rightly dividing the word of truth**"[5].

Many believers today are living as if the cross did not make any difference!

God wants us to be able to rightly divide the Word. He wants us to be astute in rightly dividing and clearly separating what belongs to the old covenant of law and what belongs to the new covenant of grace. He wants us to be able to distinguish what occurred before the cross from what occurred after the cross, and to understand the difference the cross made. Many believers today are living as if the cross did not make any difference!

There's one crucial fact that you need to recognize about the two incidents of God's fiery judgment — they both took place in the Old Testament and before Jesus' crucifixion.

Don't just take it from me that God will **not** call down the fires of judgment on you today. See for yourself what Jesus Himself said about what Elijah did. Do you remember the time when Jesus wanted to enter a certain village in Samaria, but the people there refused to receive Him? When Jesus' disciples saw that the people rejected Jesus, they said, "Lord, do You want us to command fire to come down from heaven and consume them, just as Elijah did?" Now, how did Jesus respond to them? Did He say, "That's a great idea! You are truly disciples who carry My heart"? No, of course not! Read your Bible. He turned to His disciples and rebuked them firmly, saying, **"You do not know what manner of spirit you are of**. For the Son of Man did not come to destroy men's lives but to save them."[6]

My friend, the spirit of Jesus in the new covenant of grace is not the spirit of the old covenant of law during Elijah's time. Jesus wants you to have full assurance in your heart today that He did not come to condemn or destroy you. He came to save you[7]! The devil comes to steal, kill and destroy, but Jesus came that you may have life, and have it more abundantly[8]. Hallelujah!

Bear in mind also that God almost spared Sodom because of Abraham's plea. He promised Abraham that if there were only 10 righteous men in Sodom, he would not destroy the city for their sake[9]. Later, when the angels rescued Lot, Abraham's nephew, we see that God would not have destroyed the city even if just one righteous man — Lot — remained! Notice what the angel said to Lot, "Hurry, escape there. **For I cannot do anything** until you arrive there." They had to wait until Lot was out of the city and in the safety of another city called Zoar. The Bible records that the Lord rained brimstone and fire on Sodom and Gomorrah only after Lot had entered Zoar[10].

Are the people who claim that September 11 was God's judgment upon America saying that there is not even one righteous person in America today? If God would have spared Sodom for the sake of 10 righteous men, don't you think that the terms He would give today, after Jesus' finished work on the cross, would be even better? Even if God still demands the presence of at least 10 righteous people, you would easily find millions of righteous men and women of God in America today because righteousness is a gift of grace from the Lord, and believers all over America are clothed with Jesus' perfect righteousness! Folks, what happened on September 11 was not an act of judgment from God. God is certainly not a terrorist and the Son of Man did not come to destroy men's lives, but to save them!

Filter All Prophecies Through The Cross

All prophecies that you receive today must be filtered through the cross. If you receive a "word" from someone which brings your sins to remembrance or instills an expectation of punishment for sins in your life, don't fear it, just throw it out the window. Don't allow anyone to tell you that something negative has happened to you or will happen to you because of your sins. Reject such bad news in the name of Jesus. Instead, start receiving the good news of Jesus. When you are faced with difficult circumstances, keep on believing in His love for you that was demonstrated on the cross and He will cause whatever the devil meant for evil to be turned around for good, and to His glory! When the devil throws lemons at you, God will turn them into lemonade for your enjoyment!

There was a young couple in my church who had lost their baby due to some complications. And I was furious when I learned that a so-called "prophet" had told them that they had lost their baby because there was sin in their lives. That was really cruel! The couple was grieving, and instead of being a source of encouragement and edification, this "prophet" took advantage of the situation to appear prophetic at the expense of God's precious people.

We may not have all the answers, but we can have full assurance that the negative circumstances that we may sometimes experience are not the works of God, neither are they punishments for our sins. When we have this confidence that **God is for us** and not against us, we can believe for restoration, breakthroughs and good things to happen to us.

Our church leaders told the young couple that it was not the Lord punishing them for their sins. They reminded them that all their sins have been punished at the cross of Jesus. This helped them to remove all the guilt and condemnation that they were carrying in their hearts. Since then, the Lord has blessed them with a beautiful baby.

---

*When we have this confidence that **God is for us** and not against us, we can believe for restoration, breakthroughs and good things to happen to us.*

I have also received testimonies from other couples who received God's restoration in this area. I noticed that these couples had one thing in common: After they heard the good news of the gospel of grace, it liberated them from all guilt and condemnation. Instead of believing that God was against them or punishing them, they started believing that He was for them. They started trusting aggressively in His grace and goodness. And without fail, restoration always came. Now, that's God! When He restores, His restoration is always greater in quantity or quality. But think about it: If those couples continued to believe erroneously that God was punishing them because of their sins, they would never be able to muster the courage and hope to trust God for restoration, for a new child. My friend, your sins have been punished on the cross. God is on your side. And if God is for you, who can be against you?

Let me share with you a testimony of how believing in God's love, grace and goodness brought healing to one precious lady:

Pastor Prince, early last year, I was diagnosed with a tumor on the pituitary gland in my brain. The MRI scan showed that the tumor was a macro-growth of about 1.5cm. The neurosurgeon at the Singapore General Hospital said that if I had seen him any later, the tumor would have affected my eyesight as it was pressing on my optic nerves.

I was presented with two options: Immediate surgery to remove the tumor (the risk of surgery was that besides a 20 per cent failure rate, I could become blind in one eye) or medication (I was told that medication would take a long time to work and most patients only experience a shrinkage in the tumor after a year or so).

What the doctors had found out and said about the tumor was devastating news to me and my family. I remember telling myself that if I were to lose my eyesight, I would not want to live anymore.

It was during this time that my family resolved to commit the whole thing to God, to trust and rely on Him entirely and pray for healing. We opted to go with taking medication. During this time, despite wanting to believe in God's love and goodness toward me, I was constantly plagued with questions like, "Does God love me anymore?" "Does He even care?" "Is He punishing me for something wrong that I've done?" "Should I just grit my teeth and accept the situation?"

It was only when a fellow colleague and friend at my workplace started passing me your sermon CDs to listen to that I was reminded once again of my Savior's love, grace and goodness toward me. And I believe that as I listened to the Word preached via the CDs, my body began healing.

Within a month of the medication, the level of prolactin in my blood decreased and the balance of chemicals in my body became stable. After two more months, the MRI scan showed that the tumor had shrunk to half its original size.

I was very encouraged, and most importantly, I felt confident and secure that my God was doing His work of healing in my body, that He loves and cares for me enough to know that I was hurting and to do something about it.

The best news came in early August when the MRI scan that I went for showed that the macro-tumor was GONE! The doctor was amazed and kept saying that in most cases, even when a tumor had shrunk by so much, there would still be remnants of tumor cells. But in my case, the tumor was completely GONE, with no trace of any tumor cells at all!

No words can describe how grateful and thankful I am to God. I know that it is God who has healed me. But what's more important is the fact that I stand tall as a child of God, and I know that I am the righteousness of God because of what Jesus has done on the cross for me. This deep sense of knowing that I am deeply loved and cared for by God makes me so secure in my relationship with God. I want to give all the glory and praise to God. I am what I am today — healed, whole and at peace — only because of the preaching of the good news of the gospel of grace!

Connie Ang
Singapore

David's Definition Of Blessedness

If this lady had continued to believe that God was punishing her for some sin, she would have just gritted her teeth, accepted her sickness as punishment and never sought God for healing. But praise God He brought light into her situation, and showed her how much He loved her!

"But Pastor Prince, didn't God punish King David for his sin and he lost his child?"

Don't forget that David, like Elijah, **lived before the cross of Jesus.** You will never find an example of God punishing a believer for his sins in the new covenant. Let's study the Scriptures for ourselves and not just go by what people are saying.

When David sinned against God by committing adultery with Bathsheba and plotting the death of her husband, Uriah, sin was imputed to David and he was punished. Although the punishment was tempered with God's mercy, David was punished nonetheless because he was under the covenant of law and not the covenant of grace.

Do you know who David was describing when he said, "Blessed is the man to whom the Lord shall not impute sin"?[11] Since it's clear that sin was imputed to David, he could not have been describing himself as some scholars claim. No, he was looking prophetically into the covenant of grace. He was describing you and me — a new generation of people who are under the covenant of grace!

What does "shall not impute sin" mean? Does it mean that you will never sin again? Did Jesus die on the cross to free us from committing sinful actions or harboring sinful thoughts? If He did, then allow me to conclude with reverence that He failed. You and I know fully well that we can still be tempted with sinful thoughts and tempted to commit sinful actions, and there will still be times when we fail. Can you show me a man who is free from all temptations and who never fails?

My friend, when David described the blessed man as one to whom the Lord will not impute sin, he meant that even when this man sins, God will not count his sin against him, nor punish him for his iniquity. Too good to be true? That is why David defined this man as a blessed man. And this blessed man is you and me! Today, you are blessed because the Lord no longer counts your sins against you. Because of the cross of Jesus, you will never be punished for your sins again. Your sins were imputed to Jesus, so that they would never be imputed to you. Under the new covenant of grace that was sealed with the blood of Jesus, God has already judged sin completely on the body of Jesus Christ. This means that even when you fall short of God's holy standards, the punishment for sin will not fall on you. The wages of sin is death, but Jesus has already died on your behalf. Your sins have already been imputed to His account!

Today, you are blessed because the Lord no longer counts your sins against you. Because of the cross of Jesus, you will never be punished for your sins again.

Look at what John said: "**If anyone sins, we have an Advocate with the Father, Jesus Christ the righteous.**"[12] He did not say, "If anyone sins, he will be punished for his sins!" No, under the new covenant of grace, Jesus is today your Advocate. He represents you before God and as Jesus is, so are you[13]!

Is Jesus righteous before God? Yes! Then so are you. Is He accepted before God? Yes! Then so are you. Is He well-pleasing before God? Yes! Then so are you.

Now, will the revelation of what Jesus has done for you cause you to go out and sin? Of course not! In fact, knowing that He has borne your punishment will cause you to fall in love with Him. It will give you the strength to break free from sin!

Not A Big Sinner?

"But Pastor Prince, I've never committed adultery or killed anyone. I haven't really committed any major sins. I think that I have kept all of the laws of Moses."

Well, have you ever lost your cool at somebody who cut into your lane without turning on his indicator lights? Have you ever blown your top at your spouse? If your answer to either of these questions is "yes", then you are a murderer. And have you ever undressed a woman in your mind? If you have, then you are also an adulterer.

"How dare you call me a murderer and an adulterer?"

Calm down my friend, it is not me. It is our Lord Jesus. He said, "You have heard that it was said to those of old, 'You shall not murder, and whoever murders will be in danger of the judgment.' But I say to you that whoever is angry with his brother without a cause shall be in danger of the judgment... You have heard that it was said to those of old, 'You shall not commit adultery.' But I say to you that whoever looks at a woman to lust for her has already committed adultery with her in his heart."[14]

Let's be scriptural here and not go by our own standards when determining whether we have sinned or not. Let's go by Jesus' standards. Man brought the law of Moses down to a place where he thought that he was able to keep it. But Jesus came and brought it back to its full and righteous standard. Man can attempt to keep the law outwardly (like the Pharisees), but Jesus has demonstrated that it has to be kept inwardly as well. If you fail inwardly, you fail outwardly too. Jesus showed us that it was impossible for anyone to be justified by the law. Only He could fulfill the law on our behalf and justify us by His grace!

God doesn't categorize sin. Whether it's a "minor" or "major" sin, it's still a sin. He does not grade on the curve — when you fail in one, you fail in all[15]. There is no person on the face of this planet who does not need to depend entirely on the grace of God because there is no man who has not failed in his own efforts to keep the law! The Bible declares that "all have sinned and fall short of the glory of God"[16]. By Jesus' standard, we all fail! The good news is, even when you fail, God does not judge you for your failure. All our sins have been judged at the cross. Hallelujah! Don't let anyone tell you otherwise!

Chapter 6

The Evil Conspiracy

When I was growing up as a young Christian, I was taught many things about God which robbed me of any desire to build a more intimate relationship with Him. I was told that the more I knew, the more God would hold me accountable, and my punishment for falling short of His expectations would be more severe than someone who knew less.

When I got hold of this teaching, I knew exactly what not to do. I decided not to touch the Bible, since the more I knew, the more I would be punished by God. Come on, my mama didn't raise no fool! I would rather be ignorant than to learn more about the Word and attract greater chastisement should I fail! So I left the Bible alone and refused to turn up for any Bible study classes. I simply stayed away from anything that could further "incriminate" me.

I was also taught that the closer I drew to God, the more trials and tribulations I would experience. Have you heard this one before? When I got hold of this teaching, again I thought to myself, "My mama didn't raise no fool. I'm not about to allow trials to overwhelm me!" From that point on, I didn't want to draw close to God.

Can you see how wrong teachings about God can rob you of all that He has for you?

As I grew in the Lord, He opened my eyes and I realized that the teachings that I had received were not true. Contrary to what I had been taught, I found that the closer I drew to God, the closer I was to the Answer to all my problems. I was drawing close to the miracle worker. I was drawing close to the healer. I was drawing close to the provider, my Jehovah Jireh!

As long as you continue to have a wrong perception of God and withdraw from Him, the devil can keep you bound in a life of defeat.

The more of God's truth you know, the more the truth will set you free from erroneous beliefs that are not based on His Word. In fact, it is the devil who would love for you to fear God (in an unhealthy way), so that you would stay away from your only source of help. The devil would love for you to stay away from the Bible because it is the book of your inheritance, and it tells you what belongs to you through the blood of Jesus Christ. The devil would love for you not to find out the truth, so that he can keep you in bondage, sickness and poverty. As long as you continue to have a wrong perception of God and withdraw from Him, the devil can keep you bound in a life of defeat. He loves to pull the wool over the eyes of God's sheep, and deprive them of a life of victory and liberty. There is an evil conspiracy to keep you defeated. The devil is using erroneous teachings about God to blind and confuse God's people.

Does God Chastise Us With Sicknesses And Diseases?

One of the most evil teachings that I have heard is that God will chastise His own with sicknesses, diseases, accidents and tragedies. When I was a teenager, one of the youth leaders in my previous church was involved in a horrible accident that nearly killed him. A church leader gathered some of us youths to go visit that youth leader in the hospital and we all went in the church leader's car. As he was driving, he began to lament, "Why did this happen to him? I don't understand. Why would God's chastening be so severe this time? What did he do to cause God to chasten him this way?"

As a young Christian listening to his church leader bemoaning God's chastening, can you imagine how I felt when I "realized" that God was behind the accident? Honestly, it frightened the living daylights out of me to think that God would chastise a believer using such a severe method! I remember praying, "God, please don't ever chasten me this way. Whatever it is, please, just tell me, all right? I will listen. I promise!" I became very afraid of God. I didn't want to draw near to Him because I was afraid of Him, afraid that if I made a mistake, He would not hesitate to chastise me with accidents that could leave me crippled for life or even dead!

Do you know that this erroneous teaching is actually based on the old covenant and not the new covenant? In the book of Leviticus, God says to those who fail to obey His commandments, "I will chastise you seven times for your sins."[1] But guess what? You are no longer under the covenant of law. You are under the covenant of GRACE! Jesus has already borne all your chastisement and punishment on the cross. Read it for yourself in Isaiah 53:

> Isaiah 53:4–5
> [4]Surely He has borne our griefs and carried our sorrows; yet we esteemed Him stricken, smitten by God, and afflicted. [5]But He was wounded for our transgressions, He was bruised for our iniquities; **the chastisement for our peace was upon Him**, and by His stripes we are healed.

The prophet Isaiah saw a prophetic vision of our Lord Jesus on the cross, bearing the punishment for our transgressions. He declared that the "chastisement for our peace was upon Him". Jesus has already been chastised on our behalf! When Mel Gibson's *The Passion Of The Christ* was released, people complained that the movie was too graphic and violent. The truth is that what the movie portrayed is only the tip of the iceberg when it comes to what our Lord really suffered on our behalf.

During the time of the Roman Empire, the soldiers had various instruments of cruelty and torture at their disposal. The infamous cat-o'-nine-tails was a whip with nine chains. To each chain was attached many metal shards and hooks, so that when a prisoner was beaten with it, the metal shards and hooks would latch onto his flesh and rip it apart when the whip was jerked back. That is why the prophet Isaiah described Jesus as having "no form or comeliness; and when we see Him, there is no beauty that we should desire Him"[2].

Jesus' flesh was torn apart and He was violently scourged beyond human recognition. The chastisement that we deserved came upon Jesus, so that you and I will never have to go through what He endured on our behalf. And by His stripes, we are healed!

So how can anyone have the audacity to say that God will still chastise us with sicknesses, diseases and accidents today? To say this is to negate the finished work of Jesus Christ! Under the new covenant, God will never again chastise the believer for his sins! By His stripes you are healed! Whatever condition you have today, it is not from the Lord! Look to Jesus on the cross. See Him beaten and scourged, and receive healing and wholeness from Him. He has paid the price for your total healing. Today, He redeems your life from destruction[3]!

Chastisement In The New Covenant

"Pastor Prince, how can you say that there is no chastisement and punishment in the new covenant? Hebrews chapter 12 states it very clearly:

*"[5]… 'My son, **do not despise the chastening of the Lord**, nor be discouraged when you are rebuked by Him; [6]for whom the Lord loves He **chastens**, and scourges every son whom He receives.'*

"See, Pastor Prince, here is clear evidence that God chastens believers in the new covenant!"

My friend, there is confusion in the church because the original Greek word here for "chastens" is poorly translated. The Greek word here is *paideuo*[4], which means "child training". It does **not** mean "to punish". *Pai* is where you get the word "pediatrician" (a doctor who specializes in treating children), while *deuo* means "to teach a child". You will find that the translation of the word *paideuo* as "child training" is more consistent with the context of the passage. Read on. The next verse says, "If you endure chastening, God deals with you as with sons; for what son is there whom a father does not chasten?" Even if you do not know that the Greek word for "chastens" here actually means "child training", you would be able to deduce it from this verse, which tells us that because God deals with us as sons, He disciplines us just as earthly fathers would their sons.

Would you give your son a terminal disease to teach him a lesson? Then, why do you think that your Father in heaven would do that?

Now, think about this for a moment: Would you give your son a terminal disease to teach him a lesson?

No way!

Then, why do you think that your Father in heaven would do that?

Let me give you a Bible study tip: When you read the Bible, be sure to read everything within its context because when you take the "text" out of its "context", what you are left with is a "con"! Many believers are hoodwinked into believing "cons" and erroneous teachings when something is lifted and taught out of its context.

I've never understood how people could see a terminal illness as a lesson from God. They say things like, "God gave that person a terminal illness to teach him patience". My friend, what lesson is there to learn after the person dies from that terminal illness?

You need to be alive for the lesson to be useful. There is no use for patience when one is dead!

Let me say this again to make it very clear: Sicknesses, diseases and accidents are **not** lessons from God! When you train a child, you give lessons that teach the child things that will benefit him in the future. There is **no** future if the child is dead. God would never use sicknesses and accidents to teach you and me — His children — lessons!

God's righteous anger against sin has been satisfied and today, we can expect only love from Him, not judgment. We can expect grace, not punishment. We will never be punished in the old covenant way ever again! In the new covenant, while there is no longer any punishment, there is **child training**, but God does not train His children with sicknesses, diseases and accidents any more than you and I do!

How Would You Discipline Your Children?

If you ask me whether there is correction in the Christian walk, I will say, "Yes, absolutely." But it is important that we understand that God corrects us the way a father corrects his son. Would you torture your own son with sicknesses, diseases and pains to teach him a lesson?

Would you force your son to put his hand into the fire until the smell of burning flesh fills the kitchen to teach him not to play with fire or to touch a gas stove? Can you imagine doing that and saying, "Do you know why daddy is doing this? It's because daddy loves you. Now, you know that fire can burn you, so don't play with matches anymore"?

Would you drive your car over your daughter's legs to teach her the dangers of playing by the side of the road? Can you imagine saying, "Come, girl, be strong! Daddy loves you, so he is doing this for your good. You will understand it some day"? Of course not! Parents who do such things should be incarcerated! There is a "special home" for parents who are like that.

Sadly, there are still Christians who accuse our heavenly Father of afflicting them with sicknesses and accidents to teach them lessons. With teachings like that, it's no wonder believers are wandering in the wilderness, thinking that God is angry with them and looking for opportunities to destroy them. What kind of God do you think we have? He is our *Abba*! *Abba* is the most affectionate term you can use to address a father in the Hebrew language. It means "Daddy"! Do you really think that your Daddy God will punish you this way?

If you earthly fathers know how to give good gifts to your children, how much more your heavenly Daddy who loves you! I don't have to tell you that sicknesses, diseases and accidents aren't good gifts! They are from the devil, and because of Jesus' finished work, we have been redeemed from every evil work and curse. We can receive protection from every evil occurrence, sickness and disease. By the stripes on Jesus' back, we are healed!

Read Psalm 103 and look at all the benefits that Jesus has purchased for you with His own body:

> Psalm 103:1–5
> ¹Bless the Lord, O my soul; and all that is within me, bless His holy name! ²Bless the Lord, O my soul, and forget not all His benefits: ³Who forgives

all your iniquities, who heals all your diseases, ⁴who redeems your life from destruction, who crowns you with lovingkindness and tender mercies, ⁵who satisfies your mouth with good things, so that your youth is renewed like the eagle's.

Come on, believers. Read this Psalm every day and do not forget any of the benefits of Jesus' finished work! He forgives you of all your sins, heals you of all your diseases, redeems you from destruction, crowns you with lovingkindness and satisfies your mouth with good things so that your youth is renewed like the eagle's. Don't you accuse Him of giving anyone diseases or accidents!

By the way, if the people who insist that God uses sicknesses to punish believers truly believe that, why are they going from doctor to doctor trying to get healed? That's inconsistent! On the one hand, they say that their sicknesses are from the Lord, but on the other hand, they are trying to get rid of them.

Stop believing the LIE that God gives you sicknesses, diseases and accidents to punish you or teach you a lesson.

I always tell my congregation not to leave their brains at home when they come to church. Stop believing the LIE that God gives you sicknesses, diseases and accidents to punish you or teach you a lesson. I honestly find it difficult to understand why there are believers today who fight vehemently for the right to be sick, broke and defeated when God is full of grace and mercy, and wants us to be healthy, prosperous and protected from all evil occurrences! Let's start to expect good gifts from the

Lord. Reject anything which even remotely suggests that God is angry with you, and is going to discipline you with sicknesses and accidents when you fail!

What About Paul's 'Thorn In The Flesh'?

"Pastor Prince, what about the 'thorn in the flesh' that Paul suffered from? Wasn't it a sickness?"

Well, let's see what Paul said about this "thorn in the flesh": "And lest I should be exalted above measure by the abundance of the revelations, a **thorn in the flesh** was given to me, a **messenger of Satan** to buffet me, lest I be exalted above measure."[5] Nowhere in the verse does it say that the "thorn in the flesh" is a sickness or disease.

The Bible, not human conjectures, must be used to interpret the Bible. Thorns in the Bible refer to personalities that harass you. Even in our English language, we use the phrase "a pain in the neck" to describe someone who harasses or irritates us. It is just an expression and does not refer to an actual pain or disease in our necks.

In the same sense, the "thorn in the flesh" that Paul had was not a disease. In the book of Numbers, you will find that the enemies of Israel were described as "thorns" — "But if you do not drive out the inhabitants of the land from before you, then it shall be that those whom you let remain shall be irritants in your eyes and **thorns in your sides**, and **they shall harass you** in the land where you dwell."[6] Let the Bible interpret the Bible!

Paul himself tells us what the thorn is. He called it "a

messenger of Satan". So it was clearly in reference to an evil personality who instigated people to attack, gossip and backbite Paul everywhere he went preaching the gospel. And what did God tell Paul about this thorn in the flesh? He said, "Just be cool, Paul, My grace is sufficient for you."[7] So Paul did not suffer any sickness or disease. He was so anointed with the resurrection life of our Lord Jesus that even when his handkerchief touched the sick, they were healed.

Are You Hearing The Good News?

Recently, a lady in our church attended a prophetic seminar and a so-called "prophet" told her that the reason her son had a disability was that there was "sin in her life".

Have you been fed this lie before? Have you been told that the negative things that you may be experiencing are a result of God's discipline because of your sins? My friend, that is utter nonsense and utter cruelty. God does not punish sin in the new covenant with sicknesses and diseases because sin **has already been punished** on the body of Jesus. His blood has already been shed for the forgiveness of all our sins. When you received Jesus Christ into your life, all your sins were washed away. It is a finished work.

Anyway, the lady approached our church leaders for help and they shared with her that God has already punished sin in the body of Jesus. She then went back to seek this "prophet" to ask what he meant. When he saw her, he tried to avoid her. When she finally got to speak to him and asked him what he meant, he just said, "Oh, that was what the Lord told me to tell you." (My friend, don't be intimidated when someone flippantly or conveniently uses the name of the Lord as an excuse to tell you things in your life that are not scriptural.) He then produced a name card and explained that he ran these prophetic meetings part-time — he had a day job and was only a "part-time prophet".

This is downright cruel, isn't it? God's people are precious. They are looking for solutions, answers and help, and we have "prophets" like these going around in Christian circles condemning believers, convincing them that God is angry with them, and that He punishes them with sicknesses, diseases and accidents!

The good news of Jesus always liberates and
His perfect love removes every fear.

Come, my friend, it is time to rise above all these teachings that have no biblical basis, and which are not based on the new covenant of Jesus Christ our Lord. The Lord wants believers to be "wise as serpents and harmless as doves"[8]. Open your eyes and see the evil conspiracy of the devil to keep believers in bondage with erroneous teachings about God that are not based on the new covenant of grace. Whenever you hear a teaching that puts fear in your heart, you can be sure that what you are hearing is not the gospel, or good news, of Jesus. The good news of Jesus always liberates and His perfect love removes every fear. The good news always imparts faith and exalts the finished work of Jesus Christ on the cross!

Chapter 7

The Gospel That Paul Preached

Beloved, you must eradicate this idea that forgiveness of sins is a basic teaching. Think about it: If it is really basic, why is it that so many believers miss it and are defeated by their lack of understanding?

The power of the gospel is to live each waking moment having the confidence that all your sins have been forgiven. Contrast this with living with a perpetual sense of guilt and condemnation that comes with thinking that when you sin, fellowship with God is broken, He no longer answers your prayers, He is far away from you, and until you repent and confess all your sins, the Holy Spirit will not return. Many Christians still have this impression that the onus is on them to keep God's forgiveness by their own doing. So how can forgiveness of sins be a **basic** teaching? There are too many believers and even pastors, preachers and leaders, many with wonderful titles and Bible school credentials, who are still confused about the teaching of forgiveness.

The best way to understand the gospel, therefore, is not to base it on what you have heard from various sources, but to go back to what the apostles preached in the early church. Let's examine what Apostle Paul, the apostle of the new covenant, preached. After all, Paul was the apostle whom God appointed to preach the gospel of grace. He received more revelation on the new covenant of grace than all the other apostles put together, and was responsible for writing more than two-thirds of the New Testament.

Paul's Preaching Was Full Of Power

Acts 14:8–10

[8]And in Lystra a certain man without strength in his feet was sitting, a cripple from his mother's womb, who had never walked. [9]This man heard Paul speaking. Paul, observing him intently and seeing that he had faith to be healed, [10]said with a loud voice, "Stand up straight on your feet!" And he leaped and walked.

Observe how the Holy Spirit describes this man: One, he was without strength in his feet. Two, he was a cripple from his mother's womb and three, he had never walked. The Holy Spirit used three different descriptions to emphasize how the man **could not walk** and was facing a (seemingly) impossible situation. Yet, when he heard Paul speaking, he was filled with faith to be healed!

How did the man come to be filled with faith?

The Bible says that faith comes by hearing and hearing the word of Christ[1]. The man at Lystra was filled with faith because he heard the word of **Christ**! I know that in most of your Bible translations, it says that faith comes by hearing "the word of

God". But if you study the original Greek word for "God" here, it is not *Theos* for "God", but rather *Christos* for "Christ"[2].

You see, faith does not come by simply hearing the word of God because the word of God would encompass everything in the Bible, including the law of Moses. There is no impartation of faith when you hear the Ten Commandments preached. Faith only comes by hearing the word of Christ. This doesn't mean that you should only listen to preaching from the portions in your Bible that are printed in red which indicate that Jesus spoke those words. (Putting what Jesus said in the Bible in red letters is a human convention anyway.) To hear the word of Christ is to hear preaching and teaching that have been filtered through the new covenant of grace and Jesus' finished work.

Only when Christ is preached will faith be imparted.

You **can** preach from Genesis to Revelation from the perspective of Jesus and His grace. In my church, I am known to preach and teach extensively from both the Old and the New Testaments. After all, Christ is in the Old Testament **concealed**, and in the New Testament **revealed**. In the Old Testament, you will find shadows of Christ in the five Levitical offerings, the tabernacle of Moses and even in the high priest's garments, but it takes a new covenant minister to draw Christ out. Only when Christ is preached will faith be imparted. Hallelujah! I love talking about Jesus!

What Did Paul Preach?

Let's get back to the man at Lystra. What could Paul have been preaching that was so powerful that it imparted such faith to this man so that he could believe for healing in his impossible situation?

"Well, Pastor Prince, I think that Paul was teaching divine healing."

Let's look at the passage. The Bible only says that Paul was "preaching the gospel" in Lystra³. It doesn't say that he was teaching divine healing. Don't misunderstand me. There **is** a place for teaching divine healing. I even have a whole series of teachings on divine healing. But faith for healing doesn't come only when you hear teaching on healing. Faith for healing can also come when you are simply hearing the gospel! Anyway, I wanted to know what Paul preached at Lystra, so that I could preach the same message and impart faith to people. So I asked the Lord what Paul preached. I mean, how could the Holy Spirit leave out something so important? If only He had recorded it in the Bible!

Then, the Lord told me that He **had** recorded one of Paul's sermons in the Bible. He told me to go to the previous chapter and showed me that right there, in Acts chapter 13, the Holy Spirit had preserved a sample of the gospel that Paul preached everywhere he went. So there it was, Paul's sermon recorded for us by the Holy Spirit, word for word! Paul covered quite a lot of ground, but you have to see for yourself what the main thrust of Paul's sermon was and where it climaxed:

> Acts 13:38–39
> ³⁸Therefore let it be known to you, brethren, that through this Man [Jesus] is preached to you the forgiveness of sins; ³⁹and by Him everyone who believes is justified from all things from which you could not be justified by the law of Moses.

The power of the gospel that Paul preached is found in the forgiveness of all your sins for "everyone who believes". There is no other qualification for being forgiven of your sins. The old covenant was based on justification by works (obedience to the Ten Commandments). You had to perform to be forgiven. But the new covenant of grace is based entirely on justification by faith (believing in Jesus Christ). Can you see the radical difference? The demand is no longer on you, but on Christ. This is the good news: All who **believe** in Jesus receive the forgiveness of all their sins and are justified from all things! Good news? Hallelujah! There is no better news than this!

All who believe in Jesus receive the forgiveness of all their sins and are justified from all things!

I can just imagine how the man at Lystra responded when he heard Paul proclaiming that he could be justified from all things if he only believed on Jesus. When he heard Paul preaching about the good news of Christ, faith came and filled his heart. With tears in his eyes, he must have turned away from his lame feet and rejected every thought that he had been lame from birth because he was being punished for his or his parents' sins. Instead, he must have believed with all his heart that if he believed in Jesus Christ, he would be forgiven of all his sins. Probably choked with tears, he whispered, "I believe." And at that very moment, he heard a loud voice saying, "Stand up straight on your feet!" It was Paul commanding him and before he had time to hesitate, he found himself leaping to his feet with joy, and for the first time in his life, he walked!

The Gospel Imparts Faith

Notice that Paul did not lay his hands on the man to heal him. There wasn't an altar call for those who wanted healing. The faith to be healed came from just listening to the gospel of Jesus Christ. We have experienced this time and again in our services. As people are sitting in the service, and hearing the gospel of grace and Jesus' finished work being preached, healing miracles break forth!

The more revelation you get of His finished work, the more you will receive an impartation of faith for any situation, even the seemingly impossible ones!

One of my dear friends, Marcel Gaasenbeek, shared with me about a wonderful healing miracle which took place in his car as he was driving to Romania with a few friends. Marcel is a pastor of a dynamic grace church in Holland, and on this particular day, he was on his way to Romania for a preaching engagement. He was listening to one of my sermons in his car, something that he did often.

Lulled by the monotony of the long drive, one of Marcel's friends dozed off in the back seat. This friend had been involved in a jet-ski accident some years ago and since then, he often suffered sharp pains in his back. Somehow, through the fog of sleep, he heard me preach this: "Jesus has already healed you and the devil is the one giving you lying symptoms in your body." He said "Amen!" in his heart, agreeing that Jesus **had already** healed him by taking his sin and bearing his curse. At that moment, he felt the power of God go through him, and today, he is completely healed! All the pain in his back is gone!

That's the power of hearing and hearing the gospel of Jesus. That's how faith comes! The more of Jesus you hear, the more of His grace you receive. And the more revelation you get of His finished work, the more you will receive an impartation of faith for any situation, even the seemingly impossible ones!

A Supernatural Encounter With The Chimes

In the year 2000, I preached a sermon titled, *'Aleph-Tav'* — *Jesus' Signature In The Bible*, during one of our regular midweek Bible study meetings. *Aleph* is the first letter in the Hebrew alphabet and *tav* is the last. The message was all about the person of Jesus, and how He revealed Himself to be the Alpha and Omega, the Beginning and the End. As I was preaching, I came to the two verses in Paul's sermon that we have just covered and I read them out loud:

> Acts 13:38–39
> [38]Therefore let it be known to you, brethren, that through this Man [Jesus] is preached to you the **forgiveness of sins**; [39]and by Him everyone who believes is justified from all things from which you could not be justified by the law of Moses.

The moment I finished quoting the verses, the chimes that were on the stage behind me started to play by themselves! There was nobody near the chimes. My musicians do not sit on the stage behind me when I preach. Everyone was seated in front of me as usual.

It wasn't just a soft tinkle. The chimes played beautifully by themselves, back and forth, back and forth, back and forth, from the first to the last of the chimes. This was witnessed by more than a thousand people who were at the service. Everyone in the service could hear the crystal clear notes coming from the chimes. The anointing of God swept through the auditorium. Some people started crying, while others glorified the Lord and started clapping. It was beautiful.

It was the Lord.

Exactly at the point when I had finished reading the two verses on the forgiveness of sins, the Holy Spirit fell upon our congregation and hugged us. It was as if the Holy Spirit was saying a resounding "Amen" to the two verses.

Anyone who has heard the sounds can vouch that there was no way the waves of music from the chimes could have been caused by a gust of wind or some other natural cause. It was a supernatural event. God was confirming His Word with a sign. The chimes were played very deliberately. I can just imagine an angel of God running his fingers down the length of the chimes softly, before allowing His fingers to sweep through the chimes again... and again. It's impossible for me to describe completely what had happened to you in this book. You have to hear it for yourself!

By the way, this service, like all our regular services, was captured on both audio and video recordings. If you do get hold of the recordings, you will be able to hear the chimes playing distinctly. Unfortunately, you won't be able to see the chimes in the DVD recording, even though you will see a shot of me turning to the chimes and asking the congregation to look at them. The cameraman was caught off-guard. He was completely stunned by this supernatural occurrence and just kept the camera focused on me.

Now, let me share with you why that night was particularly significant to me. During that time, there were some vindictive emails being circulated about our church and me. There were several false accusations by people who called me all sorts of nasty things. Unbeknown to me, many of our church members had read those poison emails and were very affected. That evening, after the service, many of them came to me and said, "You know, Pastor Prince, I came here tonight praying and asking God to show me if the accusations about you in the emails were true. I didn't want to hear from the people who wrote the emails, or even from you. I wanted God to speak to me."

Many of them came and shared with me what they had prayed for, and their accounts were almost identical. They had read the emails and wanted to hear from God. I was stunned! So many of my church members were asking God to speak to them, and when the chimes played so supernaturally, it was a confirmation from the Lord about the accuracy of what I had been preaching and they decided to disregard the poison emails.

Without me even knowing about the venom that was being circulated about me, the Lord had vindicated me. He is my defense. Hallelujah! Through the years, many people have written and said all kinds of horrible things about me. I have been called all kinds of names, but I have never retaliated in any way. My trust and confidence is in the Lord. I have never lifted a pen or spoken one negative word against any of my accusers. I don't come against those who oppose me. In every situation, I just pray that it redounds to the greatest glory for Jesus and to the greatest good for the body of Christ.

Persecution Against The Gospel Of Grace

In any case, I was not unprepared for the persecution. The Lord had warned me a long time ago that there was a price for preaching the gospel that Paul preached. He told me that people would call me names and persecute me. And the persecution has indeed come. But the persecution has come mainly from people who believe in justification through the law and man's self-efforts.

This is consistent with what Jesus Himself experienced. When He walked on this earth, the only people who could not receive from Him were the Pharisees, the experts on the law. They knew the law inside out, but not the author of the law who was standing right before them. Isn't that amazing? It shows us that legalism blinds people — legalistic people have eyes that do not see and ears that do not hear! In contrast, those who acknowledged that they were helpless sinners (the prostitutes, corrupt tax collectors, uncouth fishermen and social outcasts) did not know the law as the Pharisees did, but they received and welcomed Jesus with joy!

"But Pastor Prince, if what you are preaching is really from the Lord, then it will not cause division."

Let's look at what happened in Acts 13. After Paul had finished preaching, the Gentiles begged that the same sermon be preached to them the next Sabbath. On the next Sabbath, the Bible records that "almost the whole city"[4] of Antioch gathered to hear Paul preach on the forgiveness of sins, justification by faith through the cross of Jesus and the grace of God. For the whole city to show up to listen to Paul, the good news that he was preaching must have spread like wildfire across the city!

However, notice that there was one group of people that was very unhappy with what Paul was preaching — the Pharisees or what I call the "religious mafia". The Bible says that when they saw the multitudes, "they were **filled with envy**; and **contradicting** and **blaspheming**, they **opposed the things** spoken by Paul"[5]. These legalistic keepers of the law are still around today. The law blinds them. There is a veil over their eyes and they cannot see that the old covenant of the law is no longer valid. When they see believers impacted by grace, they become "filled with envy" because they have worked so hard and depended on their own efforts to achieve their own sense of self-righteousness.

Jesus did not come to bring us laws and more laws.
He came to bring us abundant life through His grace!

So when the Pharisees saw believers under grace receiving miracles, blessings and breakthroughs by the power of Jesus Christ, and being clothed with His perfect righteousness without works and without any self-effort, they were filled with envy. In their envy, they contradicted, blasphemed and opposed Paul. Division was caused not because Paul was not preaching the gospel of Jesus Christ, but precisely because he was preaching the gospel of grace which was from the Lord.

Grace contravenes the traditions of man. It makes nothing of man's own efforts and makes everything of Jesus Christ. This angered the religious mob of His day.

Paul's sermon ended with a firm warning for those who refused to believe in God's grace and forgiveness in the new covenant:

> Acts 13:41
> [41]'Behold, you despisers, marvel and perish! For I work a work in your days, a work which you will by no means believe, though one were to declare it to you.'

This warning given by Paul was not for the whole congregation. It was only for those who rejected the gospel of grace. You see, those who blindly insist on holding on to justification by the law of Moses will "by no means believe" when they hear about justification by faith, and will say in their hearts that it is too good to be true. The law is a veil over their eyes and they cannot see God's grace. But praise God that when Jesus died on the cross, the veil that had separated unrighteous man from a righteous God was forever removed. The Bible says that when Jesus yielded up His spirit, the veil of the temple was "torn in two from top to bottom"[6]. The veil is a picture of the law of Moses. Once the law was removed, man was made righteous by faith in Jesus' blood and the way into the Holy of Holies was opened! Too good to be true? It **is** true, my friend, and that's why the gospel of Jesus Christ is good news for us today. Jesus did not come to bring us laws and more laws. He came to bring us abundant life through His grace[7]!

Let's come back to the question of the gospel of grace causing division.

Is it possible to preach the gospel of grace and cause division to the extent that people would even want to kick you out of their cities? Yes! This happened in the early church. Paul was "speaking boldly in the Lord" and preaching "the word of His grace" when in the very next verse, you find that **"the multitude of the city was divided**: part sided with the Jews, and part with the apostles"[8]. There was even a "violent attempt... made by both the Gentiles and Jews, with their rulers, to abuse and stone them"[9].

Thus, it is clear that when you preach the same good news that Paul preached, it doesn't mean that everybody will be united and say, "Hallelujah!" There will be those who would want to kick you out of their cities and say all kinds of things about you to assassinate your character. But just because there was division, it certainly did not mean that what Paul preached was not true. That is precisely why Paul warned that even when God declares something so good, there are those who will refuse to believe — "you will by no means believe, though one were to declare it to you".

If you are believing the Lord for a miraculous breakthrough, then be sure that you are hearing "the word of His grace" and not the word of His law.

That is why the gospel that Paul preached is not a man-pleasing gospel. Paul did not preach to be welcomed everywhere he went. He preached the truth of the gospel even if it meant being stoned by his opponents and being expelled from cities. He did it because the gospel is THE POWER OF GOD to salvation!

Make sure that you are hearing the gospel that Paul preached. The Bible declares that the Lord bore witness to "**the word of His grace**, granting signs and wonders to be done by their hands"[10]. You see, the Lord bears witness only to "the word of His grace". If you are believing the Lord for a miraculous breakthrough or want to see more power in your life, body, finances, career and ministry, then be sure that you are hearing "the word of His grace" and not the word of His law.

By the way, look at how Paul had to preach first before the Lord could bear witness to the word of His grace with signs and wonders. Preaching the good news first is also consistent with Jesus' style. Everywhere He went, He went teaching and preaching to the multitudes **before** healing them. There are some people who come to me for prayer for their conditions before the service, and it is clear that they are not interested in hearing the gospel, or any teaching or preaching. They just want prayer. But God's way is always teaching and preaching first, followed by healing. He confirms the word of His grace with signs and wonders.

Are you faced with an impossible situation today? Are you trusting the Lord for a breakthrough? If so, I encourage you to get hold of good teachings that are full of the good news of Jesus. Faith will be imparted to you as you hear more and more of Jesus. You will stop being preoccupied with yourself, your lack and your weaknesses, and you will become fully occupied with Jesus, His beauty, His perfection and His grace!

The Gospel That Paul Preached

My only endeavor is to preach the same gospel that Paul

preached, and no other gospel. Preaching any other gospel was a serious matter to Paul. In fact, he pronounced a double curse on those who preached a different gospel. Paul said, "Even if we, or an angel from heaven, preach any other gospel to you than what we have preached to you, let him be accursed."[11] And as if that first curse was not sufficient, he reiterated, "As we have said before, so now I say again, if anyone preaches any other gospel to you than what you have received, let him be accursed."[12] Now, my mama didn't raise no fool. I decided years ago that people can say what they want about me, but I'm not coming under any curse for preaching any other gospel!

Is the gospel of Jesus Christ the power of God to salvation

  (a) for everyone who keeps the law of Moses?

  (b) for everyone who confesses all his sins?

  (c) for everyone who fasts and prays long prayers?

It is none of the above. It is (d) for everyone who believes! This is the "justification by faith" that Paul preached and this is what I will preach! Under the new covenant of grace, we are justified not by our right behavior, but by our right believing in Jesus Christ. Through this Man is preached to you the forgiveness of all your sins. Do you believe in Jesus? If your answer is "yes", then don't let anyone add more conditions to your forgiveness — you are already forgiven of all your sins simply because you believe in Jesus! Nothing more, nothing less. This is the gospel that Paul preached. And when you get a hold of this truth and simply believe it, you'll see the power of God come into your situation to turn it around for good!

Chapter 8

The Main Clause Of The New Covenant

When I was a teenager, I got hold of a teaching from a book which said that a Christian can commit the "unpardonable sin". Have you heard this "unpardonable sin" teaching before? This erroneous teaching says that all sins can be forgiven, but if you commit the sin of blaspheming the Holy Spirit[1], there is no forgiveness. That's how this sin came to be known as the "unpardonable sin".

As a young Christian, I did not understand why other believers didn't seem to be affected by the thought that they could actually commit the unpardonable sin. For me, I was really frightened. My conscience was very sensitive and the more I thought about the possibility of committing the unpardonable sin, the more I was convinced that I had committed that sin! My thoughts became increasingly negative and I even started to doubt God. This gave me even more reason to believe that I had indeed blasphemed the Holy Spirit.

I went to my church leaders at that time to seek counsel, but instead of leading me to the new covenant of grace, they told me that it was indeed possible for a Christian to commit the unpardonable sin. By then, I was getting more and more depressed. The devil was oppressing me with thoughts of guilt and condemnation. Plagued by such thoughts, I would go to Orchard Road, Singapore's main shopping belt, and I would witness to the people on the streets about Jesus, all the time believing that I had committed the unpardonable sin. I thought that if I got these people saved, God would see them when they made it to heaven and perhaps remember Joseph Prince who would be in hell. I honestly believed that! The amazing thing was that the evangelistic anointing was already flowing in me then and many did actually receive Jesus, even though I thought that I was not going to make it to heaven.

Discovering The Gospel Of Grace

The more I believed that I still had unforgiven sins, the more I believed that I had used up all of God's grace in my life. No one taught me about the blood of Jesus, or showed me that my behavior was actually dishonoring the blood of Christ and negating Jesus' work on the cross for me. No one preached the good news to me, so at that time, I really thought that my sins were greater than God's grace. I felt like I was losing my mind and on the verge of a nervous breakdown. My mind literally felt like it was about to snap and I became so afraid that I would be committed to a mental institution.

It was through this tumultuous journey that I began to understand the grace of our Lord Jesus. I now know beyond a shadow of a doubt that a Christian **cannot** commit the unpardonable sin. Be careful when you hear any teaching that gives you the impression that believers can commit the unpardonable sin of blaspheming the Holy Spirit. There are times when the devil puts negative thoughts about the Holy Spirit in your mind, or when you yourself say something negative about the Holy Spirit. This may lead you to wonder and worry if you have committed the unpardonable sin. Well, let me declare once and for all that **there is no sin that a Christian is not forgiven of**. When you understand why God sent the Holy Spirit, you will realize that the unpardonable sin is simply to consistently reject Jesus!

The Bible tells us that the Holy Spirit came to testify of and witness about Jesus Christ. Jesus said, "The Spirit of truth who proceeds from the Father, He will testify of Me."[2] To blaspheme the Holy Spirit is therefore to **continually reject the person of Christ** whom the Holy Spirit testifies of. Study the Word of God carefully. Who was Jesus speaking to when He spoke of the unpardonable sin? He was speaking to the Pharisees, who continually rejected Him as their Savior and plotted to kill Him on several occasions. They even accused Him of having an unclean spirit, saying, "He has Beelzebub. By the ruler of the demons He casts out demons."[3] Jesus' response was, "Assuredly, I say to you, all sins will be forgiven... but he who blasphemes against the Holy Spirit never has forgiveness, but is subject to eternal condemnation."[4] Why did He say that? The next verse tells us that it is "**because they said, 'He has an unclean spirit.'**"

The Holy Spirit is present even today to witness about Jesus. Therefore, to blaspheme the Holy Spirit is to keep on rejecting the gospel of Jesus and to depend on your own efforts to be saved. Jesus was warning the Pharisees not to commit this sin, and to stop rejecting Him. This clearly does not apply to the believer. You see, in reading the Bible, it is important to note who the words were spoken to and to ascertain if the words are relevant for the believer. In this case, Jesus was speaking to the Pharisees who had rejected Him and who even made claims that He had an unclean spirit. Imagine their audacity! As for you, my friend, have full assurance in your heart that it is impossible for a believer to commit the unpardonable sin. A believer has already received the gift of eternal life and will never be "subject to eternal condemnation".

Rightly Dividing The Word

There is a lot of confusion and wrong believing in the church today because many Christians read their Bibles without rightly dividing the old and new covenants. They don't realize that even some of the words which Jesus spoke in the four gospels (Matthew, Mark, Luke and John) are part of the old covenant. They were spoken **before** the cross as He had not yet died. The new covenant only begins **after** the cross, when the Holy Spirit was given on the day of Pentecost.

There is a lot of confusion and wrong believing in the church today because many Christians read their Bibles without rightly dividing the old and new covenants.

I know that our Bibles are divided into the Old Testament and the New Testament, which begins with the four gospels. However, it is important to realize that **the cross made a difference**! Some of what Jesus said **before** the cross and what He said **after** the cross were spoken under completely different covenants. You also need to see who Jesus was speaking to. At times, He was speaking to the Pharisees, who boasted in their perfect law-keeping. With them, Jesus brought the law to its pristine standard, such that it was impossible for any man to keep.

"But Pastor Prince, I believe that we should do everything that Jesus said!"

My friend, Jesus said, "If your right eye causes you to sin, pluck it out and cast it from you… And if your right hand causes you to sin, cut it off and cast it from you; for it is more profitable for you that one of your members perish, than for your whole body to be cast into hell."[5] Have you done that?

Do you think that Jesus expects us to do all that, or does He want us to rightly divide the Word, and understand who He was speaking to in that passage and what He meant? If the church were to obey everything that Jesus said in that passage, then it would look like a huge amputation ward! (I hope that I don't hear you saying, "Pastor Prince, you should have written this book earlier — I have already plucked out one eye and severed one arm!")

Come on, Jesus said all that to bring the law back to its pristine standard, a standard that ensured that no man could keep the law. He said all that so that man would come to the end of depending on himself and begin to see that he desperately needs a savior. So when we read the words of Jesus in the four gospels, it is necessary for us to rightly divide the Word and understand **who** Jesus was speaking to.

Let me give you another example. You may have heard some preachers yelling at unbelievers and using the term "a brood of vipers". But Jesus **never** called sinners — not even the prostitutes and corrupt tax collectors — "a brood of vipers". Never! Those harsh words by Jesus were reserved only for the Pharisees[6], whose fixation on the law blinded them from seeing God in the flesh — Jesus, who gave the law in the first place and who came to fulfill the law on man's behalf. So learn to rightly divide the Word of God whenever you read the Bible. Not everything that Jesus said was spoken to the church.

Feed On The Letters Of Apostle Paul

Paul's letters were written to the church and are thus for our benefit today. God raised him up to write the words of the ascended Jesus, who is seated today at the Father's right hand. That is why, when it comes to reading the Bible, I always encourage new believers in our church to begin with the letters of Paul. (Many new believers like to start with the book of Revelation or Genesis, without first getting a foundation in the gospel of grace through reading the letters of Paul.)

Have you noticed that Paul never mentioned the unpardonable sin? Not one time, in all his letters to the churches, did he warn Christians about the unpardonable sin. If Christians could commit the unpardonable sin, he should have mentioned it in every epistle that he wrote. On the other hand, Paul emphasized that Jesus, by His death on the cross, has made us "alive together with Him, having forgiven you **all** trespasses"[7]. I have checked the original Greek word for "all"[8] in this verse and guess what? "All" means ALL! Jesus, with His own blood, has forgiven you of ALL your sins, so there is **no** sin that is unpardonable! By one perfect sacrifice, Jesus has cleansed you of the sins of your entire life and you are now sealed with the promise of eternal life! Now, this is good news that will establish your heart with grace and confidence.

God does not leave you wondering whether you are saved or not. He tells you outright that you are His and that nothing can ever separate you from the love of Christ. Not even sin because His blood is greater than your sin! Knowing that all your sins are forgiven is crucial for your health, peace of mind, wholeness and wellness. My struggle with the unpardonable sin during my teenage years is a case in point. The more you believe that all your sins are forgiven by the blood of Jesus, the more you will become whole — body, soul and spirit!

Knowing that all your sins are forgiven is crucial for your health, peace of mind, wholeness and wellness.

I hope that by now, you can see the dangers of lifting the Word of God out of its context. We have to be careful not to take a verse out of its context and build a teaching or doctrine around it. Bible teachings have to be confirmed by several supporting verses and these have to be studied within their proper contexts. When you hear teachings that put fear in your heart and place you under bondage, don't just swallow them hook, line, sinker, fisherman and boots. Look at the context of the verse, and see if it is a new covenant truth or an old covenant teaching. Who was the verse spoken or written to, and how is it applicable to you today? Just remember that all new covenant truths exalt Jesus and His finished work. Hallelujah!

The Main Clause Of The New Covenant

It is sad that you hardly hear the main clause of the new covenant being preached today:

> Hebrews 8:8–12
> [8]... "Behold, the days are coming, says the Lord, when I will make a new covenant... [9]not according to the covenant that I made with their fathers in the day when I took them by the hand to lead them out of the land of Egypt... [10]For this is the covenant that I will make... I will put My laws in their mind and write them on their hearts; and I will be their God, and they shall be My people... [12]**For I will be merciful to their unrighteousness, and their sins and their lawless deeds I will remember no more.**"

"I will be merciful to their unrighteousness, and their sins and their lawless deeds I will remember no more." Memorize this, beloved, for this is the main and final clause of the new covenant!

Unfortunately, it seems that what the average Christian believes today is the complete opposite. They believe that God is **not** merciful to their sins. When something goes wrong, inwardly they think, "Well, the rooster has come home to roost. My past sins have caught up with me. All these terrible things are happening to my family and my finances because of the sins that I have committed." When they have a flat tire, they start thinking to themselves, "What sin is God punishing me for now?" This kind of thinking is so prevalent in the church because Christians don't really believe that they are under the new covenant.

The problem with the church today is **wrong believing**. I'm sorry to tell you this, but if you refuse to believe what God has said about the forgiveness of sins in the new covenant, then you are actually in disobedience. Jesus Himself defined the new covenant for us at the last supper when He said, "This is My blood of the **new covenant**, which is shed for many for the **remission of sins**."[9] The main clause of the new covenant is the forgiveness of all your sins because of the shed blood of Jesus Christ. I don't care how many good deeds you have done, how much money you have given to charity or what leadership position you hold. If you do not believe the main clause of the new covenant, you are in disobedience.

God does not keep an itemized account of all your failures.

God put the main clause of the new covenant as the last clause to show us that it is this final clause that makes everything work. If you don't believe the main and final clause, you are rejecting the new covenant and negating the finished work of Jesus. The new covenant says that God is merciful to **all** your unrighteousness, and has forgotten your sins plus your lawless deeds. If God says that He has forgotten them, then He has truly forgotten them. Who are we to contradict Him? God cannot lie!

"But how can God forget my sins?"

He can because He is God! If He said it, then He has done it. You know that sin you committed many years ago? **God has**

forgotten it. Contrary to what you might have been taught, God does not keep an itemized account of all your failures. There is no big projector screen in heaven to show all your sins from the day you were born to the day you return to heaven. All records of your sins have been incinerated by the blood of Jesus when He cried out, "It is finished!"[10] His blood has removed the sins of your entire life. When God looks at you today, He sees you covered with Jesus' blood and completely righteous.

Only the devil, you yourself and the people around you will bring your sins to your remembrance. So when you are weighed down by the mistakes of your past, run to God and lean on His grace! Why? For He will be merciful to your unrighteousness, and your sins and your lawless deeds He will remember no more. This is the main clause of the new covenant of grace!

Chapter 9

The Waterfall Of Forgiveness

I n the previous chapter, we established that the main and final clause of the new covenant is captured in Hebrews 8:12 — "I will be merciful to their unrighteousness, and their sins and their lawless deeds I will remember no more."

"Pastor Prince, if people know that all their sins have already been forgiven, won't they go ahead and sin?"

Well, I have yet to encounter such a creature. I have yet to encounter anyone who, after receiving the grace of our Lord Jesus, says to himself, "Now I can go out and sin!" However, I have encountered people who have given up and walked away from God, not because they were evil and desired to sin, but because they were sincere and had consistently failed in their attempts to keep the laws of the old covenant, and ended up feeling like hypocrites. On the other hand, because of the teaching of new covenant truths, I have received countless written testimonies and personally witnessed precious lives, marriages and families transformed by the grace of our Lord Jesus.

I had a couple come up to me one time, telling me that they would like to be married in our church. I saw that they were accompanied by a few children and asked if they had been married before. (I was thinking that the kids might have come from their previous marriages.) Smiling widely, they told me that they had in fact been married to each other before, but that they had been separated for many years.

Somehow, separately, they both started attending New Creation Church, and after listening to the teaching on forgiveness and God's grace, God began to restore their relationship and they wanted to be remarried. Isn't that wonderful? I also thought to myself that it must have been so wonderful for their children to actually get to witness their parents' wedding ceremony. (How many kids have that privilege?) My friend, that's the power of the gospel of Christ. It's about restoring marriages and mending broken lives!

The Revelation Of Forgiveness

My friend, knowing that you are completely forgiven destroys the power of sin in your life. I know how this revelation has changed me and transformed my life. Jesus Himself said that those who are forgiven much will love Him much. Those who are forgiven little (actually, these creatures do not exist because all of us have been forgiven much!), or I should say, those who **think** that they have been forgiven little will love Him only a little.

Do you remember the woman who brought an alabaster flask of fragrant oil and anointed Jesus' feet? Jesus said to Simon, a

---

Knowing that you are completely forgiven destroys the power of sin in your life.

Pharisee, "I entered your house; you gave Me no water for My feet, but she has washed My feet with her tears and wiped them with the hair of her head… Therefore I say to you, her sins, which are many, are forgiven, for she loved much. **But to whom little is forgiven, the same loves little.**"[1]

The more you realize that you have been forgiven much, actually, of **all** your sins, the more you will love the Lord Jesus. Forgiveness does not lead to a lifestyle of sin. It leads to a life of glorifying the Lord Jesus. What do you think the woman's response would have been after she had departed from Jesus? Would she have desired to continue living a life of sin, or would she, knowing that she has been forgiven much by God's grace, be strengthened to live a life that honored and glorified Jesus?

Come on, folks! All of us, including the author of this book, have been forgiven much. All of us have broken the Ten Commandments many times over. If we have not done so in action, then we have done so in our hearts and minds. Jesus said that if you are angry with your brother without a cause, you have committed murder, and if you look at a woman in lust, you have committed adultery with her in your heart[2]. So all of us have been forgiven much and there is no reason for us not to love Him much. The only reason people don't love Him much is that they **don't understand just how much they have been forgiven**. They are just like Simon the Pharisee, who was confident in his self-righteousness.

The Secret To Godliness

Many preachers are telling believers that they have to exhibit more Christian character, more self-control, more godliness and more brotherly kindness. My friend, I totally agree that all these qualities are good and necessary, but the question is, how do we develop them? How should we preachers help believers to exhibit more Christian character? When asked for the solution, most people would say, "Discipline! We need to focus more on the Ten Commandments and develop discipline, and then self-control, godliness and brotherly kindness will come." While all that sounds very good (to the flesh), that is **not** what the Word of God says, and I for one, want to go by what it says:

> 2 Peter 1:5–9
> [5]… add to your faith virtue, to virtue knowledge, [6]to knowledge self-control, to self-control perseverance, to perseverance godliness, [7]to godliness brotherly kindness, and to brotherly kindness love. [8]For if these things are yours and abound, you will be neither barren nor unfruitful in the knowledge of our Lord Jesus Christ. [9]For **he who lacks these things** is shortsighted, even to blindness, and **has forgotten that he was cleansed from his old sins**.

It is clear that if a person lacks good Christian qualities like self-control, godliness and brotherly kindness, it is not because he lacks discipline, but because he has forgotten the main clause of the new covenant. He has forgotten that the blood of Jesus has purchased for him the forgiveness of all his sins. Beloved, if you remind yourself daily that you have been cleansed from all your sins, you will exhibit more and more of these Christian qualities. Your heart will overflow with self-control, godliness, perseverance, brotherly kindness and love.

Pray like this every day and enjoy your forgiveness:

> Dear Father, I thank You for the cross of Jesus. I thank You that today, because of Jesus' blood, I have been forgiven of all my sins, past, present and future. Today, You are merciful to my unrighteousness, and all my sins and lawless deeds, You will remember no more. You see me as completely righteous, not because of what I have done, but because of Jesus. I am greatly blessed, highly favored and deeply loved by You. Amen.

The secret behind every godly man and woman is their belief in the truth that they have been forgiven.

My friend, the secret behind every godly man and woman is their belief in the truth that they have been forgiven. Their godliness stems from a revelation of their forgiveness. They are believers who believe and honor God's Word. When God says that He is merciful and that He has forgiven all their sins, they take Him at His Word. All day long, they are forgiveness-conscious. Even when they say the wrong thing, do the wrong thing or have a wrong thought, they continue to be forgiveness-conscious. They see the blood of Jesus continually washing them. They see God in His mercy and grace. Because of their forgiveness-consciousness, they experience victory over sin.

How Are You Forgiven Of Your Sins?

"Pastor Prince, are you saying that we don't have to confess our sins?"

Listen carefully: We don't have to confess our sins **in order** to be forgiven. We confess our sins because **we are already forgiven**. When I say "confess our sins", I'm talking about being open with God. I don't go before Him begging for forgiveness. No, I talk to Him because I know that I have already been forgiven. I know that I can come to Him freely — He is my God, my Daddy God. Forgiveness is not dependent on what I do, but what Jesus has done. So confession in the new covenant is just being honest about your failures and your humanity. It is the result of being forgiven and not something you do in order to be forgiven.

Let me give you an illustration that will help you. When my little daughter Jessica makes a mistake, do I forgive her only when she comes to me and says, "I am sorry, Daddy"? No, of course not! As a loving father, I have already forgiven her. I don't forgive her because of her confession or what she does. But when she says, "I am sorry, Daddy," I can tell her that I love her and have already forgiven her. In the same way, our loving heavenly Father does not forgive us only after we have confessed our sins. Fellowship with Him is not broken because our forgiveness is not contingent on what we do. It is contingent on the finished work of Jesus. We do not confess our sins to be forgiven. We confess or speak openly to our gracious Father because we **have already been** forgiven.

My friend, understanding this difference determines whether you experience "heaven on earth" or "hell on earth"!

Let me explain what I mean. When I was growing up as a

young believer, I was taught that unless I confessed all my sins, I would not be forgiven. I was even told that if someone dies without having confessed all his sins, he would end up in hell. Such teachings made the forgiveness of sins man's responsibility, instead of something that was dependent on what Jesus' blood had already accomplished. My friend, such teachings are based on man's traditions and not the Scriptures.

Such teachings put me in severe bondage when I was a teenager. Again, I didn't understand why it didn't seem to bother other Christians. But it really bothered me. I was really sincere and wanted to always be "right with God" and not have any sin that was not forgiven. I did not want fellowship with God to be broken. So everywhere I went, I would confess my sins, and I mean EVERYWHERE!

I would be playing soccer with my friends and as the goalkeeper, I would yell at the defenders, "Hey, you, what do you think you are doing? Watch out for that striker… Hey, come on!" Sometimes, in the midst of the game, I would get angry and feel like scolding one of the players. I would catch myself and think, "I am a believer. How can I think such thoughts?" So right there and then, I would close my eyes and start confessing my sins, whispering my confession under my breath. The next thing I knew, the ball would streak past me and go right into the net. I was left wondering, "God, what happened? Here I am getting right with You and You allowed the opposing team to score?"

This "keeping short accounts with God" continued even when I was drafted into the military, which is mandatory for all male citizens in Singapore. One day, I overheard my bunk mates talking about me among themselves: "He's really strange…"

said one. Another replied, "Yeah, why does he do that? Have you seen him whisper under his breath as he's running or doing something?" At that point, I realized that I wasn't being a very good testimony for Jesus. All my military friends must have thought that Christians, to put it mildly, were a strange bunch. But I was in serious bondage. I really believed that I had to confess every bad thing that I thought I had done, all the time. Since all this happened during the time when I believed that it was possible for Christians to commit the unpardonable sin, I confessed as much as I could just to be "safe". I took 1 John 1:9 to the limit and it nearly drove me insane. But what does 1 John 1:9 really say and to whom was it actually written?

1 John 1:9
⁹If we confess our sins, He is faithful and just to forgive us our sins and to cleanse us from all unrighteousness.

People have taken this verse and built a whole doctrine around it when actually, chapter 1 of 1 John was written to the Gnostics, who were unbelievers. John was saying to these unbelievers that if they confessed their sins, God would be faithful and just to cleanse them from all unrighteousness.

We are not to live from confession to confession, but from faith to faith in Jesus Christ and His finished work.

For us believers, the moment we received Jesus, all our sins were forgiven. We are not to live from confession to confession, but from faith to faith in Jesus Christ and His finished work. You see, there are no two ways about it. If you believe that you have to confess your sins to be forgiven, then make sure that you confess everything! Make sure that you don't just confess the "big sins" ("big" in your own estimation). Make sure that you also confess your sins every time you are worried, fearful or in doubt. The Bible says that "whatsoever is not of faith is sin"[3]. So don't just confess what is convenient for you. Make sure that you confess **everything**.

If you really believe that you need to confess all your sins to be forgiven, do you know what you would be doing? You would be confessing your sins **ALL THE TIME!** How then can you have courage before God? How can you enjoy liberty as a child of God? I tried it and it is impossible!

Let's not build a whole doctrine on one verse. If confession of sins is vital for your forgiveness, then Apostle Paul, who wrote two-thirds of the New Testament, has done us a great injustice because he did not mention it even once — not once — in any of his letters to the church. When there were people in the Corinthian church living in sin, he did not say, "Go and confess your sins." Instead, he reminded them of their righteousness, saying, "Do you not know that your body **is** the temple of the Holy Spirit who is in you?"[4] Notice that in spite of their sins, Paul still considered them temples of the Holy Spirit and he reminded them of this truth.

The Waterfall Of Forgiveness

My friend, this is the assurance that you can have today: The day you received Christ, you confessed all your sins once and for all. You acknowledged that you were a sinner in need of a Savior, and He is faithful and just to cleanse you from all unrighteousness. All the unrighteousness of your entire life was cleansed at that point!

Entire doctrines have been built around 1 John 1:9, but John actually made it clear in the same chapter that when it comes to believers, people who "walk in the light", the blood of Jesus Christ cleanses them from all sins:

> 1 John 1:7
> ⁷But if we walk in the light as He is in the light, we have fellowship with one another, and **the blood of Jesus Christ His Son cleanses us from all sin**.

Notice that for us, believers who "walk in the light", it is **not our confessions** that cleanse us from all sin, but the **blood of Jesus**! Notice also that this verse says "walk **in** the light" and not "walk **according to** the light". Walking in the light means walking in the realm of light which Christ's death has already translated us into. Christians often misconstrue this to mean walking according to the light, thinking that darkness will decrease and light will increase if we try to stay in the light. But that is not what the verse is talking about! It's talking about us **already being** translated out of the realm of darkness into the realm of light. One little word makes all the difference! When we understand this verse, we realize that even when we sin, we sin in the realm of light! So, if we sin in the light, we are cleansed in the light, and we are kept in the light. This idea of us going into darkness when we sin is not from the Bible.

The Bible is so rich and full of treasures! Did you know that even the word "cleanses" in 1 John 1:7 is really beautiful? In the Greek, the tense for the word "cleanse" denotes a present and continuous action, which means that from the moment you receive Christ, the blood of Jesus **keeps on cleansing** you[5]. It is as if you are under a waterfall of His forgiveness. Even when you fail, this waterfall never stops. It keeps on keeping on, cleansing you from ALL your sins and unrighteousness.

Knowing that you are forgiven of all your sins will give you the power to reign over every destructive habit and live a life of victory!

Beloved, confessing your sins all the time will only make you more sin-conscious. But knowing that you are under Jesus' waterfall of forgiveness will keep you forgiveness-conscious. And knowing that you are forgiven of all your sins will give you the power to reign over every destructive habit and live a life of victory!

In 1 John 2:1, John addressed the believers as "My little children" (he never addressed the unbelievers whom he was writing to in chapter 1 as "My little children") and went on to say, "These things I write to you, so that you may not sin. And if anyone sins, we have an Advocate with the Father, Jesus Christ." Notice that John did not tell the believers, "If anyone sins, make sure that he confesses his sins." No, his solution for a believer who sins is to point him to the finished work of Jesus. Jesus is our Advocate before God and it is because of His blood that we have forgiveness of all our sins. It is time to stop being robbed by traditional teachings and to start enjoying the waterfall of His forgiveness, which perpetually cleanses us. It never stops. It keeps on cleansing us. You know that negative thought that you had of me a few minutes ago? Well, that has been cleansed too!

Let me tell you a story about a little boy who used to play in the woods just a short distance away from the dilapidated hut that he lived in. His parents were too poor to buy him any toys, so he had to make do with whatever he could find. One day, he chanced upon a stone that was unlike any that he had ever seen. The polished surface of the stone glistened in his hands and winked at him each time he turned it around in the sunlight. It was his very own treasure and he loved it. The boy did not dare bring it back to his home as there was nowhere in the hut he could hide it. He decided to dig a deep hole under some bushes and hide his precious possession there.

The next day, the boy couldn't wait to retrieve his stone and ran to its hiding place as soon as the sun arose. But when his fingers finally found the stone in its muddy hideaway, it was all grubby and stained, without any of the luster that he loved so much. The boy took the stone to the stream and carefully dipped it in, allowing the dirt to be washed away. Finally, it was clean again and the boy's heart swelled with pride at his coveted find. But all too soon, the time came for the boy to head home and he had to return the stone to its hiding place.

Every day, the boy would rush to the spot where he had hidden the stone. And every day, he would find its shiny surface smeared with mud and he would trek to the river some distance away to wash it. This happened for a while before he decided to solve the problem. That day, when it was almost time for him to head home, the little boy took his stone to a small waterfall and wedged it carefully between two rocks, right in the middle of the steady flow of the waterfall. That night, the stone experienced a continual washing. And that little boy never had to wash the stone again. Every time he retrieved it, it gleamed in his hands, completely cleansed.

What the little boy did with the stone initially can be likened to what happens under the old covenant. Each time you sinned, you had to be cleansed. But before you knew it, you would sin again, and you would have to bring your sin offering of either a bullock or lamb to the priests to be cleansed again. Some believers still think that this is our covenant today, but let me declare to you that Jesus' blood is far greater than the blood of bulls and goats. The blood of Jesus Christ, the Son of God, bought us eternal forgiveness[6]. The blood of bulls and goats in the old covenant could only offer temporal forgiveness, and that's why the children of Israel had to keep bringing animal sacrifices to the priests over and over again, every time they failed.

Jesus, however, died on the cross once and for all[7]. When you were born again, you became a living stone and God placed you right under the waterfall of His Son's blood. Hence, every thought you have that is amiss, every feeling that is not right, every action that is not correct, is washed away! You are always kept clean and forgiven because of the continuous cleansing of Jesus' blood!

Understanding The Holy Communion

"Pastor Prince, what about the times we partake of the Holy Communion? Aren't we expected to confess all our sins so that we don't partake of it unworthily?"

Let's read what Paul actually said about partaking of the Holy Communion:

1 Corinthians 11:27–30

^{27}Therefore whoever eats this bread or drinks this cup of the Lord in an **unworthy manner** will be guilty of the body and blood of the Lord. ^{28}But let a man examine himself, and so let him eat of the bread and drink of the cup. ^{29}For he who eats and drinks in an **unworthy manner** eats and drinks judgment to himself, **not discerning the Lord's body**. ^{30}For this reason many are weak and sick among you, and many sleep.

Down through the years, the body of Christ has mistakenly believed that to partake of the Holy Communion in an "unworthy manner" is to partake with sin in your life. So we are told not to partake of the Communion when we deem ourselves "not right with God", lest we become weak, sickly and die before our time. But we have turned what was meant as a blessing into a curse. When I received this erroneous teaching as a teenager, I would always let the Communion elements pass me by, thinking, "My mama didn't raise no fool!" I was always concerned that I would be partaking unworthily. Now, by doing so and being "safe", I did not realize that I was robbing myself of the blessings and benefits of Jesus' broken body and His shed blood.

I now know that this is **not** what the Bible teaches. To partake unworthily does not refer to you partaking as an unworthy person because of your sins. Come on, Jesus died for unworthy people! What the verse really refers to is the **manner** in which you partake. To partake unworthily is to fail to discern that the bread which you hold in your hands is the body of Jesus Christ that was beaten for you, so that your body may be healed and whole. This was what was happening in the early church. There were believers who were just eating the bread because they were hungry, or taking the bread as a ritual without discerning the Lord's body and releasing faith.

Therefore, to partake in an unworthy manner is not about you failing to examine yourself and confess all your sins to make sure that you are worthy to partake. It is not about the one partaking. It is about the act or manner in which one partakes. It is about discerning the Lord's body and releasing faith to see the bread as His body, striped for your healing. It is about seeing the wine as the blood that was shed for the forgiveness of all your sins. Therein is the secret to God's divine health and wholeness. Many fail to discern the body of Jesus and see for themselves how He has suffered in His body on their behalf. This is the reason "many are weak and sick". So it is not about looking at yourself and confessing your sins. It is about looking to Jesus and seeing what He has accomplished on the cross for you!

In our church, we partake of the Holy Communion every week. And by teaching the people to discern the Lord's body, we have experienced one amazing healing miracle after another. There was a lady in our church who suffered from deep vein thrombosis while on her way to Israel with one of our church groups. (We organize regular tours to Israel for our church members.) She had fallen asleep on the flight after taking some medication, and did not move around enough to allow her blood to circulate freely and sufficiently throughout the long flight. As a result, she went into a coma upon arrival in Israel and had to be hospitalized immediately.

I happened to be in Israel at that time with my pastoral team. We visited her in the hospital and partook of the Holy Communion by her bed, proclaiming the finished work of Jesus over her. Miraculously, after a couple of days, she awoke from the coma and from what medical practitioners considered a potentially fatal condition! Praise be to God, she was completely healed. She was so full of the resurrection life of Jesus that she joined the next group that had just arrived in Israel. Hallelujah! Praise the Lord!

If you are interested to learn more about the Holy Communion, get hold of my book titled, *Health And Wholeness Through The Holy Communion*. There are more testimonies in the book and the book will liberate you to partake of all the benefits of the Holy Communion. Remember, it is not about examining yourself for sin and making yourself worthy to partake. It is all about discerning the Lord's body! It is all about Jesus and nothing about man's own efforts.

Consciousness Of Jesus' Blood Brings Victory

Perhaps you are going through some challenges right now and you are wondering, "How can the blood of Jesus bring me healing, prosperity and victory in my marriage?"

My friend, all you need to know is that you are being constantly cleansed of all your sins. Once you believe that all your sins are indeed forgiven and that God does not hold anything against you, faith will spring forth. Faith will be there for healing. Faith will be there for prosperity. Faith will be there for restoration in your marriage and family. The continuous washing of Jesus' blood qualifies you for **any** miracle that you need in your life right now. Jesus said to the paralytic man, "Son, your sins are forgiven you," before He said, "Arise, take up your bed, and go to your house."[8] Why? Because Jesus knew that unless the man had the assurance that all his sins had been forgiven, he would not have faith to be healed. This is what people need to hear. This is what we need to teach in the church!

The devil's strategy is to make you feel like you are not qualified to enter God's presence. He will bombard you with thoughts of condemnation, accusing you of being unworthy for having wrong thoughts or saying harsh words against someone. He will give you a thousand and one reasons why you don't qualify for God's blessings. But the truth is that whatever wrong feelings you had or whatever bad habit you had succumbed to, the blood of Jesus keeps you clean. The blood of Jesus qualifies you to have constant access to the Most High God. Because you are under this waterfall of forgiveness, every prayer that you make avails much.

The blood of Jesus qualifies you to have constant access to the Most High God.

We overcome the devil by the blood of the Lamb. When Monday comes and Tuesday rolls by, and your pastor is not there to preach to you, do you know what you need to remind yourself of? 1 John 1:7 — "... the blood of Jesus Christ His Son cleanses us from all sin." His blood keeps on keeping on cleansing you from every sin. Twenty-four hours a day, seven days a week, His blood is cleansing you. And any time and every time you pray, your prayer hits the mark.

My friend, cease from depending on your own efforts to maintain your forgiveness and begin to enjoy the extravagant waterfall of God's forgiveness every moment of the day. You'll find peace for your soul and the faith to reign in life will well up on the inside of you. You'll see miracles begin to unfold in your life!

Chapter 10

The Ministry Of Death

I didn't write this book to tell you what is so wrong about you and to point out where you have fallen short. On the contrary, I wrote this book to declare to you what is so right about you (in spite of all your weaknesses) because of Jesus Christ. This book is about the good news of Jesus Christ. He did not come to condemn you. He came to take your condemnation upon Himself, so that you will never be condemned again.

Has Jesus died on the cross for us?

Has His blood been shed for our forgiveness?

Then, why is it that so many believers are still living in condemnation even though He has already been punished for their sins?

Did the cross make a difference or not?

Jesus Christ has already delivered all believers from the covenant of law which condemns. But there are believers who choose to continue living under its condemnation instead of receiving the grace that has been purchased by the blood of Jesus Christ. Rather than put their trust in the unmerited goodness of God through Jesus Christ, they have chosen to put their trust in their ability to abide by the Ten Commandments. Simply put, they have chosen the ministry of death.

"Sacrilegious! I would have you know that the Ten Commandments are God's holy laws. How dare you call them the ministry of death!"

Take it easy, my friend. I'm not the one who came up with that. The Bible states it very clearly:

> 2 Corinthians 3:7–9
>
> ⁷But if the **ministry of death, written and engraved on stones,** was glorious, so that the children of Israel could not look steadily at the face of Moses because of the glory of his countenance, which glory was passing away, ⁸how will the ministry of the Spirit not be more glorious? ⁹For if the **ministry of condemnation** had glory, the ministry of righteousness exceeds much more in glory.

It is the Bible that describes the Ten Commandments, which were written and engraved on stones, as the "ministry of death"! Some have argued that the "ministry of death" refers exclusively to the "ceremonial laws" of Moses, such as those pertaining to animal sacrifices. Therefore, they say that while we may no longer be bound by the ceremonial laws, we are still under the "moral laws" or Ten Commandments. However, this cannot be true because the ceremonial laws were never "written and engraved on stones". They were written on parchment. Only the Ten Commandments were written and engraved on stones, and the Bible calls them the "ministry of death". That's why the Bible also says in the preceding verse that "the letter kills, but the Spirit gives life"[1]. The covenant of law kills, but the covenant of grace gives life!

The Covenant Of Grace Is Much More Glorious

I used to think that Moses put a veil over his face because his face shone so bright that he did not want to frighten the people. Actually, the Bible says that Moses put on the veil because he did not want the people to know that the glory was departing or "passing away"[2].

Moses represents the law, the Ten Commandments. He represents the ministry of death and condemnation. While the law, the ministry of condemnation, had glory, the Bible declares that "the ministry of righteousness exceeds **much more** in glory". Praise be to God that you and I are under the new covenant, the covenant of grace and righteousness!

How is the covenant of grace more glorious than the covenant of law?

The law **demands** righteousness from sinful man, whereas grace **imparts** righteousness to sinful man. Let me illustrate what I mean. The law says to a man who is balding, "Thou shall not be bald!" The poor guy grabs what little hair he has left on his scalp and says, "I can't help it! It keeps falling off!" Grace, on the other hand, says, "Receive the hair!" and the guy gets new hair!

You see, the law **demands perfection, but will not lift a finger to help**. And, as shown in the case of the balding chap, man has no ability in himself, no matter how hard he tries, to fulfill the law's demand, and is thus cursed for breaking the law. Grace, on the other hand, **imparts perfection and does everything for man** through Jesus Christ, and all that man needs to do is to believe. Which do you think is more glorious? The ministry of death which demands or the ministry of grace which imparts?

The Ten Commandments Kill

When God gave the law on Mount Sinai, it was on the first Pentecost, exactly 50 days from the Passover when the Lord delivered the children of Israel from slavery in Egypt. Do you know what happened when the Ten Commandments were given? At the foot of Mount Sinai, 3,000 people died[3]. Now, let's compare this with the New Testament. When the Day of Pentecost had come, God poured out His Holy Spirit upon all flesh and what was the result? Peter stood up to preach the gospel and 3,000 people were saved that day[4].

The power for the church to overcome sin is actually found in being under grace and not in reinforcing the law.

Even today, when you go to Israel, the Jewish people celebrate the Day of Pentecost as the day that God gave the Ten Commandments. For us, we celebrate the Day of Pentecost as the birthday of the church and the day God gave us the Holy Spirit. Unfortunately, there are some believers who are still celebrating the Ten Commandments instead of rejoicing in the Spirit of the new covenant, not realizing that the law kills, while the Spirit gives life!

Now that you know that the Ten Commandments is the ministry of death, think with me: What do you think happens when the church remains bound by the law? What happens when we preach a series of sermons on the Ten Commandments? Can you see why the body of Christ is sick and depressed today, or why believers don't have the power to overcome sin?

For generations, the church has believed that by preaching the Ten Commandments, we will produce holiness. When we see sin on the increase, we start to preach more of the law. But the Word of God actually says that "the strength of sin is the law"[5]. It also says that "sin shall not have dominion over you, for you are not under law but under grace"[6]. So the power for the church to overcome sin is actually found in being under **grace** and not in reinforcing the law. Preaching more of the law to counteract sin is like adding wood to fire!

So who has hoodwinked us all this time and sold us a lie? Why is the body of Christ so wary of preachers of grace when grace is the antidote to sin? Come on, church, it is time to see that it is the devil who benefits from all this. The devil is the one using the law to bring about death and condemnation, and to put believers under oppression!

Am I An Antinomian?

I know that I have stepped on a few toes because of what I have just said. But please understand that it is not Joseph Prince who is finding fault with the old covenant of law. The Word of God says, "For if that first covenant had been faultless, then no place would have been sought for a second."[7] God Himself found fault with the old covenant of law and the Ten Commandments. He sent Jesus Christ as our Mediator of "a better covenant, which was established on better promises"[8]. And indeed, the new covenant of grace is established on better promises and is more glorious than the ministry of death, for it is no longer dependent on us, but is completely dependent on Jesus, who CANNOT FAIL! By cutting a new covenant of grace, God "has made the first obsolete"[9]. In other words, with the advent of the new covenant of grace, **the Ten Commandments have been made obsolete.** We are no longer under the ministry of death, but under the ministry of Jesus which brings life!

Over the years, I have developed a better understanding of why Apostle Paul declared, "I am not ashamed of the gospel of Christ, for it is the power of God to salvation"[10]. I used to wonder why Paul had to announce that he was not ashamed of the gospel. Why should anyone be ashamed of the good news? But I now realize that not everybody is willing to accept how good the good news truly is. Because I preach the gospel of Jesus and teach that we are no longer under law, my name has been dragged through the mud. Today, people don't throw stones, they shoot poison emails.

One of the things which I have been accused of is being an antinomian (someone who is against the law of Moses). The truth is that I have the **highest regard for the law**. And it is precisely because I have the highest regard for the law that I know that no man can keep the law. We have to depend totally on God's grace! Those who accuse me and other grace preachers of being antinomian are the same ones who pick and choose the laws that are convenient for them to keep. They claim that they have a high regard for the law, but they are actually lowering the standard of God's law to a place where man thinks that he can actually keep the law. So they choose the laws which are convenient for their personalities or which are in line with their denominations. Come on, it is us grace preachers who have the highest regard for the law! We recognize that it is impossible for man to keep the law perfectly.

You cannot pick and choose which laws you want to keep. The Bible says that if you want to keep the law, you have to keep all of it, and if you break one law, you break them all[11]. The law is a composite whole. God does not grade on the curve. Also, you cannot just keep the law outwardly. You have to keep it inwardly as well. Do you know anyone (other than God Himself) who can keep God's laws perfectly all the time?

Let me say this explicitly so that there is no misunderstanding: **I am for the law, for the purpose for which God gave the law** (and you can quote me on this). You see, God did not give the law for us to keep. He gave the law to bring man to the end of himself, so that he would see his need for a Savior. There is nothing inherently wrong with the law. The law is holy, just and good. But it is time to realize that while the law is holy, just and good, it has no power to make you holy. It has no power to make you just and it definitely has no power to make you good.

God gave the law to bring man to the end of himself,
so that he would see his need for a Savior.

Do you remember the analogy I used earlier about the law being like a mirror that exposes your flaws? My friend, if you look in the mirror and see someone ugly, don't blame the mirror. Don't get mad and punch the mirror! It's not the mirror's fault. The purpose of the mirror is simply to expose your flaws. In the same way, the law is not at fault. Its rightful purpose is to expose your sins. It was not designed to take away your sins! In fact, the Bible states that the law was given to magnify your sins — "the law entered that the offense might abound"[12].

Without a mirror, you would have no knowledge of your flaws. Similarly, the Word of God says that "by the law is the knowledge of sin"[13]. It also tells us what the role of the law is: "Wherefore the law was our schoolmaster to bring us unto Christ, that we might be justified by faith."[14] What do all these verses tell you, my friend? They tell you that the law was designed to lead you to the end of yourself, and cause you to despair in your own efforts to achieve God's standards, so that you will see for yourself that you need a savior!

The law justified no one and condemned the best of us, but grace saves even the worst of us. Yet, there are still people today trying to use the Ten Commandments to remove their sins. That is like rubbing the mirror on their faces to remove their pimples. It just doesn't work! My friend, only the blood of Jesus can remove sins. His blood was shed on Calvary so that your sins can be forgiven. Start believing the good news today!

The Knowledge Of Good And Evil

There are two trees in the garden of Eden that you need to be familiar with. The first is the tree of the knowledge of good and evil. This is the tree that Adam and Eve were forbidden to eat from. Have you noticed that this tree was not called the tree of the knowledge of **evil**? It was called the tree of the knowledge of **good and evil**. This is because the tree is a picture of God's law or the Ten Commandments. The law is the knowledge of **good** and **evil**. God did not want man to partake of the law. He wanted man to partake of the tree of life, which is a picture of our Savior Jesus Christ. Whoever partakes of this tree will have eternal life[15].

"But Pastor Prince, what's so wrong with knowing good and evil? What is wrong with knowing the law?"

The danger is this: You can know the law inside out, and yet be miles and miles away from God. Under the law, all you will have is **religion**, not a **relationship** with God. But God is after a relationship with us, one that is dependent on His goodness and His goodness alone. When man partakes of the tree of the knowledge of good and evil, he becomes dependent on his self-efforts to do good and keep away from evil. And when man is depending on his own efforts, he is bound to fail. On the other hand, when man partakes of the tree of life, he is completely dependent on Jesus and Jesus alone.

God is after a relationship with us, one that is dependent on His goodness and His goodness alone.

Now, who planted the tree of the knowledge of good and evil in the garden? The serpent? No, it was God. In fact, when God had created everything in the garden of Eden, He saw everything that He had made and said that it was good. This included the tree of the knowledge of good and evil. The tree of the knowledge of good and evil was from the Lord. But while the tree was good in itself, it was not good for man to partake of it.

Likewise, while God's law is holy, just and good, it was not meant for man to keep. Man has no ability to keep it. Also, man cannot pick and choose which laws to keep — if he fails in one, he fails in all. God does not grade on the curve. The Bible says that the wages of sin is death. Therefore, once man fails in one facet of the law, he is condemned to die and can no longer partake of the tree of life, which would give him eternal life. This is why when Adam and Eve sinned, God had to drive them out of the garden, and place cherubim and a "flaming sword which turned every way, to guard the way to the tree of life"[16].

What's the significance of all this? Well, there is a principle in Bible interpretation known as the "law of first mention", which says that every time a word is mentioned for the first time in the Bible, the meaning of the word in that instance has special significance for how we are to understand that word throughout the Bible. In this instance, it is the first time the word "sword" is mentioned in the Bible. In the context of this verse, we see the sword here as God's judgment. It is a restless sword turning every way so that there is no way that sinful man, having disobeyed God, can ever return to Him.

Now, let's look at the last mention of the word "sword" in the Old Testament. It is found in Zechariah chapter 13:

> Zechariah 13:7
> "Awake, O sword, against My Shepherd, against the Man who is My Companion... Strike the Shepherd, and the sheep will be scattered..."

The Shepherd mentioned in the verse refers to Jesus, our good Shepherd, and how all His disciples fled when He was struck on the cross. It shows us that the restless sword of judgment, which for so many generations had barred sinful men from a holy God, was finally sheathed in the bosom of our Lord Jesus when the full judgment and vengeance of God for all our sins came upon Him on the cross. Jesus was smitten on the cross for our sins.

By sacrificing Himself and absorbing the full brunt of the judgment that was meant for you and me, Jesus stopped the sword of judgment that prevents us from partaking of the tree of life. He sacrificed His own body to open the way to the tree of life. God will never condemn us because His only begotten Son has already been condemned on our behalf. The cross at Calvary has become the tree of life for us in the new covenant. We can freely partake of His righteousness and live each day without guilt, condemnation and shame. Hallelujah!

There is no more judgment for you when God looks at you.

What does this mean, my friend? This means that there is no more judgment for you when God looks at you. Stop depending on the tree of the knowledge of good and evil for your justification. Jesus has redeemed you from the ministry of death by dying on the cross. Enjoy what He has purchased for you today and partake of the finished work of Jesus, our tree of life.

You are no longer under the ministry of death.

Jesus came that you may have life, and have it more abundantly[17]!

Chapter 11

Unearthing The Deepest Root

O nce, when I was preparing to preach, the Lord showed me an inner vision of a sickly plant with each of its leaves representing a particular condition. But I really sat up and took notice when He showed me the roots of the plant. Some of the roots were just beneath the surface of the ground and could be unearthed easily. The main root, however, was embedded much deeper in the soil.

When dealing with any problem in life, we want to get to its root.

What the Lord shared with me next was most powerful. He showed me that the deepest root represented the fundamental tactic that the devil uses against man. He unveiled this truth to me because He wanted me to expose the devil's strategy against His people, so that He could equip them to counter the devil's attacks. You see, when we are dealing with any problem in life, we want to get to its root. If you were growing a plant, and the plant was getting weak and sickly, it would be foolish to attempt to nourish and restore the plant by dealing with superficial elements such as its leaves. To resolve the problem, you would have to go after its root.

In the same way, chronic sicknesses, mental depression, perpetual anxiety, financial lack or marital disharmony are all like the withering leaves of the sick plant. You can cut away one leaf, but it's just a matter of time before another leaf becomes sickly. So what we want to examine in this chapter is the root of some of these problems that believers face. When you are able to identify and deal with the root, the fruits and the leaves, or the outward manifestations, will take care of themselves. In other words, if the root is healthy, the rest of the plant will naturally be healthy too.

Stress Is One Of The Roots

The world has found out that many sicknesses and diseases are linked to a root called stress. An article on the Mayo Clinic website warns that stress may disrupt almost all of your body's processes and make you more vulnerable to life-threatening health problems[1]. I am sure you have read articles in the newspapers about how stress can erode health and cause human ailments[2]. Scientific research has linked excessive stress to various conditions, including cardiovascular diseases, hypertension, elevated cholesterol levels, stroke, skin eruptions, migraine, sexual impotence and infertility[3].

Fear Is A Deeper Root Than Stress

The world has also identified fear as the root cause of stress. They have found that in many cases, stress is preceded by fear. Fear can manifest itself in the form of panic attacks or a perpetual state of anxiety. It can also result in prolonged insomnia, constant unrest and a disturbed state of mind. But while fear sounds like a critical root that needs to be addressed, it is still not the deepest root. The Lord showed me a root that was deeper than stress and fear. He showed me that the biggest and deepest root exists in the spiritual realm, and that it can only be destroyed by the power of Jesus' finished work.

Are you interested to find out what this root is?

Are you interested to go further to find out what is deeper and more insidious than stress and fear?

Condemnation Is The Deepest Root

The Lord showed me that the deepest root is **condemnation**.

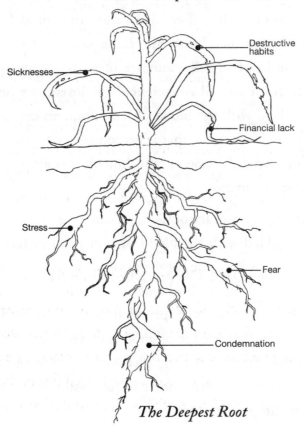

The Deepest Root

It all began in the garden of Eden when the first man, Adam, partook of the tree of the knowledge of good and evil. From that point onwards, man developed a conscience. Your conscience is that which is within you that knows good and evil. Your conscience understands justice. It understands that when there is sin, sin must be punished. This has also led man to punish himself for his sins.

A conscience that typically expects punishment is a conscience that is under condemnation.

There are both believers and unbelievers who are defeated by guilt and condemnation. But the difference is that a believer, who has Jesus Christ and the power of His finished work, can reject any accusation, guilt and condemnation thrown at him by the devil and by his own heart. The Bible says, "Let us draw near with a true heart in full assurance of faith, having **our hearts sprinkled from an evil conscience**"[4]. Beloved, our hearts have been sprinkled with the blood of Jesus from an evil conscience. An evil conscience is one that is perpetually conscious of sin and failure, and typically expects punishment. It is a conscience that is under condemnation.

However, by the grace of God, we can have a good conscience that is sprinkled with the blood of Jesus, and instead of being sin-conscious, we can be forgiveness-conscious. We can always be conscious of our righteousness in Christ Jesus, even when we fail. A good conscience sprinkled by the blood of Jesus does not feed on the knowledge of good and evil. A good conscience feeds on the life of Christ and gives you the confidence to draw near to God with a "true heart in full assurance of faith" that God is not angry with you.

Condemnation robs you of intimacy with God. But the Word of God says, "Worshippers, once purified, would have had no more consciousness of sins."[5] Unfortunately, many believers do not rely on the power of the cross to eradicate condemnation from their lives. They depend on their own efforts — do right and do more — to be free from guilt and condemnation.

The Accuser Of The Brethren

That is why condemnation is the deepest root. It is a root that man cannot overcome through self-effort. Condemnation demands a payment for all your failures and sins, but without Jesus, there is no payment. For some time now, there has been talk about guilt and how it can cause various adverse symptoms to appear in the human body, but that is just skimming the surface of the matter. While experts may be able to identify guilt and condemnation as the sources, they have no solution to destroy them. They cannot see that people are actually faced with a spiritual problem, for the devil insidiously uses condemnation to afflict people today. In Hebrew, the devil's name is *ha-satan*, which literally means "the accuser"[6]. He is a prosecutor at law and an expert in condemning you, always pointing out your faults and shortcomings. That is why the Bible calls him "the accuser of our brethren"[7].

Even when you do something right, the accuser will say, "It's not good enough." Like the constant sound of dripping water, he will keep on accusing and spewing condemnation toward you. His crowning achievement would be to bring about accusations in your life and leave them undetected. Many a time, believers under condemnation would even think that it is the Holy Spirit convicting them of their sins and pointing out their faults. They begin to entertain negative thoughts about themselves. They begin to **believe** that they ought to have negative feelings about themselves because of all their sins and unworthiness. Hence, the devil's crowning achievement is to bring about condemnation in your life, concealing it in a fog of deception, so that you would be the last person to think that you are under condemnation.

Some people whom I've counseled for being under condemnation have told me, "Pastor Prince, I don't have a condemnation problem. I am just under stress." I don't deny that stress is a genuine problem. In fact, I have a number of sermons on overcoming stress, one of which is a best-selling series called *Live The Let-Go Life*. But what I am saying is that in many instances, there is a deeper root than stress or fear, and that root is condemnation. The accuser's most effective tactics are always very subtle. The world has no solution for his tactics, but as believers, we do. We have the power of the finished work of Jesus. His blood was shed and He was condemned on our behalf, so that we will never need to live in condemnation.

Does The Holy Spirit Convict You Of Sin?

"But Pastor Prince, how can I differentiate between the Holy Spirit convicting me of sin and the accuser hurling condemnation at me?"

That is a very good question and the answer is really simple. Now, pay attention to this because it will liberate you. The bottom line is that **the Holy Spirit never convicts you of your sins.** He NEVER comes to point out your faults. I challenge you to find a scripture in the Bible that tells you that the Holy Spirit has come to convict you of your sins. You won't find any! The body of Christ is living in defeat because many believers don't understand that the Holy Spirit is actually in them to convict them of their **righteousness in Christ**. Even when you fail, He is ever present in you to remind you that you are continually cleansed by the blood of Jesus. That's the Holy Spirit.

Wouldn't you agree that you don't actually need the Holy Spirit to point out your faults and tell you when you have sinned? Come on, your spouse already does a good job at that! Even non-believers, who clearly do not have the Holy Spirit in them, are fully aware when they have failed because they too have a conscience. You don't need anyone's help to point out your sins. You are already aware of them because you have a conscience.

When you've failed, the Holy Spirit convicts
you of righteousness, not your sin.

It does not take a revelation from the Holy Spirit to see that you have failed. However, when you know that you've failed, what you **do** need is for the Holy Spirit to convict you of your righteousness. You need Him to show you that even though you have failed, you are still the righteousness of God in Christ. To know and believe that God still sees you as righteous even when you have sinned certainly takes a revelation from the Holy Spirit. Can you say "Amen" to that? In fact, God's inexhaustible grace in our lives and the power of the cross can only be understood by revelation. That is why a non-believer can never be convicted of righteousness. That privilege is reserved for you and me, born-again believers who are gloriously washed by the blood of Jesus!

Understanding The Work Of The Holy Spirit

"Pastor Prince, what about John 16:8? Doesn't it say that the Holy Spirit came to convict the world of sin?"

I am glad that you brought up this verse. Let's examine it together:

> John 16:8–11
> [8]And when He [the Holy Spirit] has come, He will convict the world of sin, and of righteousness, and of judgment: [9]of sin, because they do not believe in Me; [10]of righteousness, because I go to My Father and you see Me no more; [11]of judgment, because the ruler of this world is judged.

It is important to always read Bible verses in their context. Many people end up misinterpreting Bible verses because they fail to do this. One way to read Bible verses in their context (and this is a key Bible interpretation principle) is to identify who the verses are talking about. So who was Jesus talking about in John 16:8? Was He talking about believers or unbelievers?

When He said that the Holy Spirit would come to "convict the world of sin" because they do not believe in Him, it is clear that He was referring to unbelievers because they are of "the world". And notice that the Holy Spirit does not convict the world of "sins" (plural). It is only one "sin" (singular) that the Holy Spirit convicts the world of, and that is the sin of unbelief, the sin of rejecting Jesus and not believing in His finished work.

Jesus died for the whole world, but that does not mean that the whole world is automatically saved. Each individual must make a personal decision to receive Jesus as his Savior. Being born into a Christian family does not automatically make you a born-again believer, anymore than walking into McDonald's makes you a Big Mac or being in a garage makes you a car! No, every person must make a personal decision to receive Jesus as his Savior. So the Holy Spirit is present to convict unbelievers of that one sin of unbelief. But when people take John 16:8 out of its proper context, they start to believe erroneously that the Holy Spirit is here to convict believers of their sins. Like I said earlier, none of us need help in that department. We all know when we have failed.

If the Holy Spirit never convicts you the believer of your sins, then what does He convict you of? Jesus says that the Holy Spirit convicts you "of righteousness, because I go to My Father and **you** see Me no more". Now, who was Jesus referring to here? Clearly, with the use of the second person pronoun "you", Jesus was referring to His believers, as represented by His disciples whom He was talking to. This tells us that the Holy Spirit was sent to convict believers of righteousness.

Now, are you made righteous by your works or by faith in Jesus? By now, you should know that you are made righteous by faith, for righteousness is not **right doing**, but **right standing** before God because of your right believing! So when you miss it, the Holy Spirit comes to convict and remind you that you are the righteousness of God because of Jesus Christ. He is present to remind you of the main clause of the new covenant — that God will be merciful to your unrighteousness, and your sins and your lawless deeds, He will remember no more[8].

The Holy Spirit is your Helper[9]. He was sent to live in you to help you, not to nag at you and point out all your faults. Nobody can live with a nag. The Holy Spirit is not a nag. No, He was sent to help you by convicting you of your everlasting righteousness.

Awake To Righteousness And Sin Not

I have come across ministers who hold back from teaching believers that they are righteous in Christ because they are afraid that believers will go out and sin once they realize this truth. Once, I met a minister who told me that after hearing my sermons, he checked the Scriptures and confirmed that we are indeed made righteous apart from our works because of Jesus. But he told me that he could not preach this because he was afraid that if believers knew that they were forever righteous, they would go out and sin.

This is sad because the power to overcome sin is found in knowing that you are righteous. When a believer is struggling with sin, it is a case of mistaken identity: He thinks that he is still a dirty rotten sinner and as a result, he will continue to live as a dirty rotten sinner. But the more he sees that he has been made righteous apart from his works, the more he will be empowered to live righteously.

Your answer lies in right believing.

Believers are struggling with sin today precisely because they do not realize that they are righteous. The Bible says, "Awake to righteousness, and sin not."[10] This means that the more a believer realizes that he is indeed righteous, the more he will start to behave like a righteous person. It is time to awake to righteousness!

Now, commit this to memory: **Right believing leads to right living**. Say it out loud with me for this is a powerful revelation that you cannot afford to miss:

"Right believing always leads to right living!"

To understand this truth, you need to realize that everything that you see in creation came out of the spirit realm. God, who is a Spirit, spoke all the things that He created into being. In the same way, long before your blessing manifests physically, it is first in your spirit. The Bible says, "A good man out of the good treasure of his heart brings forth good things."[11] In other words, your life today is a reflection of what has been hidden and carried in your heart all this time. **So if you don't want your life to remain the same, the solution is not in changing your circumstances, the solution is in changing your heart, changing what you believe.** My friend, for every area of weakness, failure and defeat that you may be experiencing right now, I assure you that there has been some wrong believing in that area. Search the Scriptures for Jesus and the truth. Your answer lies in right believing.

For generations, the body of Christ has been defeated and put under a constant siege of condemnation from the accuser because they believe wrongly that the Holy Spirit convicts believers of their sins. Start believing rightly today. Read this chapter over and over again. Meditate on the verses that I have pointed out. Let the truth sink in and be set free by the knowledge that the Holy Spirit is your Helper, given by God to convict you of righteousness. You are the righteousness of God in Christ!

Right Believing Leads To Right Living — A Testimony

There is a precious brother in my church whose life started to turn around when he received Jesus as his Lord and Savior. However, he was still struggling with a smoking habit. He had been smoking for many years and not a day passed without him going through at least one pack of cigarettes. He shared with me that he felt really lousy every time he smoked. He felt condemned and constantly heard the voice of the accuser bombarding him with accusations:

"How can you call yourself a Christian? Look at you — you are still a smoker!"

"Give up! You are not worthy to be a Christian."

"You are such a hypocrite."

He kept hearing these accusations and the more he heard them, the more he smoked. He said that he really tried to muster all his willpower to overcome this destructive habit, but he just could not do it. He knew that his body was a temple of God and he sincerely wanted to glorify the Lord, but there was no power to do so. He started to condemn himself and was prepared to throw in the towel.

Then, he heard me preach on how the Holy Spirit is present in him to convict him of **righteousness**, and how the more he believed that he was righteous because of Jesus Christ, the more his behavior would start to line up with what he believed. So he began to confess this daily: "I am the righteousness of God through Jesus Christ." Every day, he would wake up, stare at himself in the mirror and say, "I see a righteous man standing in front of me." Even when he succumbed to the temptation and lit up, he would still confess, "I am the righteousness of God through Jesus Christ. Even right now, the Lord sees me righteous."

This brother really believed that he was righteous, not because of what he did, but because of what Jesus had done. And the more he believed that he was the righteousness of God, the more the power of his nicotine addiction faded. He began to have a supernatural strength to cut down his daily tobacco intake within a short span of time. He began to replace the voice of the accuser which said, "You are a hypocrite. How can you call yourself a Christian?" with the voice of the Holy Spirit which declared, "You are righteous in God's eyes. God sees you as righteous as Jesus Christ today." The voice of the Holy Spirit became louder and louder until it completely drowned out the voice of the accuser.

This precious brother finally stopped hearing the voice of condemnation and heard only the voice of righteousness, and one day, he woke up and realized that the desire for cigarettes was no longer there! Hallelujah! He was delivered from his destructive habit simply by believing the voice of the Holy Spirit and seeing himself as the righteousness of God every day. Just being faithful in believing and confessing, "I am the righteousness of God in Christ," caused a power to be released in his life that made the craving for cigarettes fall away. This is powerful, my friend!

His Grace Is Greater Than Your Addictions

Are you overwhelmed by an addiction today? It may be smoking, pornography, alcohol, drugs or gambling. Whatever it may be, my friend, God's grace is greater than any addiction in your life. His grace will swallow up your addiction. Today is your day of freedom and liberty. Today is the day that the Lord will set you free from every lie, guilt and condemnation that the accuser has been bombarding you with. Now, I want to pray this prayer with you:

> "Lord Jesus, I thank You for the cross. I thank You that when You died for me, Your blood cleansed me from all my unrighteousness and the sins of my entire life. You are my Lord and Savior. I give You all my addictions today. I am sick and tired of being defeated and condemned by the accuser. Today, I confess that because of the blood of Jesus Christ, I am right now the righteousness of God. By the supernatural strength and power of the Holy Spirit who is present to convict me of my righteousness, I will be reminded every day that I am the righteousness of God through Jesus Christ. Amen!"

Hallelujah! When you start believing that you are righteous apart from your works, the voice of the accuser who comes to condemn you will have no more dominion over your life. I look forward to hearing your testimony on how the Lord has delivered you from your addiction. The contact information for my ministry is at the end of this book. Write to us!

Come on, my friend, it is time to awake to righteousness and sin not. Right believing leads to right living. Believe that you are righteous and you will start living like a righteous man or woman of God. Condemnation may be the deepest root, but today, you have found the solution — simply believing that you are the righteousness of God because of Jesus Christ.

Is There Judgment For The Believer?

From John 16, I have established that the Holy Spirit came to convict the world (unbelievers) of the sin of unbelief in Jesus. But for the believer, the Holy Spirit came to convict him of his righteousness in Christ. Today, there are some believers who believe that the Holy Spirit is in them to convict them not just of their sins, but also of God's anger and judgment toward them. This is just not true either.

I have established in the earlier chapters that God's anger and judgment for all our sins have been exhausted on the body of Jesus when He hung on the cross. So what judgment is there for the believer today? When Jesus said, "… of judgment, because the ruler of this world is judged," who was He referring to? Believers or unbelievers? The answer is neither. He was referring to "the ruler of this world", as plainly stated in the verse.

"So who is the 'ruler of this world'?"

The "ruler of this world" is the devil, the accuser himself. When God created Adam and Eve, He gave them dominion over the world. But when Adam sinned, he handed this dominion over to the devil. That's why we live in a fallen world today, where we see sicknesses, diseases, wars, earthquakes and floods around us. These are **not** the "acts of God". They are the acts of the devil! Jesus did not come to destroy lives, but to save lives[12]. So anything that you see in the world that is destructive is the work of the "ruler of this world". But guess what? His lease on this world is running out, and we are edging closer and closer to the day when Jesus will return for us. Hallelujah!

My friend, we've seen in this chapter that the Holy Spirit has come to one, convict unbelievers of the sin of unbelief; two, convict believers of righteousness apart from works; and three, remind us that the devil has been judged at the cross. Now, this is called rightly dividing the Word! Confusion occurs when believers read the Scriptures and do not rightly divide whom the speaker is speaking to. All of God's Word is written for our benefit, but not all of it is written **to** us. The Holy Spirit will never call you a hypocrite, nor will He say, "What kind of Christian are you?" These are the words of the accuser, whose strategy is to spew condemnation on you to disqualify you and make you feel unworthy to enter God's presence. The Holy Spirit is called the **"Comforter"**[13]. He is here to comfort you and to point you back to the cross of Jesus every time you fail. The only thing that He will convict you of is your righteousness in Jesus Christ!

Believe that you are the righteousness of God in Christ and enjoy the blessings that are on the head of the righteous!

Today, beloved, believe that you are the righteousness of God in Christ. Start walking in the freedom from condemnation that Christ has purchased for you and enjoy the blessings that are on the head of the righteous[14]!

Chapter 12

Condemnation Kills

The accuser is an astute legal prosecutor who will not hesitate to use the Ten Commandments to condemn you. That's why the Word of God declares that the Ten Commandments are not just "the ministry of death", they are also "the ministry of condemnation"[1]. Remember, there is nothing unholy about the Ten Commandments. They are holy, just and good, but they have no power to make you holy, just and good. The law is an unbending and inflexible standard. It cannot compromise. When you fail, it cannot show you grace. If it does, then it is no longer the law!

That's why Apostle Paul said that "the commandment, which was to bring life, I found to bring death. For sin, taking occasion by the commandment, deceived me, and by it killed me"[2]. Notice that sin "by the commandment" deceived him and killed him. What that means is that when Paul came under the old covenant of law, he too came under the ministry of death and condemnation.

The law always ministers condemnation. If you are under the law, every time you fail and fall short of God's standards, you will be condemned. Grace, on the other hand, always ministers righteousness. That's why it is called the ministry of righteousness, which exceeds the ministry of condemnation in glory by much more.

> 2 Corinthians 3:9
> [9]For if the **ministry of condemnation** had glory, the **ministry of righteousness** exceeds much more in glory.

When you are under grace, even when you fail and fall short of God's standards, God still sees you as righteous because of Jesus Christ. God did not give the law for man to be made right through his own obedience. He gave the law so that man would have knowledge of sin. Without the law, sin was dead. Paul described it most aptly when he said, "I would not have known covetousness unless the law had said, 'You shall not covet.' But sin, taking opportunity by the commandment, produced in me all manner of evil desire. For apart from the law sin was dead."[3]

The law always ministers condemnation.
Grace, on the other hand, always ministers righteousness.

The Law Stirs Up Sinful Desires In Man

There is nothing wrong with the law. The problem is with man's flesh. It is like a group of teenage boys walking down a long street, just hanging out and having fun. They pass by a greenhouse and no one thinks anything of it — it is just another greenhouse. Then, they walk on to the end of the street where there is another greenhouse similar to the first one they just saw. But this time, all around the greenhouse are huge signs with big red letters saying:

"Do not throw stones or you will be handed over to the police."

Now, the first greenhouse had no signs and the boys didn't think twice about it. The second greenhouse had warning signs all around and now, the boys have stopped in their tracks because something inside them has been stirred. They look around to see if anybody is watching them, and then guess what?

The next thing you hear is the sound of glass breaking, followed by the sounds of footsteps scampering away.

When the boys were walking down the street, was the desire to commit mischief in them? Yes, it was there all along. But because there were no laws, the desire to sin that was in them was not stirred up. That's what the law does. It stirs up sin in us.

Let me give you another scenario. If you are the only person in a room and there is a door with a sign that says, "Private: Do Not Enter", what would happen? Very likely, you would look around the room to make sure that there are no hidden cameras, and slowly, you would be stirred to peer behind that door!

That is the effect the law has on all of us. There is nothing wrong with the law. There is nothing wrong with the Ten Commandments. Listen carefully to what I am saying. When you are dealing with the law of God, you have to be very precise, so let's keep to the language of the Scriptures. Paul said that the law was designed to bring forth the offense — "Moreover the law entered that the offense might abound."[4]

The law stirs up sinful desires in man's flesh. Let me tell you that as long as you are in your current body, you will have the propensity to sin. I did not come up with this. It was Paul who said, "For what I will to do, that I do not practice; but what I hate, that I do."[5]

What does this mean? It means that as long as you are in this body, even though you hate to lose your temper and be angry, trust me, you will. No matter how hard you try not to, you will fail. And when you fail, the devil will be ready to use God's law as a weapon to condemn you. He knows that if he is able to put you under condemnation, you will start to fear. That fear will bring stress, and then all kinds of psychosomatic sicknesses and oppression can start to make inroads in your life. This is no joking matter — condemnation kills!

The Secret To Overcoming Condemnation

So what is the solution to the accuser's barrage of condemnation?

Paul was faced with the same struggles that you and I are faced with today. His lament is recorded in Romans 7: "For the good that I will to do, I do not do; but the evil I will not to do, that I practice... O wretched man that I am! Who will deliver me from this body of death?"[6]

But Paul does not stop there. He goes on to show us in the first verse of Romans 8 how we can counter the accuser's attacks:

> Romans 8:1
> [1]There is therefore **now no condemnation** to those who are **in Christ Jesus**.

There is NOW NO CONDEMNATION to those who are IN CHRIST JESUS! This is such a powerful verse. I encourage you to commit this verse to memory for with it, you can repel all of the accuser's attacks! Are you in Christ Jesus today? Yes! Then, there is no condemnation over your life!

If you are in Christ Jesus today,
there is no condemnation over your life!

"But Pastor Prince, you always talk about interpreting scriptures in their context, and my Bible says that there is a condition for having no condemnation — we need to walk according to the Spirit, not according to the flesh. So it means that there will be no condemnation only if we do not sin."

I am so glad that you brought this up. Let's look at the entire verse of Romans 8:1 in the New King James Version (NKJV):

> Romans 8:1, NKJV
> [1]There is therefore now no condemnation to those who are in Christ Jesus, who do not walk according to the flesh, but according to the Spirit.

That's how it appears in your NKJV Bible right? But do you know that the last part, "who do not walk according to the flesh, but according to the Spirit", was added by the Bible translators and does not appear in the original Greek manuscripts[7]? It is almost as if the translators could not believe that the declaration of no condemnation comes without any conditions. Don't take my word for it, check it for yourself.

For a more accurate translation, look at the New American Standard Bible (NASB):

> Romans 8:1, NASB
> ¹Therefore there is now no condemnation for those who are in Christ Jesus.

That is it, my friend — no condemnation for those in Christ Jesus, **period**. There are no conditions and no prerequisites. It's all about Jesus' finished work and none of man's efforts. Hallelujah!

Yet, there are people who will argue that there is no condemnation only when we do not sin. My friend, if there is no sin, why would there be any condemnation to begin with? Paul's statement would be superfluous if there is no sin. So the good news that he was declaring is that even when there is sin, there is NOW no condemnation for those who are in Christ Jesus. Why? Because Jesus has already been condemned for all our sins. Amen!

When the word "therefore" appears in a scripture, always find out why it is there for. When Paul said, "There is **therefore** now no condemnation..." he was referring to how "sin, taking occasion by the commandment", had deceived and killed him. When Paul was struggling under the law, he was condemned again and again (you will find Paul's account of his struggle in Romans 7). In fact, he said, "O wretched man that I am! Who will deliver me from this body of death?" That was a rhetorical question. Look at his own reply: "I thank God — through Jesus Christ our Lord!"[8] It was because of Jesus Christ that Paul could declare that there is therefore now no condemnation to those who are in Christ Jesus!

Let me give you a practical tip on how you can grow in this revelation of "no condemnation": Learn to see the Ten Commandments (the law of God) and condemnation as the same thing. Whenever you read or think about the law, think "condemnation".

I was talking to a brother in church recently and he told me that his understanding of "obeying the law" was that one has to "do right". While it is true that the law tells you to do right, you will nevertheless always end up being condemned by the law. The law is called the "ministry of condemnation" because it wasn't designed to make you do right, but to condemn you. And you know what? The more you come under the law and attempt to be justified by it, the more you will fail and be condemned by it. This is not God's way. He doesn't want to see you living in guilt and condemnation because as I said earlier, condemnation is the deepest root that breeds fear, stress and all kinds of sicknesses. Condemnation literally kills you!

When the accuser comes to condemn you for all your faults and says things like, "How can you call yourself a Christian?" or "You are the biggest hypocrite in the world!", **that** is the time to start seeing yourself free from any condemnation. The opposite of the ministry of condemnation is the ministry of righteousness, which exceeds much more in glory. Begin to see yourself righteous not because of what you have done or not done, but because of what Jesus has done, and because His blood cleanses you continually. Remind yourself that the Holy Spirit was sent to convict you of your **righteousness** apart from works. The devil will use the law as a weapon to condemn you. But praise be to God, there is therefore now NO condemnation for those who are in Christ. When is there no condemnation? The Word of God says NOW!

Boldness To Go To His Throne Of Grace

"But Pastor Prince, what happens when I sin?"

Well, does "NOW" cover the moment when you sin? Of course it does. "There is therefore **now** no condemnation…" is a "now" verse. The declaration is true every moment, every day. It is true in the morning. It is true in the night. And when tomorrow comes, it is still true. There is presently, continuously, no condemnation for you because you are in Christ!

What will give you the boldness to go to God is the knowledge that He sees you completely righteous.

"Shouldn't we be at least a little bit condemned when we fail, so that we would return to God?"

When Adam was condemned, he hid from God. Beloved, when you fail, condemnation and guilt will cause you to run **from** God's presence. It is a lie that condemnation and guilt will lead you back to God. What will give you the boldness to go to Him is the knowledge that today, He is ever gracious and He sees you completely righteous. What will cause you to go boldly before His throne of grace is the knowledge that He will never condemn you because you are **in** Jesus Christ!

The Father's Heart Of Grace

Do you want to see how your heavenly Father responds when you have failed?

Look at the parable of the prodigal son which Jesus shared:

Luke 15:11–24

[11]"A certain man had two sons. [12]And the younger of them said to his father, 'Father, give me the portion of goods that falls to me.' So he divided to them his livelihood. [13]And not many days after, the younger son gathered all together, journeyed to a far country, and there wasted his possessions with prodigal living. [14]But when he had spent all, there arose a severe famine in that land, and he began to be in want. [15]Then he went and joined himself to a citizen of that country, and he sent him into his fields to feed swine. [16]And he would gladly have filled his stomach with the pods that the swine ate, and no one gave him anything. [17]"But when he came to himself, he said, 'How many of my father's hired servants have bread enough and to spare, and I perish with hunger! [18]I will arise and go to my father, and will say to him, "Father, I have sinned against heaven and before you, [19]and I am no longer worthy to be called your son. Make me like one of your hired servants."' [20]"And he arose and came to his father. But when he was still a great way off, his father saw him and had compassion, and ran and fell on his neck and kissed him. [21]And the son said to him, 'Father, I have sinned

against heaven and in your sight, and am no longer worthy to be called your son.' 22"But the father said to his servants, 'Bring out the best robe and put it on him, and put a ring on his hand and sandals on his feet. 23And bring the fatted calf here and kill it, and let us eat and be merry; 24for this my son was dead and is alive again; he was lost and is found.' And they began to be merry.

We see a father who runs toward his prodigal son to embrace him the moment he sees him from a distance. Do you know that the father's behavior is actually contrary to the law of Moses? I was studying this sometime back and I found that according to the law, if a man has a stubborn and rebellious son who refuses to heed his parents, that man is supposed to bring his son to the elders of the city, and all the men of his city are to stone his son to death, so that they can put away the evil from among them, and all Israel shall hear and fear[9]. That's the law of Moses.

When Jesus shared the story of the prodigal son, all the Jewish people who heard Him would have been familiar with this law. However, instead of the condemnation and punishment that the rebellious son deserved under the law, Jesus revealed the Father's heart of grace and forgiveness in the new covenant. At that point, Jesus had not yet died to establish the new covenant of grace and the people listening to Him were all still under the law of Moses. Jesus was giving them a taste of what was to come. He was showing them the reality that we enjoy today. Hallelujah!

Did the son sin against his father? Yes, most definitely. But did the father heap guilt and condemnation on his son before he received his son? No, he did not. In fact, the father did not even give his son the opportunity to finish his rehearsed speech. The father interrupted his son before he could ask to be made one of his hired servants. The father interrupted him not to condemn him for sinning against him, but to instruct his servants to bring out the best robe, put a ring on his son's hand and sandals on his son's feet!

Did it matter to the father that his son's intentions may not have been all that good? We all know that the son was not returning to the father's house because he had realized his mistake. He was returning because he was hungry! When he was feeding the pigs, he remembered that even the hired servants in his father's house had more than enough food to eat. **That** was when he decided to head back to his father's house. But the father did not care what his son's intentions were. When the prodigal son "was still a great way off" (and the father had no way of determining why his son was returning), his father saw him and had compassion, and ran and fell on his son's neck and kissed him. What a wonderful picture of God's heart of love!

Who was the one sharing the parable of the prodigal son? It was Jesus. I think Jesus knows His Father really well, wouldn't you agree? We are hearing an eyewitness account of what God the Father is like, and Jesus should know! See how He described God's response to those who have sinned. How is it that the father saw his son even when he was still a great way off? That's because the father had been waiting and longing for his son to return. He must have kept his eyes on the horizon daily, hoping that each day would be the day his beloved son returned home.

Can you see His heart of love for you even when you have failed Him? You just have to take one step toward God and your loving Daddy in heaven will run toward you with no condemnation. He wants to fall upon you, kiss you, and lavish you with His love and blessings! He is waiting to clothe you with the robe of righteousness, put the signet ring of authority back in your hands and shod your feet with the sandals of right standing. He wants to reinstate you, wash you and throw a party because you came home! Our God is a God who will run toward you with NO CONDEMNATION.

Let's cast aside our religious ideas about God. Take that one step toward your Daddy even when you have failed, and He will run to you and embrace you. He loves you and accepts you just as you are. He has all the power to help you when you fail and feel defeated.

Rejoice, my friend — there is now no condemnation for you because you are in Christ Jesus!

Your Daddy loves you and accepts you just as you are, and He has all the power to help you when you fail and feel defeated.

Chapter 13

The Gift Of No Condemnation

When I had just completed my studies, I decided to take on a part-time job teaching in an elementary school, while waiting for my academic results to be released. I was made the teacher in charge of a class of about thirty 10-year-old students.

One morning, one of the girls in my class did not turn up. I didn't think much of it as it was common for students to be absent from school for a day or two for various reasons. But as I was praying at home that day, the Lord brought this particular girl to my mind. I prayed regularly for my students, but it was usually a general prayer for all of them. Because it was so specific this time, I knew that it was the Lord leading me to pray for her, so I prayed for the blood of Jesus to cover her. Even though my understanding of the blood of Jesus was rather limited at that time, I knew enough to know that His blood protects, so that was what I prayed for.

Several days after that, the girl still had not returned to school. Then, her name and picture appeared in the news. Her story was covered on national television and in all the major newspapers. This student of mine had actually been kidnapped by a notorious local serial killer by the name of Adrian Lim. A murderer who was involved in the occult, Adrian Lim kidnapped children and offered them as human sacrifices to the idols that he worshipped.

To the surprise of many, this girl was actually released by the serial killer! When interviewed by the press, the girl shared that she had been taken to a small room reeking of burning incense. The room was very dimly illuminated, but she could see Adrian Lim performing some kind of ceremonial rite and offering prayers before his idols. Suddenly, he stared at her and said with disgust that his gods did not want her. She was then set free, becoming the only girl to have been released by Adrian Lim. The other children who were kidnapped had been brutally murdered. When I heard that, I knew that it was the Lord who had protected her. No other god could have her because she was covered by the blood of Jesus! Today, this girl is all grown up and happily married with kids. Praise the Lord!

The Blood Protects You From Condemnation

At that point in time, I did not know what the main function of Jesus' blood was or why it provided protection. I just covered everything with the blood of Jesus. I am not against Christians applying the blood of Jesus for protection, but today, I have a deeper understanding of His blood.

Do you know what Jesus said about His blood on the night that He was betrayed? During the last supper, when Jesus held the cup in His hands, did He say, "This is the blood of the new covenant, shed for your protection"? No! He said, "This is My blood of the new covenant, which is shed for many for the remission of sins."[1] His blood was shed **for the forgiveness of all your sins**. Does the blood of Jesus protect? Yes, of course it does! But even though His blood protects us from the schemes of the devil, that's not the main reason His blood was shed.

Knowing you are protected from condemnation will cause you to reign over that sin, addiction or depression that is holding you in bondage today.

My friend, the main reason our Savior's blood was shed was for the forgiveness of our sins. This means that the blood of Jesus also offers us protection from any form of condemnation. When you have a revelation that Jesus' blood has made you righteous and that all your sins are forgiven, you are protected from condemnation from the accuser. It's imperative that you understand this because it will give you the confidence to come before the throne of God boldly and see Him as a loving Father. It will cause you to reign over that sin, addiction or depression that is holding you in bondage today.

My Struggle With Condemnation

I wished that somebody had shared this revelation with me when I was going through the ordeal of thinking that I had committed the unpardonable sin. The condemnation that I felt and the belief that I had blasphemed the Holy Spirit were actually from the accuser. It was a terrible season for me and all the teachings that I received then did not help.

Today, I understand that it is impossible for a believer to commit the unpardonable sin — the sin of constant and consistent rejection of Jesus Christ. So if you are a believer, you have already received Jesus and there is no way you can commit the unpardonable sin.

But there I was, a young man with almost no knowledge of the new covenant of grace, no revelation of my righteousness in Christ and no understanding of the main function of the blood of Jesus. Without these truths, I fell for the great deception. I believed that I had sinned irrevocably against God. I thought that I had blasphemed against the Holy Spirit because I had bad thoughts about God and the Holy Spirit. I was relentlessly bombarded with feelings of guilt and condemnation, until I felt like my mind was about to snap.

All that condemnation was from the devil. The accuser had put negative thoughts in my mind about God and I did not know how to resist him, so I took the thoughts as my own, and received his lies and condemnation for those thoughts. Back then, I did not even know that God had a call on my life. How could I? I really believed that I was not even going to make it to heaven because of the unpardonable sin that I had committed!

Plagued by the overwhelming sense of condemnation, I went to a man of God for prayer, hoping that he would be able to free me from my fears and oppression. His name is Percy Campbell and at that time, he was overseeing one of the prominent Bible schools in Singapore.

Percy laid his hands on me and prayed over me. Even now, I can still remember exactly how Percy, with his distinctive New Zealander accent, said, "Joe, I see you in the spirit. I see you preaching to thousands of people." Now, at that time, I was still in high school, and could hardly speak in front of a crowd without stammering and stuttering. In fact, there was this really cruel teacher who would always get me to stand up and read in class. All the girls would end up giggling and laughing at me as I stammered and stuttered, trying desperately to get one sentence out. My face would turn red and my ears would burn. Those were painful moments indeed. So when I came to Percy for deliverance from my oppression, but received instead his prophecy that I would speak to thousands, it actually scared me.

In 2004, Percy visited our church and saw for himself just how much our church had grown by God's grace. When we finally spoke after the service, it was with tears in his eyes that he said, "The prophecy has come to pass." He remembered what he had spoken over me many years ago when I was still a teenager struggling with oppression and condemnation. All glory to Jesus!

My friend, I know what it means to be under guilt and condemnation from the accuser. He is using the same strategy to afflict believers today. The devil will come at various times to make you feel guilty for anything you can think of. He makes you feel guilty in your role as a father. He makes you feel guilty as a provider. He makes you feel guilty as an employee. He makes you feel guilty as an employer. He will even make you feel guilty for being sick!

By the way, a believer should never feel guilty for being sick. We have to be careful not to create a culture in the church where people think that you will never be attacked by symptoms of sickness if you are walking with God. Having a sickness or disease does not mean that you have sinned or that God is teaching you a lesson. It just means that your healing is on its way!

When Jesus and His disciples saw a man born blind, His disciples asked Him if the man was born blind because he had sinned or because his parents had sinned. Jesus answered, "Neither." He went on to say, "I am the light of the world," and proceeded to open the man's eyes[2]. I love Jesus' style!

My friend, when there is a problem, deal with it. Don't ask whose fault it is! Don't ask if it is your father's fault, your grandfather's fault or your great-grandfather's fault. No, let's learn to handle situations Jesus' way. When faced with a man who was blind, Jesus declared that He was the light of the world and proceeded to heal the man. So don't let the devil make you feel guilty for being sick. It is guilt that will keep you sick!

Eradicate All Condemnation From Your Life

The devil is smarter than many psychiatrists and psychologists because he does not deal with what is peripheral. He does not get distracted by superficial details. Do you know what the devil's name is? His name is not "murderer", even though he kills. It is not "thief", even though he steals. It is not "destroyer" either, even though he destroys. His name is Satan. In Hebrew, it means "the accuser"[3]. He is the prosecutor against you. A prosecutor never talks about any of your good points. He is there to prosecute you for every one of your failures. He will bring back every piece of dirty laundry and show you evidence after evidence of your failures.

While we are trying to deal with stress and fear, the devil goes straight for the deepest root, and uses the law to heap guilt and condemnation on you. He knows that when you are under **condemnation**, fear, stress and all kinds of sicknesses will follow, so he goes straight for the jugular.

When you are under condemnation,
fear, stress and all kinds of sicknesses will follow.

What should we do then? We should kill condemnation at its very root and eradicate it from our lives. So when you hear the voice of the accuser, remind yourself that there is now no condemnation to those who are in Christ[4]. Why? Because no matter what the devil condemns you of, the truth is that the blood of Jesus has been shed for the forgiveness of all your sins. There is not a sin, not one iota of guilt or condemnation that the devil can throw at you today that Jesus' blood has not completely removed.

No wonder Isaiah chapter 54 says that no weapon formed against you shall prosper. What is the weapon that the devil uses against you? We have learned that it is the law. The devil uses the law to condemn believers and remind them that they have fallen short. But the Word of God declares, "No weapon formed against you shall prosper, and **every tongue which rises against you in judgment** you shall condemn."[5] The devil uses his tongue to speak words of guilt and condemnation to you, but by the blood of Jesus, you have the authority and the power to condemn every word of judgment that comes against you!

The Gift Of No Condemnation

"Pastor Prince, if believers know that there is now no condemnation for them, won't they go out and sin?"

Well, it is obvious that Jesus did not think so. Do you remember what He said to the woman who was caught in adultery?

John 8:10–11
[10]When Jesus had raised Himself up and saw no one but the woman, He said to her, "Woman, where are those accusers of yours? Has no one condemned you?" [11]She said, "No one, Lord." And Jesus said to her, **"Neither do I condemn you; go and sin no more."**

Now, pay close attention to this: Jesus gave her the gift of "no condemnation" **before** He told her to go and sin no more. Yet, the church today says, "Go and sin no more first, and only then will we not condemn you." That's the reason people are shying away from churches. It is not because they are rebelling against Jesus. It is because they have not been introduced to the Jesus who gives the guilty sinner **the gift of no condemnation**!

Too often, non-believers have only been introduced to Christianity as a set of rules that only judges and condemns them. If you conduct a poll among non-believers to find out what they know about Christianity, many of them would probably be familiar only with the Ten Commandments. They know only about the law that kills and not the Person who came to bring life!

But my friend, Christianity is not about laws. It is about Jesus and how He shed His blood for the forgiveness of our sins, for without blood, the Bible says that there is no forgiveness of sins[6]. That is why Christianity is a relationship based on the shed blood of Jesus Christ. His blood washed away all our sins, and the laws that we were supposed to fulfill, He fulfilled on our behalf. Even Jesus Himself came against legalism. His strongest words were said to the religious Pharisees and not the sinners. I challenge you to find any instance in the Bible where Jesus called tax collectors or prostitutes a "brood of vipers"!

Now, let's come back to the story of the woman caught in adultery. Let me ask you a question: Was the woman guilty? Yes, she was, absolutely. There is no doubt about that. The Bible states that she was "caught in adultery, in the very act"[7]. But instead of condemning her according to the law of Moses, which required her to be stoned to death (the law of Moses always ministers condemnation and death, it cannot save the guilty sinner), Jesus showed her grace and gave her the gift of no condemnation.

Jesus believed that when someone really has a revelation that God does not condemn them, they would have the power to get out of the vicious circle of sin.

Do you think that the woman would go off, look for her lover, and jump back into bed with him after she had received the gift of no condemnation? No, of course not! It is obvious that Jesus believed that when someone really has a revelation that God does not condemn them, they would have the **power** to get out of the vicious circle of sin. They would have the power to "go and sin no more"!

What are you going to put your trust in today? Jesus' grace which swallows up sin? Or man's fears that believers would use "grace" as a license for them to sin?

Condemnation Perpetuates The Cycle Of Defeat

Let me tell you this: If you are under condemnation, you are doomed to repeat your sin. Why? Because when you are under condemnation, you feel guilty and condemned, and you believe that fellowship with God is broken. And since you believe that God is far away, you will end up committing that sin again. You may do something good that makes you feel that you have restored fellowship with God, but when you fail again, you start receiving condemnation again, and the cycle of defeat continues.

Jesus' method of countering sin is completely different. When you sin, He says to you, "Neither do I condemn you, go and sin no more." When you receive the gift of no condemnation from Him, you will know beyond any doubt that fellowship with God is never broken because the blood of Jesus continually cleanses you. Believing that you are the righteousness of God through Christ Jesus and simply receiving the gift of no condemnation give you the power to go and sin no more.

Do Not Back Away From Grace

"Pastor Prince, I know of someone who says that he is under grace, but is clearly living in sin. Can a person be under grace and still live in sin?"

My friend, do not back away from the gospel of grace just because you see some negative examples. Go to the person and confront him! If he says, "Well, I am under grace," but still lives a lifestyle of sin, this is what I'll say to him: "No, you are **not** under grace. The Bible says that sin shall not have dominion over you when you are **not under law but under grace**[8]. So if you are living in sin, you are **definitely** not under grace. You are not enjoying the gift of no condemnation and the free, unmerited favor of God. That is why sin has dominion over you. You cannot claim to be under grace when you continue to live in sin!" Such people become agents that the devil uses to instill suspicion and fear against the gospel of grace. But our part is not to back away from the gospel that Jesus preached just because a very small group of people use grace as an excuse for their lifestyle of sin.

If someone has really known and experienced grace and the gift of no condemnation, he will NOT want to live in sin. Sin will be the last thing on his mind! Let me put it very clearly: **Anyone who is living in sin is not under grace** and has not experienced the gift of no condemnation. Grace always results in victory over sin!

The Power To Sin No More

I believe that most believers desire to live lives that are glorifying to God and that most of us normal, rational human beings are NOT looking for an excuse to sin. But there is a struggle which Paul himself wrote about: "For what I will to do, that I do not practice; but what I hate, that I do."[9]

I am writing to believers who have this genuine struggle with the law and who like Paul are crying out, "O wretched man that I am! Who will deliver me from this body of death?"[10] If this is your cry, then this is written especially for you: The person who will deliver you is Jesus. His amazing grace will save every "wretched man". In all your helplessness, weaknesses and vulnerabilities, Jesus looks at you with His tender loving eyes and says to you, "Where are those accusers of yours? Has no one condemned you? Neither do I condemn you. Go and sin no more."

Every time you fail in thought, word or deed, receive this afresh: There is now no condemnation to those who are in Christ. When Jesus died on the cross, all your failures were already condemned in His body. Today, you are free to live a victorious life not because of your obedience to the law, but because of your obedience of faith in Jesus' blood and righteousness.

Every time you fail in thought, word or deed, receive this afresh: There is now no condemnation to those who are in Christ.

Paul said, "For **what the law could not do** in that it was weak through the flesh, **God did** by sending His own Son in the likeness of sinful flesh, on account of sin: He condemned sin in the flesh."[11] What the law could not do, God did (notice the use of the past tense) by sending His Son. The law could not save the "wretched man" that we were. It could only condemn us. But God saved us by placing all the guilt, punishment and condemnation for our sins on Jesus' body at Calvary.

Your inheritance today is no longer guilt, punishment and condemnation for your sins, but righteousness, peace and joy through Jesus Christ. This is God's way for you to experience effortless success in your life. He has already done it all on your behalf. Your part is simply to believe and receive. That is how you walk in victory over sin, addictions, negative thoughts and every cycle of defeat that has you in bondage. Good news? That is the gospel of Jesus Christ!

Chapter 14

No More Consciousness Of Sin

One of the things that I was taught during my formative years as a Christian was that I had to search my heart for sin before I could worship the Lord. I was told to bow my head and search my heart for sin. Each time I did so, I felt like I was entering a dark and dingy storeroom filled with cobwebs. I pictured myself peering around and searching for all my sins with a little torchlight. And the more I searched, the more I felt unworthy to worship the Lord. The more I probed, the more I found, and I would start to feel too condemned to even think that I was qualified to enter His holy presence.

So instead of being more conscious of the love of my Savior, I became more and more self-conscious — more conscious of my sins, uncleanness, guilt and unworthiness. Initially, my hands would be raised and I'd be all ready to praise and worship God, but the more I searched my heart for sin, the more my hands would hang down with dejection and my head bow down with disappointment. How could I worship God? How could I have the courage and audacity to enter His courts with praise?

Come To Him Just As You Are

As I grew and matured in the things of God, I realized that the idea that you had to be "right" before you could worship Jesus is man's **tradition**. The woman in Luke chapter 7, who came to Jesus with an alabaster flask of fragrant oil, simply fell at His feet and worshipped Him. She washed His feet with her tears and wiped them with her hair before anointing them with the oil. The Bible clearly records that the woman was a sinner, but it says nothing about her searching her heart or confessing her sins before she worshipped Jesus. She worshipped Him just as she was, and after that, Jesus said to her, "Your sins are forgiven."[1]

Whatever your need is, come to Jesus. He is your Savior, your healer, your provider and your peace. He is your "I AM".

I think that the devil has tried to rob us of this tremendous truth. Whatever your need is, whether you are mired in debt, trapped in a particular sin or fearful for your future, come to Jesus. He is your Savior. He is your healer. He is your provider. He is your peace. He is your forgiveness. He is your "I AM", which means that He is the great "I AM" for whatever situation you are facing in your life.

Whatever lack you may be facing right now, He is your solution. Come and worship Him just as you are, and He **will** meet you at your point of need. You don't have to worry about your sin because you are worshipping your forgiver. You don't have to worry about your sickness because you are worshipping your healer. If believers really knew this truth, even wild horses would not be able to stop them from coming to worship God!

Do you know anyone who cleans himself before he takes a bath? Sounds ridiculous, right? Yet, there are people who avoid going to Jesus because they feel that they should "straighten things out" in their lives first. Can't they see that what they're really saying is that they need to clean themselves before they can take a bath? Come on, Jesus is the "bath" that makes us clean! He **is** the solution and He will help us straighten out what we will never be able to straighten out on our own.

The lie that you have to clean yourself first is so entrenched in the church that many believers say, "Pastor, I don't want to come to Jesus until I make my life right." If that is your refrain, then the sad truth is that you will **never** come to Jesus because you will never come to a place where you can make your life "right". Come to the bath and the bath will make you clean. Come just as you are with all your sins, and Jesus will wash you clean of all guilt and condemnation.

The world needs to hear this truth, and not be given a bunch of do's and don'ts. Preach the truth and the world will come flocking to churches for their answers. They are searching for the real thing and that's what we can offer them. But the real thing is not found in two pieces of stone. You cannot have a relationship with the cold, hard and impersonal law engraved on stones. But you can definitely have a relationship with our Savior Jesus Christ. He is warm, loving and full of grace. People will flock to where the true gospel of Jesus is being preached — the gospel that God commissioned Paul to preach, the gospel of grace, forgiveness and no more condemnation!

God's Grace Will Teach You To Deny Ungodliness

Do you know what can produce character, godliness and the fruit of the Holy Spirit in the body of Christ? Contrary to what some preachers of the law are saying, it is the unadulterated gospel of the **grace** of God that will produce all these good fruit. The Bible states it plainly: "For the **grace of God** that brings salvation has appeared to all men, teaching us that, **denying ungodliness and worldly lusts,** we should live soberly, righteously, and godly in the present age."[2] Clearly, it is the "grace of God" that will produce sober, righteous and godly living!

Grace is not a teaching. It is not a doctrine. It is not a topic in Bible school curricula. Grace is a person and His name is Jesus.

What I love about preaching the gospel of grace is that God's Word is always being preached in its context. I honestly don't understand how those who oppose grace can still teach within the context of the Scriptures. It is not the "law of God" that appeared to teach man how to deny ungodliness and worldly lust. Yet, this is what you hear being preached all the time.

It is time to emphasize what the Bible emphasizes. The new covenant is all about the grace of God that brings salvation. And grace is not a teaching. It is not a doctrine. It is not a topic in Bible school curricula. Grace is a person and His name is Jesus. Grace "appeared to all men" teaching us the secret to godliness, character and holiness. He showed us that it is all found in Him and His work on the cross. When you have Him, you are godly. When you have Him, you are made righteous. When you have Him, good character will manifest. When you have Him, you are made holy!

Understanding Holiness

What is holiness? The conventional understanding of holiness is that it is about doing right. But check the word "holiness" in the original Greek and you will find that it is the word *hagiasmos,* which means "separation to God"[3]. Therefore, being holy means that you have been set apart, made **uncommon** from the rest of the world of unbelievers.

In the old covenant, when God set the children of Israel apart from the world, He insulated them from the plagues that were brought against Egypt. God takes care of His own. In the old covenant, He provided for the Israelites and protected them because they were made holy and set apart unto Him by the blood of bulls and goats. How much more for us in the new covenant, who are made holy and set apart unto God forever by the blood of the everlasting sacrifice of Jesus Christ!

What this means is that even when the world is facing a financial crisis, we who are made holy by Jesus' blood will have more than enough in our storehouses. It means that even when there are all kinds of pestilences, sicknesses and diseases in the world, like mad cow disease and bird flu, we are made holy and set apart to enjoy God's protection and divine health!

My friend, God does not require you to search your heart and locate your sins before you can worship Him. When the psalmist David cried out, "Search me, O God, and know my heart,"[4] he was asking **God** to search him. He was not searching his heart himself. In any case, today, all that God will find if He searches you is your righteousness in Jesus Christ, for He sees you as righteous, holy and forgiven. He has already declared,

"Your sins and your lawless deeds I will remember no more."[5]

How do you see yourself today? Are you more conscious of your sins, or are you more conscious of your righteousness and what Jesus' blood has done? Tradition has taught us to be occupied with self, but grace teaches us to be occupied with Christ. The more you are occupied with yourself, the more dejected, oppressed and depressed you become. From whichever angle you see yourself, you'll see ugliness, unworthiness and disqualification.

To be occupied with Christ is to turn away from self and to see Jesus. He is like a precious diamond. When you hold Him up in the light of God's Word, whichever way you turn Him, He sparkles with rays of beauty, perfection, righteousness, holiness and wholeness. Can you see that? Look away from your own frailty and see Jesus because the Word of God says, **"As He is, so are you in this world."**[6] Is Jesus holy? Then so are you!

Just **how** holy are you? Earlier on, I explained that you are not made holy by your thoughts and actions. You are made holy because of Jesus' sacrifice on the cross. Now, let's go just a little deeper to examine the sacrifice that was made on your behalf.

The book of Leviticus talks about the five offerings of the old covenant: The burnt offering, peace offering, meal offering, sin offering and trespass offering. These offerings are shadows or typologies of what our Lord Jesus accomplished when He offered His life for us on the cross. Jesus, as our sacrificial offering, did such an amazing work that it takes five offerings to depict the one act of His sacrifice on the cross! I will just focus on two of the more important offerings in this book — the burnt offering and the sin offering.

The Sin Offering

Let's focus on the sin offering first. According to the law, a man must bring a sin offering to the priest whenever he sins. Imagine that you are living in Old Testament times. You have sinned and you are now bringing a lamb as your sin offering to the priest.

The first thing that will happen is that the priest will examine the lamb to ensure that it has no blemishes. The lamb must be without blemish and perfect because it speaks of Jesus' perfection. Jesus knew no sin and committed no sin. He is the true sacrificial Lamb without blemish.

After the priest has examined your sin offering, you must lay your hands on its head.

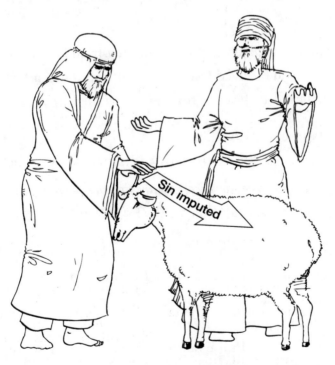

The Sin Offering

Why must you lay your hands on the lamb's head? Laying hands on the animal that you bring to the priest is an act of identification. When you lay your hands on your sin offering, your sins are transferred to the innocent lamb. After you lay your hands on the lamb, you must kill it. The lamb must die because all your sins have been transferred to its body. And because it dies bearing your sins, you can go free.

In the same way, Jesus had to die on the cross with your sins so that you might go free. He was not murdered. He came to lay down His life for you and me[7]. He chose to become our sin offering on the cross. That is why, when John the Baptist saw Jesus, he said, "Behold! The Lamb of God who takes away the sin of the world!"[8] That is why Apostle Paul said, "For He made Him who knew no sin to be sin for us."[9]

Do you know what all this means, my friend? It means that the moment you received Jesus Christ into your life, **all** your sins were transferred to Jesus... **forever**! Jesus died in your place as your sin offering, so that you might go free. What a wonderful Savior we have!

By Jesus' one sacrifice, you are forever perfected, every single day for the rest of your life.

But there is a big difference between the sin offering in the Old Testament and Jesus' sacrifice for you on the cross. In the Old Testament, the blood of bulls and goats could only provide a temporal covering for sin. Every time man failed, he had to offer another sin offering. Praise be to God that in the new covenant, the Bible declares that "by one offering He has **perfected forever** those who are being sanctified"[10].

The blood of bulls and goats could never take away sins, so the sacrifices had to be offered repeatedly. But Jesus' sacrifice was **"once for all"**[11]. It is a complete and finished work, and He never needs to be sacrificed again! Jesus **is** the perfect sin offering. His blood does not just cover your sins temporarily. **All** your sins have been removed permanently! Even if you fail tomorrow, Jesus would not need to be offered again. His sacrifice has perfected you... for how long? Forever! You are **forever** perfected, every single day for the rest of your life. The blood of Jesus is continually cleansing you. You are now under the waterfall of forgiveness and you are sanctified perpetually. Hallelujah!

The Burnt Offering

The sin offering speaks of your sins being transferred to the body of Jesus on the cross. That is why God does not want you to be conscious of your sins today. He wants you to be conscious of your forgiveness.

Let's look at the burnt offering now. The burnt offering is beautiful because while the sin offering speaks of Jesus taking your sins on His own body, the burnt offering speaks of the righteousness of Jesus being transferred to you at the cross.

When you read the book of Leviticus, you will see that of the five offerings, God put the sin offering last and the burnt offering first. Man puts it the other way round — we first come to God with all our sins, and all our sins are judged as a sin offering at the cross of Jesus. There is nothing wrong with this order, but God does not expect us to stop there. He wants us to know that

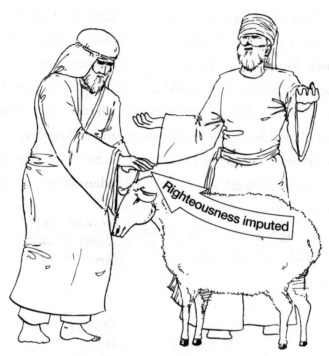

The Burnt Offering

Jesus did not just die for our sins, He also died as our burnt offering to make us well-pleasing, righteous and favored before God. That is why when the burnt offering is offered, it ascends as a "sweet aroma" to the Lord[12]. (There is no sweet aroma in the sin offering.) The sweet aroma from the burnt offering speaks of Jesus' beauty, perfection and loveliness to the Father.

This may be the first time you are hearing all this, so let me reiterate the difference. The sin offering speaks of your sins being transferred to Jesus, while the burnt offering speaks of Jesus' worthiness before God, His acceptance before God and His delight before His Father **being transferred to you**. Today, God favors you in exactly the same way He favors His Son.

Unfortunately, there are believers today who only understand that they have been forgiven. They do not understand that they have been made righteous as well by the cross of Jesus. Because of this, they have allowed themselves to come under condemnation. If this describes you, then rejoice — let the truth that God sees you clothed with the righteousness of His Son, because Jesus became your burnt offering at the cross, set you free today from every guilt and condemnation!

If you believe that you don't deserve success but deserve to be punished, you will unconsciously punish yourself and cause yourself to fail.

Self-Condemnation Is Destructive

The reason that some believers are sick, depressed and oppressed is that instead of being conscious of their righteousness in Christ, they have sin on their conscience. The moment they sin, they unconsciously feel that **someone** (usually themselves) must pay.

If this describes you, then pay attention because I am going to tell you what happens to you when you are conscious of your sins, instead of your forgiveness and righteousness. When you sin and come under condemnation, your mind and body begin to say, "He wants to punish himself, so let's make him pay." Your body will respond to this need for punishment, and you may start to develop depression and sickness in your body.

Many believers are sick today not because of sin, for sin has already been punished on the body of Jesus, but **because**

of condemnation. In the earlier chapters, we looked at condemnation from the accuser, but now I am talking to you about self-condemnation and your unconscious desire to inflict punishment on yourself when you know that you have sinned.

My friend, self-condemnation is destructive. When you fail to see that Jesus has already borne your punishment, you will punish yourself, or take it out on your family with verbal or even physical abuse. If you believe that you deserve to be punished and that you do not deserve success, you will unconsciously activate a self-sabotaging mechanism to punish yourself and cause yourself to fail. You could be on the brink of a lucrative business contract, or about to embark on an exciting career opportunity, but somehow, you find yourself doing something that sabotages the entire deal and causes it to crumble before your eyes. Why? Because deep down you think that you do not deserve it.

Self-condemnation also manifests itself with destructive effect in relationships. If you are in a wonderful relationship with somebody who really loves and cares for you, you will inevitably do something that sabotages the relationship because again, something inside tells you that you do not deserve to be loved by this person.

Psychiatrists will tell you that a person with such behavior is driven by guilt and has a perpetual sense of wanting to punish himself. The world has all kinds of fancy terms to describe people who exhibit an unconscious desire for punishment, but it cannot show you how to overcome it. It takes a revelation of the finished work of Jesus to overcome it.

Beloved, wake up and realize that Jesus has already been punished on your behalf. Stop condemning and punishing yourself because Jesus has already been condemned and punished on your behalf! If you say that you believe that God has forgiven you of all your sins, then why are you still feeling guilty? The existence of guilt and condemnation in your life tells you that you do not really believe that all your sins have been forgiven.

In the Old Testament, the Israelites had a consciousness of sins because their repeated sacrifices reminded them of their sins. The blood of bulls and goats just could not take away sins[13]. However, today, believers have no business living with sin-consciousness because Jesus, their once-for-all sin offering, has already taken away all their sins! And because of the burnt offering of Jesus, they should be living with righteousness-consciousness!

Pay Attention If You Desire To Glorify God

Let me just qualify that I am writing to believers who have a desire to glorify God in their lives, but are struggling with guilt and condemnation. If you are living in sin and have no desire to leave this kind of lifestyle, that's a different story. You can try not to be sin-conscious all you like, but you will not succeed simply because you are living in sin (for example, staying in an adulterous affair with no desire to terminate it). Get out of that lifestyle of sin by the grace of God!

Do you understand that there is a distinction? You can be struggling with sin-consciousness even though you are not living in sin. I am writing to those of you who desire to break out of the cycle of defeat that self-condemnation brings. I am writing to those of you who are trapped in the lie that you do not deserve success in life. I am writing to those of you who want to stop sabotaging yourself because of guilt and condemnation. I am writing to those of you who are not living in sin, but are nevertheless struggling with sin-consciousness.

Beloved, I am writing to those of you who have been robbed of the boldness to enter God's presence and worship Him because after "searching your heart", you have convinced yourself that you do not qualify. If I am describing you, my friend, I pray that today will be the day of your freedom.

Jesus Was An Overpayment For All Your Sins

You and I owed God a sin debt that we could never pay. But Jesus has already paid our debt. In fact, He OVERPAID it so that we would never have the debt on our conscience ever again! Let me share an illustration with you that I pray will open your eyes to just how fully paid your debt is.

I'm going to use two of my pastors for this illustration — Pastor Henry and Pastor Lawrence. Let's say that you borrowed US$50,000 from Lawrence and promised to pay him back in a month. But as time went by, you simply could not pay him the money. Now, even if Lawrence does not ask you for the money, what would happen to your relationship with him because of this **debt on your conscience**? Would you be going up to him and slapping him on the back, saying, "Hey, brother, how are you?" No way! If you ran into Lawrence, you would probably sheepishly mutter something like, "Oh, hi... er... sorry, I have to go now, see you around… er… sometime." Most of the time, you would probably go out of your way to avoid him.

Now, imagine that one day, Henry hears about your debt to Lawrence. And let's say that Henry is a billionaire and a good friend to you. He needs to fly off to Paris, but before he leaves, he goes to Lawrence to find out how much you owe him. Lawrence tells him that you owe him US$50,000. Henry gives him US$1 million! Of course, Lawrence is shocked. He protests, saying that you do not owe him that much money. But Henry insists on giving him US$1 million because Henry loves you and wants to make sure that you will never feel the debt on your heart ever again.

So your debt is more than paid. But two things could still happen that would result in the debt remaining on your conscience. Let's imagine that Henry had to rush off to Paris and had no time to speak to you, so he tasks one of his assistants to inform you that your debt has already been paid. But when the assistant speaks to you, he fails to fully convey the fact that your debt has been paid, and that Lawrence has in fact, been enriched by Henry because of the debt you owed him. The assistant says, "Er… I was told to tell you that your debt has been paid. But I'm not very sure of the details, so maybe it would be good for you to continue paying Lawrence whatever you can."

What happened in this scenario? The messenger failed to convey the good news, and you are left with no assurance that your debt has really been paid and that you are free of it. This is sad, but do you know that this is precisely what is happening in the body of Christ? People are being told by preachers that Jesus did cry out "It is finished!" on the cross, but they are also being told that they still have to continue paying for their sin debts!

Let me ask you, once you have finished repaying the bank loan that you took for purchasing your house, do you still have to send in the monthly payments? Of course not! You should stop sending your checks to the bank because your debt has already been paid. If you continue to send those checks, you are wasting your time and money!

Let's look at another possible scenario. Let's say that Henry could not get in touch with you before flying off to Paris, so he tells a good friend of yours to tell you the good news that your debt has been fully paid. Your friend is so excited for you that he drives to your house even though it's midnight and tells you, "Hallelujah! I've got good news for you! Your debt has been paid. In fact, it's more than paid! You owed Lawrence US$50,000, but Henry gave Lawrence US$1 million to settle your debt!"

The messenger has conveyed the good news to you. It's now up to you, the hearer, to believe the message. You can respond in disbelief, asking, "Are you sure? I've owed this debt for such a long time and now you're telling me that it's all paid up? You're pulling my leg!" Or you can shout, "Hallelujah!" and rejoice over this unmerited gift from Henry that has cleared your debt completely!

> *When the messenger has conveyed the good news to you,*
> *it's now up to you to believe the message.*

Let me ask you this: If you don't believe the good news, is your debt still paid?

One more time: If you refuse to believe that your debt has already been paid, is it still paid?

Yes! Your unbelief does not change the fact that your debt has been fully paid. BUT your unbelief means that you will still have debt on your conscience, and this will affect you negatively because every time you see Lawrence, you will still feel ashamed and want to avoid him! In contrast, if you believe the good news, you will not be avoiding Lawrence. In fact, knowing that he has become a millionaire because Henry overpaid your debt, you may even be bold enough to call him up and ask him for a treat!

My friend, Jesus has already paid your sin debt fully. Do you know what you are doing each time you allow that debt to remain on your conscience? Every time you are sin-conscious, you are insulting the payment of our Lord Jesus Christ. You are saying that it is not enough. You are saying that the cross is not enough. And you know what? You are also insulting the One who received the payment for your sin debt. Each time you try to pay off your sin debt which has already been paid, you are saying that God is not satisfied with Jesus' payment even though the truth is that He is more than satisfied with Jesus' overpayment. Jesus is the beloved Son of the living God. How can you say that His sacrifice is not enough?

Does it really matter if you condemn yourself and allow your sin debt to remain on your conscience even after Jesus has overpaid it? Yes, it matters because apart from dishonoring the work of Jesus on the cross, sin-consciousness makes you avoid God, and can produce in you condemnation, sicknesses, diseases, depression and a cycle of sin!

Listen closely, my friend, because of who Jesus is and the value of that one Man, the price that He paid for our sins was an **overpayment**. All the sinners put together cannot compare with the value of that one Man. Believe the good news and draw near to your Savior today! The Word of God declares to you that you can have "boldness to enter the Holiest by the blood of Jesus"[14]. It declares to you that you can draw near with a true heart in full assurance of faith, having your heart sprinkled from an evil conscience and your body washed with pure water[15]. Rejoice, beloved!

Listen More To The Gospel Of Jesus

"Pastor Prince, I want to stop being so conscious of my sins, but how can I do that?"

The way out of sin-consciousness is to hear more teaching on the finished work of Jesus, and how His blood has cleansed and forgiven you of all your sins. When you receive Jesus as your sin offering, your heart will be sprinkled with His blood from an "evil conscience" because your sins have already been punished on His body. An evil conscience is a conscience that is constantly conscious of your sins. As you listen to Christ-exalting teachings, you will begin to be more conscious of your forgiveness than of your sins. And the moment you stop carrying sin-consciousness and condemnation in your mind and heart, you will be washed with the pure water of God's Word, which will begin to affect your physical body and bring healing to every part that is not well!

Some Christians are not able to receive healing because they are not able to receive forgiveness. They are still sin-conscious and doubt their forgiveness. They believe that God may have forgiven their past sins, but not the sins of their whole life. God knows that people need the assurance that their sins are forgiven before they can receive healing in their bodies, so the Bible makes this very clear. In Psalms 103, when the psalmist lists the "benefits" from the Lord, he starts with "who forgives all your iniquities" before moving on to "who heals all your diseases".

When the man sick with the palsy was lowered through the roof and placed before Jesus, Jesus said, "Son, your sins are forgiven you," before telling him to arise, take up his bed and go to his house[16]. Your sins are forgiven you, beloved. Stop punishing and condemning yourself. It's time for you to freely receive your miracle from God!

"But I have sinned. How can there be no punishment for my sin?"

I do not deny that sin must be punished, but I am declaring to you that **all** your sins **have already been punished** on the body of Jesus. He is your perfect sin offering and we who have received His forgiveness should have no more consciousness of sins. Stop examining yourself and searching your heart for sin. Remember that when someone brings his sin offering to the priest, the priest does not examine him. He examines the sin offering. The priest is a picture of God. When you go to Him today, God does not examine you. He examines your sin offering. He examines Jesus, who is completely perfect and sinless, without spot, wrinkle or blemish. God accepts Jesus as your sin offering, and every one of your sins has been transferred onto His body!

Stop punishing yourself. Jesus has already been punished for your sins. Believe it and let your conscience be satisfied! Start enjoying all His benefits because they are your blood-bought rights. Read Psalm 103 and realize that forgiveness is yours. Healing is yours. Redemption from destruction is yours. Being crowned with lovingkindness and tender mercies is yours. Renewal of youth is yours. Hallelujah! Simply believe that your sin debt has been settled and walk in these blessings today!

Stop punishing yourself. Jesus has already been punished for your sins. Believe it and let your conscience be satisfied!

Chapter 15

The Road To Emmaus

Whatever your need is today, whether it is physical, emotional, mental, social or financial, your solution is found in a greater revelation of Jesus. When Jesus is unveiled in all His magnificence, the poor will prosper, the weak will be made strong and the sick will be healed. In Luke chapter 4, He declared, "The Spirit of the Lord is upon Me, because He has anointed Me to preach the gospel..."[1] Jesus was anointed to preach good news to you. So whenever you hear Jesus preached, good news will be proclaimed over your life, finances and marriage, and your entire household will be blessed beyond measure.

Whatever your need is today, your solution
is found in a greater revelation of Jesus.

When Jesus rose from the dead, He ministered comfort to two disciples who were walking back from Jerusalem to a village called Emmaus. When He drew near to them and walked with them, they were feeling sad and discouraged as they conversed about the events that had transpired. The Bible says that the disciples' eyes were restrained, so they did not recognize Jesus in His resurrected form.

Jesus asked them, "What kind of conversation is this that you have with one another as you walk and are sad?"² The disciples then began to narrate the events that had happened to Jesus, and how He was condemned to die and was crucified. From the way they spoke, you could tell that they did not believe that Jesus would be resurrected. They said that they were **hoping** that it was Jesus who was going to redeem Israel and were **astonished** when certain women of their company, who had gone to Jesus' tomb, told them that they could not find His body. When they finished, Jesus said:

> Luke 24:25
> ²⁵"O **foolish** ones, and **slow of heart to believe** in all that the prophets have spoken!"

These are the two indictments against the body of Christ today. The first is that we are "foolish", that is, we are suffering from ignorance and the lack of knowledge of and revelation from the Word of God. The second is that even when we do have knowledge of the Word, we are "slow of heart to believe". Now, our Lord Jesus is so loving that He would not just tell them what their problem was without giving them the solution. Look at what Jesus did immediately after He pronounced the two indictments:

> Luke 24:27
> ²⁷And beginning at Moses and all the Prophets, He expounded to them in all the Scriptures **the things concerning Himself.**

This is amazing! Right there, on the road to Emmaus, Jesus began to expound the Scriptures. He started at Moses, which refers to the first five books of the Bible (Genesis, Exodus, Leviticus, Numbers and Deuteronomy), before moving on to the rest of the Old Testament, which would include the major and minor prophets. He expounded to them all "the things concerning Himself" in every single book, showing them pictures of Himself in every page. What a tremendous time of Bible study it must have been!

This tells us that every page in the Bible is about Jesus. Jesus is in the Old Testament **concealed**, and in the New Testament **revealed**. There are no insignificant details in the Bible and everything in it is there to point to Jesus.

I can just imagine their excitement when Jesus began to unveil to them that He was the promised seed in the garden of Eden who would crush Satan's head. Then, He would have moved on to share about how each of the five Levitical offerings depicted His one perfect work on the cross. He would have shared about the high priest and how even the high priest's garments spoke of Himself as our perfect representative before God. Can you imagine it?

Jesus would even have unveiled all the typologies embedded in the Old Testament stories. He would have told them how He was typified in Joseph's character — how He was rejected by His own Jewish brothers, but would become the bread of life to the Gentile world and marry a Gentile bride (that's the church today — we are His Gentile bride!). He would have expounded all that and much, much more! One day, when I am in heaven, I will ask the Lord to show me a video of this wonderful Bible study that the Lord led the disciples through on the road to Emmaus!

Jesus Showed Us How To Study The Bible

I used to wonder why the Lord restrained the eyes of the two disciples from seeing that it was Him when He first spoke to them. Then one day, the Lord spoke to me about this. He said, "I didn't want them to see Me as the risen Jesus because I wanted them to hear the Scriptures first. I didn't want them to have faith in Me simply because they saw Me. I wanted them to have faith in Me because they heard the Scriptures talking about Me. And that's the same privilege I am giving the church today." I was so glad when I heard that. Today, we don't have to wish that we were living in the days of Jesus or that Jesus would appear to us — His way is for us to see Him in the Scriptures!

In expounding the Scriptures to the two disciples, I believe that Jesus showed us **how** we are to study the Bible. He does not want us to read the Bible to find out what to do and what not to do. He wants us to study the Bible to see **Him** and all the things in the Scriptures concerning **Himself**.

We don't have to wish that Jesus would appear to us —
His way is for us to see Him in the Scriptures!

And you know something? Ever since our church experienced the Gospel Revolution, studying the Word has been so exciting! I've found myself preaching even from the book of Leviticus on a Sunday morning. Can you believe that? For most believers, the pages of Leviticus are usually still stuck together even after their Bibles have been in use for a few years!

When you begin to see Jesus in every page of the Bible, it all comes alive. In our church, we go deep into the Word of God to search out all the hidden gems and truths about Jesus from Genesis to Maps! We have fun in the Word, for when the person of Jesus comes forth in the Word, Bible study is no longer dry and academic, but alive and **exciting**, and we love it!

Our Hearts Burn Within Us

Jesus' solution for those who are "foolish" and "slow of heart to believe" is for them to study the Bible to see more of Him. At the end of the disciples' journey, the Bible says that they said to one another, "Did not our heart burn within us while He talked with us on the road, and while He opened the Scriptures to us?"[3] My friend, when Jesus is unveiled in the Scriptures, our hearts will **burn** within us. In fact, the root word for "Emmaus" in Hebrew means "warm baths" or "warm springs"[4]. When Jesus expounded on the Scriptures, the disciples' hearts experienced "warm baths". Their hearts were strangely warmed and comforted.

On one of our trips to Israel, I took a group of my leaders on this journey to Emmaus. During the walk, our Israeli guide shared with us that during Jesus' time, there was actually a natural hot spring along the road to Emmaus[5], and people used to take advantage of its medicinal qualities while enjoying a warm bath.

Immediately after our guide shared that, I was really excited because I got this revelation from the Lord: He showed me that when you are sitting under anointed ministries that unveil Jesus in the Scriptures, not only will your heart be bathed in the warmth of His love, but even your physical body will be healed and restored! There are medicinal qualities and healing virtues in seeing Jesus in the Scriptures, as His words are truly "life to those who find them, and health to all their flesh"[6].

The Bible says that Emmaus is seven miles from Jerusalem[7]. This means that the disciples studied the Bible with Jesus for several hours! The Bible also says that when the disciples realized that it was Jesus talking to them after they had arrived in Emmaus, they "rose up that very hour and returned to Jerusalem"[8]. This means that the disciples walked for seven miles all the way to Emmaus and then walked another seven miles to get back to Jerusalem!

I believe that something supernatural must have happened to their bodies. The disciples got filled with so much life that they could walk all the way back — 14 miles in all, back to back. When I saw that several years ago, the Lord spoke to me saying, "Son, when you sit under anointed teaching of the Scriptures about Me, your body responds, life comes, and profound and boundless energy flows." No wonder David said, "Quicken me according to Your Word,"[9] which means, "Give me life through Your Word."

When you see Jesus unveiled and hear Him preached to you, it is no wonder your body receives healing, because the divine resurrection life of Jesus is imparted to you. That's what happened to the man at Lystra who was lame from birth. All he did was to hear Paul preach about Jesus and his legs became infused with so much life that when Paul commanded him, he leaped and walked[10]!

Ministry Of A New Covenant Preacher

This is the true ministry of any new covenant Bible teacher or preacher — he seeks to unveil Jesus to you and qualify you by the blood of Jesus. He does not come to unveil your faults or bring your sins to remembrance to disqualify you from entering God's presence and enjoying His blessings. That is what an old covenant preacher does. In the Old Testament, the widow of Zarephath said to Elijah, "What have I to do with you, O man of God? Have you come to me to bring my sin to remembrance…?"[11]

Every which way you turn yourself, you will find faults. But every which way you turn Jesus, you will find that like a precious diamond, there is brilliance, beauty and perfection. The accuser wants you to be conscious of yourself, and keeps telling you to look at your every wrong deed and thought. Even when you have done something "right", like spending time in the Word and praying every day, he will say to you, "It is not enough! You only read five chapters a day. Do you know that so-and-so reads 10 chapters a day? And you only pray for one hour a day! So-and-so wakes up early every morning and prays for four hours!"

The devil wants you self-conscious,
but God wants you Jesus-conscious.

My friend, don't play his game. Turn away from his accusations and from yourself, and see Jesus. God is not judging you today based on you. He has placed you **in Christ**, and He sees the excellence, beauty and perfection of Jesus when He looks at you. The devil wants you self-conscious. God wants you Jesus-conscious. It is in your best interest to find out as much as you can about Jesus — who He is, His titles, His official glories, all that He possesses — because all that He is, God has set to your account. You are a joint heir to all that He has and all the inheritance that is due to Jesus is yours as well[12]!

Unfortunately, instead of looking at Jesus, many Christians fall into the trap of thinking that God looks at them based on who they are and what they have done. The moment you think like that, you have come under the law. You see, the law, with its focus on your doing or not doing, makes you self-conscious. You may not even realize that the moment you focus on yourself and your performance, you have just placed yourself under the law. The moment you feel condemned for not doing more, for not doing better or for not doing anything at all, you have placed yourself under the law. Instead of looking toward what Jesus has done, you are looking at what **you** have done.

It Is All About Seeing Jesus

The **law** is all about you looking at **yourself**. The new covenant of **grace** is all about you **seeing Jesus**. The Pharisees committed large portions of the Word of God to memory and yet they could not see the Word of God in the flesh, standing before them. We should not be interested in just accumulating Bible knowledge. We should be opening the Scriptures to see more of Jesus. Some people think that if they knew Hebrew and Greek, they would understand the Bible better. Well, the Pharisees knew Hebrew and that did nothing for them. What we need is for the Holy Spirit to unveil to us revelations and hidden gems about Jesus and His finished work. I like what Smith Wigglesworth said:

"Some people read their Bible in Hebrew, some in Greek. I like to read mine in the Holy Ghost."

Beloved, it is all about seeing Jesus because from Him comes every supply and provision. Even as I preach, I look to Jesus. I look to Him for the Word. I look to Him for direction. I look to Him all the time. As long as Peter kept his eyes on Jesus, he could walk on water. But once he looked away from Jesus, and looked instead at the storm, the challenges and the stressful circumstances, he started to sink.

Once people look away from Jesus, they will stop attending church, and start looking to themselves and their own resources to make things happen. They think to themselves, "I need more time. I need to work harder. I have to put in more overtime work and work on Sundays as well." Why don't you enjoy your Sundays in church and with your family, and trust the Lord to see you through? God can accomplish much more in you through the anointed preaching of Jesus than what you can accomplish through your own strength and your working overtime. Let's come together more to see more of Jesus!

Typologies Of Jesus In The Bible

Now that you are all excited to see Jesus in the Scriptures, let's look at some Old Testament scriptures and unveil Jesus. If you are not familiar with the use of typology in interpreting the Scriptures, let me assure you that it is biblical and that Jesus Himself used typology in His teachings. The first time He used typology in the book of John, He said, "And as Moses lifted up the serpent in the wilderness, even so must the Son of Man be lifted up, that whoever believes in Him should not perish but have eternal life."[13]

"Pastor Prince, are you comparing Jesus to 'the serpent in the wilderness'?"

Well, you read it yourself. Jesus Himself drew that comparison and that is what we call a "typology". The Old Testament is filled with typologies. The Bible says, "It is the glory of God to conceal a matter, but the glory of kings is to search out a matter."[14] God has hidden the mysteries of His beloved Son and His finished work throughout the Bible, and it is our glory to search out all these things concerning Himself. Are you ready?

Jesus, The True Bread Of Life

Let's go to Numbers chapter 21 and see what Jesus is typified as here. The Bible tells us that as the children of Israel journeyed in the wilderness, "the soul of the people became very discouraged", and they began to murmur and complain against God and His appointed leadership, Moses, saying, "Why have you brought us up out of Egypt to die in the wilderness? For there is no food and no water, and our soul loathes this worthless bread."[15]

Can you imagine this? God delivered them from a life of slavery in Egypt with His mighty hand, protected them from Pharaoh's army with a pillar of fire and parted the Red Sea for them to pass through. And instead of being grateful, they complained and even referred to the manna from heaven as "worthless bread". In the King James Version, it says "light bread", implying that they saw the manna as something which was of little value and which did not satisfy.

According to the psalmist David, the manna was "angels' food"[16]. It was so good that when the children of Israel ate this food for 40 years in the wilderness, their feet did not swell and there was not one feeble among them. God provided them with food for champions, food that kept them free from sicknesses and diseases, food that descended daily from heaven. All they had to do each morning was to collect enough for their consumption. Yet, they despised the manna.

The church today needs to be careful not to make the same mistake that the children of Israel made when they called the manna from God "worthless bread". The manna that He gave them was a picture (or type) of Jesus. Jesus said, "I am the bread of life. Your fathers ate the manna in the wilderness, and are dead. This is the bread which comes down from heaven, that one may eat of it and not die."[17]

We should be careful not to consider Jesus as "worthless bread" by relegating Him to the periphery of our teachings.

In many places, there is an under-emphasis on Jesus Christ, and an over-emphasis on all sorts of doctrines and principles that can be extracted from the Word. I am not saying that churches should not be using the Word to teach on financial principles, keys to wisdom, leadership and so on. I teach all these in my church as well. What I am saying is that churches must be careful not to consider Jesus as "worthless bread" by relegating Him to the periphery of their teachings.

Anybody who doesn't focus on Jesus Christ and His finished work has neither the wisdom of God nor the power of God, because the Bible says that Christ crucified is the wisdom of

God and the power of God[18]. He is the true bread from heaven and only He satisfies! The devil is afraid of any church that preaches Jesus Christ on the cross because he knows that when people know how God sent His only begotten Son to die on the cross for them, they will see that they have a merciful God who loves them unconditionally. They will know the Truth and the Truth will set them free!

Let me add one more thing. Do you know that every morning, the children of Israel had to go out to collect fresh manna? The manna could not be stored overnight as it would turn stale and breed worms. Ever wondered why God didn't just give them a week's supply of manna? Well, that is because God wants us to open the Scriptures every day to collect fresh manna of Jesus. He doesn't want us to live on past and stale revelations of Jesus, for His mercies are new every morning. Hallelujah!

Jesus, The Bronze Serpent In The Wilderness

Let's continue with what happened after the children of Israel murmured and complained. In your Bible, it says that "the Lord sent fiery serpents"[19], and they bit the people and many of the Israelites died. Now, it is important to recognize that the serpents were always there in the wilderness. All God did was that He lifted His protection when they murmured against Moses. Remember this happened under the old covenant of law! Praise the Lord that in the new covenant of grace that you and I are under, God WILL NEVER lift His protection over us. Always bear that in mind when you read the Old Testament. It is necessary to **rightly divide the Word**.

The people then came to Moses and he prayed for them. Then, the Lord said to Moses, "Make a fiery serpent, and set it on a pole; and it shall be that everyone who is bitten, when he looks at it, shall live."[20] So Moses made a bronze serpent and put it on a pole, and "if a serpent had bitten anyone, when he looked at the bronze serpent, he lived"[21].

In the new covenant, God will never lift His protection over us.

The bronze serpent on the pole is a picture of Jesus on the cross. Now, why did Jesus liken Himself to a serpent when He is not like one in any way? He is beautiful, matchless, flawless and altogether lovely. You see, on the cross, Jesus became cursed with the curses that we deserved for our sins. He who knew no sin became sin. On the cross, Jesus became a serpent — a picture of a cursed creature — so that you and I could go free.

By His sacrifice on the cross, the guilty creature that brought death in the garden of Eden became a symbol of His grace. Isn't it like God to turn something that is so ugly into something that is so beautiful? That's what happens when you let His grace come into your life. He takes all the ugly things in you and makes them beautiful.

Now, why a bronze serpent? Why didn't Moses just put a real snake on the pole? Because that would have spoiled the typology. Jesus did not come in "sinful flesh". He came in the "**likeness** of sinful flesh"[22]. There is a huge difference. Jesus knew no sin and in Him is no sin. Hence, He cannot be depicted as a real serpent. He was depicted as a bronze figure which was made in the **likeness** of a serpent.

But why **bronze?** Throughout the Bible, bronze speaks of judgment. For example, the altar of burnt offering for the animal sacrifices was made of acacia wood and overlaid with bronze. Its utensils and grate were made of bronze[23]. So to see Jesus as the bronze serpent is to see a picture of God's judgment falling upon Jesus at the cross.

God does not want us to look at ourselves, our afflictions, or even our sicknesses and diseases. Just one look at Jesus on the cross, bearing all our sins, curses and judgment, and you and I will live. The bronze serpent was raised on a pole, and Moses would have lifted it to a high place so that all the children of Israel could see it. In the same way, God lifted Jesus up on the cross for the whole world to see Him. Whosoever looks on Jesus and sees their sins, curses and sicknesses punished on His body shall be saved. They shall be healed. They shall live! The Bible does not say to look at Moses (the law). It says to look at Jesus, and not just the Jesus who walked among us, but the Jesus who was crucified as a bronze serpent on our behalf. Jesus Christ and Him Crucified — that is our solution.

Don't look at yourself, your afflictions or your disease.
Look at Jesus and you will live.

My friend, stop being preoccupied with yourself and your self-efforts, and disqualifying yourself. Start being occupied with Jesus and His finished work. Begin to search the Scriptures for all the things concerning Himself and feel your heart burning within you as the Holy Spirit unveils to you just how beautiful He is.

You have a wonderful Savior. Look away from your own wounds and hurts, and look to Jesus, who will save you!

Chapter 16

The Secret Of David

Have you ever wondered why God called David "a man after My own heart"[1]? What was David's secret? What was it about David that God would bless him so much, making him king over all Israel?

I have heard some people say that God called David a man after His own heart because he was quick to repent. However, there were other people in the Bible who were quick to repent, so this would not have set David apart. Moreover, God called David a man after His own heart **before** he committed his sin with Bathsheba, so it cannot be because of his quick repentance.

David's secret is the key to the fullness of God's blessings in your life.

There must be something unique about David which caused him to stand out. Would you like to know what his secret was? I believe with all my heart that this secret is the key to the fullness of God's blessings in your life.

Turn with me to Psalm 132, where you will find David's secret. David wrote this psalm when King Saul was hunting him down. Saul was jealous of David and afraid that he would one day become king in his place, so Saul pursued David into the wilderness. Against this backdrop, David wrote:

> Psalm 132:1–5
> ¹Lord, remember David and all his afflictions; ²how he swore to the Lord, and vowed to the Mighty One of Jacob: ³"Surely I will not go into the chamber of my house, or go up to the comfort of my bed; ⁴I will not give sleep to my eyes or slumber to my eyelids, **⁵until I…**

David was making a vow to God in the wilderness that he would neither sleep nor rest until he did something. Now, hold your horses. Before I show you what he vowed to God, I want to show you something that he himself said about how God saw him:

> 1 Chronicles 28:4, KJV
> ⁴Howbeit the Lord God of Israel chose me before all the house of my father to be king over Israel for ever: for He hath chosen Judah to be the ruler; and of the house of Judah, the house of my father; and among the sons of my father **He liked me** to make me king over all Israel:

David said, "God liked me." Oh, I love that! I love the way the old King James Version captures what he said: "God liked me to make me king over all Israel." Do you know that even in Israel today, when they say, "I like you," they use the same Hebrew word here, which is *ratsah²*? "I *ratsah* you" means "I like you".

What Made David A Man After God's Own Heart?

Would you like to find out why God **liked** David? What made him so special? I believe that God liked David because he got hold of something that was of the greatest importance to God's heart. He got hold of a divine thought and objective in God's heart. This was revealed in the vow he made to God in the wilderness in Psalm 132 — "I will not give sleep to my eyes or slumber to my eyelids, **until I find a place for the Lord, a dwelling place for the Mighty One of Jacob.**"[3]

What was David talking about? To get a better picture, read on. David says in the same psalm, "Arise, O Lord, to Your resting place, You and the ark of Your strength."[4] David was talking about bringing the ark of the covenant back to Jerusalem! I've included an illustration of the ark of the covenant below:

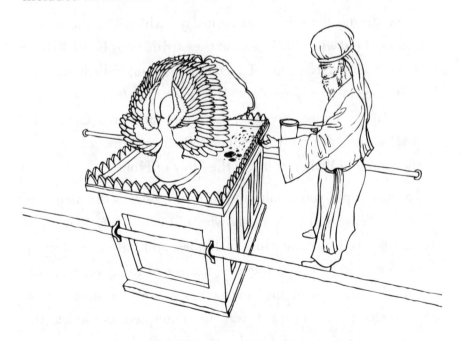

The Ark Of The Covenant

This was what David was after, and because he placed such importance on bringing back the ark, God considered him a man after His own heart.

Now, in the days of the old covenant, God dwelled between the two cherubim, which are on the ark of the covenant[5]. This was the throne of God. Whenever the children of Israel brought the ark to battle and Israel was in alignment with God, God would give them victory over their enemies.

Let me tell you just how important the ark of the covenant was, in case the only other time you've heard of the ark was when you watched the movie *Indiana Jones And The Raiders Of The Lost Ark*. By the way, if you saw the movie, let me just say that it was not an accurate depiction of the ark — there were no spirits living inside the ark as the movie portrayed!

Now, during the Old Testament days, which was the holiest country to God when He looked at the earth? It was Israel. Which was the holiest city in all of Israel? Jerusalem. Which was the holiest place in all of Jerusalem? It was the temple on the temple mount. In the temple precinct, there was the Outer Court, the Holy Place and the Holy of Holies. Which was the holiest place in the temple? Obviously, it was the Holy of Holies.

In the temple, you would find furniture such as the menorah, altar of incense and table of showbread in the Holy Place. But behind the veil was the Holy of Holies, and only one piece of furniture could be found there — the ark of the covenant. This means that the ark of the covenant was the holiest object on earth at that point in time. It was the centerpiece of God, at the center of the universe and in the center of God's heart.

In the Old Testament, God said that He would speak to the high priest "from between the two cherubim"[6]. This place was actually the "mercy seat". The mercy seat was also the place where the high priest would place the blood of the animal sacrifice, every year on the Day of Atonement. The Day of Atonement was the only time in the entire year when the high priest could go through the veil into the Holy of Holies.

Are you still with me? Hang on tight, we're coming to the exciting part!

Typology Of The Ark Of The Covenant

In the previous chapter, I shared with you about the road to Emmaus where Jesus expounded on all the Scriptures, beginning at Moses and all the prophets, the things concerning Himself. Are you ready for some unveiling of Jesus in the Old Testament that will make your heart burn within you? Let's dive right in.

The ark was so important to God that He gave the Israelites very specific instructions on how it was to be constructed[7]. Even though we can only skim the surface, every detail of the ark allows us to get a clearer picture of Jesus since there are no insignificant details in the Bible. From the start, I want you to know that the ark of the covenant points to the person and the work of our Lord Jesus Christ. He is the centerpiece of God's heart and as you read on, I know that you will fall in love with Him more and more!

For now, look at the illustration I provided earlier. We're about to look more closely at some components of the ark of the covenant. The box portion of the ark is made of acacia wood and overlaid with gold. Wood in the Bible speaks of humanity[8]. Acacia wood is known in Israel as incorruptible wood, so this speaks of Jesus' incorruptible humanity. Jesus came in the likeness of sinful flesh as a man, but there was no sin in Him. Gold in the Bible speaks of divinity and deity[9]. So the wood overlaid with gold speaks of the person of Jesus — He was completely human and at the same time completely God.

What Is In The Ark Of The Covenant?

Let's look at the lid of the box. The entire lid was made from a solid slab of gold and it covered the box. In Hebrew, the lid is called the *kapporeth*, which means "mercy seat"[10]. Let's see what the mercy seat was used to cover from view.

Three items were kept in the ark of the covenant. The first was the stone tablets on which God wrote the Ten Commandments. The tablets speak of our rebellion and inability to keep God's laws perfectly. The second was Aaron's rod. Aaron's rod was not just any ordinary rod. It was placed overnight in the tabernacle and not only did it shoot forth branches, it also bore fruit and flowers[11]. Do you know why God did that? It was because the people were complaining against God's appointment of Aaron as the high priest, so God caused Aaron's rod to bud supernaturally to show the people that it was He who had appointed Aaron. Aaron's rod thus speaks of man's rebellion against God's appointed leadership.

The final item in the ark was the golden pot of manna. The Bible calls manna "angels' food"[12] and when the children of Israel ate it while they were in the wilderness, none of them were sick for 40 years. Yet, they called it "worthless bread"[13]. So the golden pot of manna speaks of man's rebellion against God's provision.

Can you see that every item in the ark speaks of our sins and rebellion against God? But what did God do with our sins and rebellion? He put them all into the ark of the covenant and covered them with the mercy seat where the blood of the animal sacrifices was placed. By doing this, He was saying that He did not want to see man's sins and rebellion. When He looks down, He cannot see man's sins and rebellion because they are all covered by the blood on the mercy seat!

God cannot see your sins when they are covered by the blood.

Let me say it one more time to make sure that you did not miss it: God **cannot** see your sins when they are covered by the blood. That is why in the Old Testament, Israel rejoiced every time their high priest went into the Holy of Holies on the Day of Atonement and placed the blood of the animal sacrifice on the mercy seat. When the blood was on the mercy seat, God could not see the rejection of His laws in the Ten Commandments. He could not see the rejection of His appointed priesthood in Aaron's rod. And He could not see the rejection of His provision in the golden pot of manna. He could not see the people's sins and rebellion. He only saw the blood on the mercy seat!

Mercy Triumphs Over Judgment

There's more. The mercy seat also speaks of the person of Christ. The Bible says that "He Himself is the **propitiation** for our sins"[14]. This means that Jesus became our sacrifice to divert God's wrath meant for us to Himself. "Propitiation" is a beautiful word. On the cross, Jesus became the propitiation for our sins. If you study the word "propitiation" in the Septuagint (a Greek translation of the Old Testament), you will find that it is the same word as "mercy seat"[15].

So when Apostle John said that Jesus is our propitiation, he was saying that Jesus is our mercy seat. The mercy seat was made of one solid slab of gold that was beaten into shape. In the same way, for Jesus to take our place and be our mercy seat, He had to be brutally beaten and scourged, so that by His stripes, we are healed.

When you look at the illustration of the ark of the covenant, you will also see the crown on the mercy seat. This crown typifies Jesus' majesty, glory and kingship. He was the only King who came not to be served, but to serve. He became a servant-King for us on the cross.

So the ark of the covenant is a shadow of our Lord Jesus Christ, His person and His work. Because of His blood, **all** our sins have been cleansed. That is why it was dangerous for anyone back in those days to lift the mercy seat to uncover the sins and rebellion that God had covered. The mercy seat was not to be lifted at any time and the consequences for doing so were severe. The Bible records that when the people in a village called Beth Shemesh lifted the mercy seat to look inside the ark, many of them were destroyed[16].

Nobody was supposed to even take a peek at the Ten Commandments. God doesn't want the law to be exposed because it represents our rebellion, and it will only minister death and condemnation. The peculiar thing is that people have made the Ten Commandments into posters that are hung in homes today, when even in the Old Testament, God kept the law hidden under the mercy seat!

Don't you think that believers today should be exalting God's mercy and His grace above the law? Notice that the mercy seat is placed over the law. This tells us that God's mercy triumphs over judgment[17]! God's grace is above God's law. God executes judgment because He is just, but His delight is not in judgment. His delight is in mercy and grace. The Bible tells us that God's anger lasts only for a moment, but His mercy endures forever[18].

The way some people portray God today creates the false impression that His mercy lasts only for a moment, but His anger endures forever! That is just not true. His anger ended the moment it was exhausted on Jesus at the cross. In fact, even His judgment demonstrates His grace because instead of judging us for our sins (which we deserved), the judgment fell on His Son, Jesus Christ, in whom was no sin! That's grace, my friend. The judgment that we deserved fell on Jesus, while the blessings that He deserved fell on us! That is the undeserved, unmerited and unearned favor of God.

Don't uncover your sins or the sins of others.
They have been completely forgiven by the blood of Jesus.

So my friend, don't lift the mercy seat to uncover your sins or the sins of others. They have been completely forgiven by the blood of Jesus. Hallelujah!

Bring The Ark Of The Covenant Back

Let's get back to what David vowed to do — bring the ark of the covenant back to Jerusalem. For more than 20 years, the ark had been in a hilly place called Kirjath Jearim, which means "the fields of the woods"[19]. David had heard about the ark since he was a young boy growing up in Bethlehem Ephrathah (the same Bethlehem where Jesus would be born), which is why he said, "We heard of it [the ark] in Ephrathah; we found it in the fields of the woods,"[20] referring to Kirjath Jearim.

Growing up, David must have wondered why nobody made a move to bring the ark back to Jerusalem where it belonged. Saul was king at that time, but he never had the heart or desire to bring the ark back to Jerusalem. He simply left it there in Kirjath Jearim. So David made it his passion to bring the ark to Mount Zion in Jerusalem, for the Lord had chosen Zion as His dwelling place. God Himself said of Zion, "This is My resting place forever; here I will dwell, for I have desired it."[21]

Do you know why God chose Mount Zion and not Mount Sinai? This is because Mount Zion represents His grace, while Mount Sinai represents His law. On the first Pentecost, 50 days after the first Passover, God gave the Ten Commandments at Mount Sinai, and 3,000 people died[22]. On the day of Pentecost after the resurrection of Jesus, God gave the Holy Spirit at Mount Zion, and 3,000 people were saved and the new covenant church was born[23]. The law kills, but the Spirit brings life. The law condemns, but grace saves. God has chosen grace over the law, Mount Zion over Mount Sinai!

When you understand the typology of the ark of the covenant, you will see that bringing back the ark of the covenant is the same as bringing Jesus Christ back into a place of prominence, and making Him and His finished work the center of all our teaching and preaching.

A long time ago, the Lord said this to me, "Son, bring Jesus Christ back to the church."

You know, it saddens me that in many churches today, you hardly hear the name of Jesus being mentioned. Instead, you hear psychology being taught. You hear motivational teachings. You hear "doing, doing, doing", "vision, vision, vision" or "calling, calling, calling". You hear very little of Jesus Christ and His finished work being taught. Is this what Christianity is about? Your doing, your calling and your vision?

There is a popular verse from the book of Revelation, which Christians use for unbelievers. It says, "Behold, I stand at the door and knock. If anyone hears My voice and opens the door, I will come in to him and dine with him, and he with Me."[24] When you look at the context of this verse, it is actually not written to unbelievers, but to the church of the Laodiceans[25]! Now, why is the Lord standing outside the church and knocking?

It Is All About Unveiling Jesus

When I travel around the world to preach the gospel of Jesus, my greatest reward as a pastor is to be able to meet precious believers and unveil Jesus Christ to them all over again. There is no greater reward than to know that I have opened their eyes to see more of Jesus, His grace, His beauty and the perfection of His work, because I know that this is my calling in life from the Lord.

I still remember how Wendy and I were living in a very small place when we first got married. It was our first apartment. Our study room was so tiny and it didn't even have a chair at that time. As I sat on the floor of my study room reading the Scriptures, God spoke to me. He began to show me more clearly than I had ever seen before that Jesus Christ was not being given central place in the body of Christ, and as a result, the fullness of His blessings was not flowing as it should.

When Jesus Christ is not given central place in the body of Christ, the fullness of His blessings is not flowing as it should.

When He showed this to me, I said, "Lord, if I preach sermons that are full of Jesus, and if all my sermons are about Jesus, I think that nobody would want to listen to them." Then, I heard Him say this: "Son, will you still be willing to do it even if nobody comes? Even if nobody wants to hear them, will you still preach every sermon full of Jesus?" I was stunned by His question and I thought through it for a while because as a young pastor, I was ambitious and wanted to grow the church. Then, I said this to Him, and I will never forget what I said: "Lord, even if our church becomes smaller after that, I am willing to do it." So I didn't care whether people would accept it or not. I just began to preach about Jesus Christ and His finished work.

Many years have passed and I now know that the question was a test from the Lord. Our church did not become smaller. No, it exploded right after that encounter with the Lord. From only a few hundred people at that time, we have grown to more than 15,000 people as of this writing. I still remember exactly where I was sitting in my study room when God gave me that challenge. From that point onwards, He has given me everything I need to fulfill this calling. He has given me an amazing wife, a wonderful daughter (when He spoke to me, Jessica was not even born yet) and great leaders to support this call. Everything that He has given me in my life has been to bring me to a place where Jesus can be exalted.

Many have told me that I am called to preach grace, but my main calling is not just to teach on grace. It is to bring Jesus back into the central place of the church and His grace is part of that. You cannot separate Jesus from His grace anyway. The Bible says that "the law was given through Moses, but **grace and truth came through Jesus Christ**"[26].

It is actually not easy to preach grace because when you preach grace, you make nothing of man and everything of Jesus. And man does not like that. Man likes to think that he has fasted 40 days and 40 nights to get the anointing. He wants to be able to say, "I paid the price for spiritual power." Hey, my friend, Jesus paid the price already. It is not about your fasting. It is all about the work of Jesus Christ!

Bringing Jesus Back To Mount Zion

Let me explain to you what it means to bring Jesus back to Mount Zion. Bringing Jesus back to Mount Zion is to bring Jesus back to the place of grace. Have you heard sermons where they preach about Jesus, but the sermons are very hard?

As a teenager growing up in my previous church, I remember one sermon that really frightened me. The preacher said, "Jesus Himself said that unless your righteousness exceeds the righteousness of the scribes and Pharisees, you will never enter the kingdom of heaven." Then, he said, "If the Pharisees had this standard, then we must have even higher standards than them." I felt really condemned. What hope was there for me, since I did not even measure up to the standard of the Pharisees?

Even though that preacher was preaching from Jesus' words, he never brought Jesus into the context of grace. He made Jesus appear hard and legalistic. He did not bring the ark back to Zion. Now, let's interpret what Jesus was really saying in the context of grace. He was saying that the only way to enter heaven is to have HIS righteousness that exceeds all other standards of righteousness. His righteousness is far above the self-righteousness of the scribes and Pharisees! And guess what? HIS righteousness is a gift to be freely received. It is yours today!

Be A Man After God's Own Heart!

This is the secret to David's blessings. He pursued the ark of the covenant and God called him a man after His own heart. Today, you too can be the man or woman after God's own heart. You can pursue Jesus and bring Him back into the center of your life. Make Jesus the centerpiece of every aspect of your life. The Bible says that where two or three are gathered in His name, He will be there in the midst of them[27].

If your marriage is breaking down, let me tell you this, most likely, you are putting your demands on your husband to supply you what only Jesus can give, or you are looking to your wife to give you what you should get only from Jesus. You end up over-pressurizing each other. Every marriage needs a "third party". His name is Jesus. He must be in the midst of every marriage.

Today, you can be the man or woman after God's own heart by making Jesus the centerpiece of every aspect of your life.

Make Jesus, His finished work and His grace the center of everything in your life. Make Him the center of your marriage, family, career and finances, and allow the fullness of His blessings to flow in your life today!

Chapter 17

Picture Of Pure Grace

When my daughter Jessica was about five years old, I asked her, "What is a Bible?" She replied, "It is a book that is all about Jesus, with a red string in it." Oh, I love that! Isn't it so precious to see things from a child's perspective? She did not describe the Bible in religious terms that we adults are fond of. She just saw the Bible in its simplest and purest form — a book that is all about Jesus, with a red string in it! Of course, I had to explain to her that the red string is a bookmark. But you know what? There is indeed a "scarlet thread" that runs through this book, from the beginning in Genesis to the end in Revelation. It **is** all about Jesus and His finished work at the cross.

When new believers read the Old Testament for the first time, they might wonder what all the slaughtering of animals, sacrifices and sprinkling of blood are about. Well, when you understand that without the shedding of blood there is no forgiveness of sins, you will begin to appreciate the value of the blood, especially the blood that Jesus shed for our sins.

The Bible says that after Adam and Eve sinned by partaking of the tree of knowledge of good and evil, God "made tunics of skin, and clothed them"[1]. The first time an animal was sacrificed to cover man's sins happened right there in the garden of Eden. All the animal sacrifices in the Old Testament are shadows of Jesus Christ, who is the substance. The blood of bulls and goats under the old covenant all pointed to the substance of Christ, whose blood was shed on the cross of Calvary. As John the Baptist said, Jesus is the "Lamb of God who takes away the sin of the world"[2]. In the book of Revelation, John heard a voice saying, "Behold, the Lion of the tribe of Judah," but when he turned to look at the Lion, he saw instead a "Lamb as though it had been slain"[3]. Everything in the Bible from Genesis to Revelation points to Jesus' death on the cross. It is because of His sacrifice that we are under the new covenant of grace today.

Everything in the Bible from Genesis to Revelation points to Jesus' death on the cross.

The old covenant will always cause you to look at yourself, whereas the new covenant will always cause you to turn and look at Christ crucified. Old Testament prophets call your sins to remembrance, while New Testament preachers call your righteousness to remembrance. Old Testament preachers tell you what is wrong with you, while New Testament preachers tell you what is right with you because of what Jesus has done, in spite of what is wrong with you. The **first miracle of Moses**, who represents the law, was to turn water into blood, resulting in death[4]. The **first miracle of grace** was Jesus turning water into wine, resulting in celebration and life[5]. The law kills, but the Spirit gives life.

Pure Grace From Egypt To Sinai

When God liberated the children of Israel from the bondage of slavery in Egypt, He did not do so because they had kept the Ten Commandments. The Ten Commandments had not even been given yet. The children of Israel came out of Egypt by the blood of the Lamb.

The Lord showed me something a number of years ago that ushered me into the Gospel Revolution. I was sitting in my living room, just spending time in the Word, when He spoke to me and said, "Son, study the journey of the children of Israel from Egypt to Mount Sinai for this is a picture of pure grace. Not a single Israelite died during this period although they murmured and complained."

I had never heard anyone preach that before and neither had I read it in any book. So, feverishly, I turned to that portion of the Scriptures, trying to find someone who had died, so that I could prove God wrong! Have you been there before, trying to prove God wrong? Well, you can never succeed, and indeed, I could not find any Israelite who died even though the people murmured and complained.

Even though God had rescued the children of Israel from their Egyptian slave masters by performing great signs and wonders, the children of Israel failed to honor God, and murmured and complained over and over again. When the Egyptian army came thundering toward them from behind and the Red Sea was before them, the children of Israel cried out to Moses saying, "Because there were no graves in Egypt, have you taken us away to die in the wilderness?"[6]

That was a complaint against God, and murmuring and complaining are sins. But what was God's response? He opened up the Red Sea and they crossed over to dry land on the other side, safe from their enemies. Even after God had brought them safely to the other side of the sea, the murmuring continued. At Marah, they complained about the bitter waters. What was God's response? He made the bitter waters sweet[7]. In the wilderness, they cried out against Moses when they were hungry. What was God's response? He rained bread from heaven[8]. But still, the children of Israel complained. When there was no water again, they cried out against Moses, saying, "Why is it you have brought us up out of Egypt, to kill us and our children and our livestock with thirst?"[9] What was God's response? He brought water out of the flinty rock.

Study the Bible yourself. You'll find that every time the children of Israel murmured and complained, it only brought forth fresh demonstrations of God's favor, supply and goodness. Why? Because during that period, the blessings and provisions they received were not dependent on their obedience or goodness. They were dependent on God's goodness and faithfulness to the Abrahamic covenant, which was a covenant of grace.

The Exchange Of Covenants At Mount Sinai

Then, something tragic happened right at the foot of Mount Sinai. In Exodus 19:8, your English Bible says that the people cried out to Moses, saying, "All that the Lord has spoken we will do." In the original Hebrew text, this is actually a statement of pride. They were saying, "All that God requires and demands of us, we are well able to perform." In other words, they were saying, "God, stop assessing or blessing us based on Your goodness. Start assessing, judging and blessing us based on **our obedience**." So they effectively exchanged covenants, from the Abrahamic covenant which is based on grace, to the Sinaitic covenant which is based on the law.

All this while, God was with them and had fought for them. He opened up the Red Sea, rained manna from heaven and brought water out of the flinty rock, even though they kept murmuring and complaining. But the moment they said those prideful words, God had to change His tone. He told Moses to instruct the people not to go near the mountain, for "whoever touches the mountain shall surely be put to death"[10].

Why do you think God changed His demeanor here? It was because man presumed on his own strength and entered into a covenant based on his obedience. This is what we call self-righteousness. Since the people wanted to be judged based on their performance, in the very next chapter, God gave them the Ten Commandments. From then on, since they boasted that they could do all that God commanded, God had to assess them based on His laws. He would bless them if they kept His commandments, but they would be cursed if they failed to do so. What the people did not understand was that they had to obey all of the Ten Commandments perfectly because if they failed in one, they would be guilty of all[11]. You see, the law is a composite whole and God does not grade on the curve.

Now, let's see what happened when the children of Israel placed themselves under the law. After they boasted that they could fulfill all that God demanded of them, the works of the flesh were **immediately** manifested. They broke the very first commandment — "You shall have no other gods before Me"[12] — by fashioning a golden calf and worshipping it as their god[13]! Isn't that sad? So be careful when you boast of keeping or defending the law because the works of the flesh will follow soon after.

From that point onwards, every time the children of Israel murmured and complained, many of them would die. Observe this: **Before Sinai, none died. After Sinai, the moment they murmured, they died.** Before Sinai, every failure brought forth a fresh manifestation of God's favor. But now that the Israelites were under the covenant of law, sin had to be punished. Their blessings and provisions no longer depended on God's goodness, faithfulness and grace. Under the covenant of law, their blessings depended on their perfect obedience, and every failure and sin would result in judgment and punishment.

That is why the law of Moses is called the ministry of death and condemnation. It is an inflexible standard that had to minister death and condemnation to the Israelites whenever they sinned. You would think that after 2,000 years, people would learn, but there are believers today who are still using the same refrain as the children of Israel at the foot of Mount Sinai. They are bragging, "All that the Lord has spoken we will do."

We Are No Longer Under The Old Covenant

Can you see what the Lord was showing me? The Israelites' journey from Egypt to Sinai was **a picture of pure grace**. It was not dependent on their goodness but **His goodness**, not on their faithfulness but **His faithfulness**. Before the law was given, they were under grace and nobody was punished even when they failed. But immediately after the law was given, nobody was spared when they failed. The good news is that we are no longer under the old covenant of law. We have been delivered from the law through Jesus' death on the cross. Because of Jesus Christ, we are now under the new covenant of grace, which means that today, God does not assess us based on our performance, but on **His** goodness and faithfulness.

If you are still trying to be justified by your obedience to the law, you are effectively negating what Jesus has already done for you on the cross!

Why are there believers today living as though the cross did not make a difference? Instead of enjoying the new covenant of grace, they are still fighting to be under the old covenant of law and the Ten Commandments. I declare to you that the cross of Jesus **did** make a difference. If you are still trying to live under the law, trying to be justified by your obedience to the law, you are effectively negating what Jesus has already done for you on the cross!

Under the old covenant, God said, "I will by no means clear the guilty."[14] However, in the new covenant, God says, "I will remember your sins no more."[15] Can you see the contrast? It is the same God speaking, so what happened? The **cross** happened, my friend. The cross made the difference. Today, God does not remember your sins or hold them against you because He has already judged them in the body of His Son. Believers get confused when they do not realize that the cross has made a difference. Consider this: If we are still supposed to be under the Ten Commandments as many argue, then what did the cross of Jesus accomplish?

Grace Has Done What The Law Could Not

"Pastor Prince, are you insinuating that there is something wrong with the law?"

No, of course not! There is nothing intrinsically wrong with the law. As Apostle Paul said, "What shall we say then? Is the law sin? Certainly not! On the contrary, I would not have known sin except through the law..."[16] I am saying exactly the same thing that Paul said. It is through the law that we have the knowledge of sin, but that is all that the law can do. It exposes your sins. It cannot cover, cleanse or remove your sins. The law was designed to show forth our sins to bring us to despair and lead us to the realization that by our own efforts, we can never save ourselves. It was designed to show us that we all need a Savior who can cleanse and remove our sins. That is the purpose of the law.

The law condemns the best of us, but grace saves the worst of us.

While the law is holy, just and good, it has no power to make us holy, just or good. Only Jesus' magnificent grace and the splendor of His love can make you holy, just and good. And His blood has already made you holy, just and good! God has already done what the law could not do. How? By sending His own Son to be condemned on your behalf, so that you could be made the righteousness of God. That is your position today — you are made righteous in Christ.

With the advent of the new covenant, the Bible says that God has made the old covenant obsolete[17]. Stop fighting to hold on to something which the Bible has declared to be obsolete! The law condemns the best of us. Even David was condemned under the law and I personally esteem him to be the best of those under the old covenant. The law condemns the best of us, but grace saves the worst of us. Under law, if you break one law, you will be guilty of all. By the same token, under grace, if you do one thing right, and that is to believe on the Lord Jesus, then you will be justified from all[18]!

The True Gospel Always Produces Peace In Your Heart

Several years ago, I had the privilege of counseling one of Wendy's close friends. Wendy had invited her to join us for what was supposed to be a simple dinner, but it ended up stretching over a few hours. Wendy's friend was a young Christian who did not attend our church. Over dinner, she shared that one of her spiritual leaders had told her that the Christian life was difficult, and that she had to suffer for the Lord and pay her dues. She was told that she had to work hard, pray hard and make sure that she read the Bible every day so that God would be pleased with her.

We don't read the Bible to qualify for God's blessings. We read the Bible to find out about our blessings and inheritance in Christ.

Once she shared all that with us, I felt that it was my responsibility to tell her the good news. So I shared with her that we do not read the Bible because we want to qualify for God's blessings. We read the Bible to **find out** about our blessings and inheritance in Christ. See the difference? I told her that if I stopped reading the Bible for a few days, I should **not be feeling guilty**, I should be **feeling hungry**. God is not pleased with us on the condition that we read the Bible, pray long prayers and pay our dues. No, absolutely not! He is pleased with us because our trust is in **Jesus**, who qualified us.

The Bible never said that it is our works that qualify us. It says, "Giving thanks to the Father who has qualified us to be partakers of the inheritance of the saints in the light."[19] It is **the Father** who has qualified us, and He qualified us by sending His Son to save us. He has qualified us to be partakers of His favor, healing, prosperity, love, joy, peace and well-being in our families. All these blessings are the inheritance of the saints, purchased by the blood of Jesus Christ. We partake of our inheritance by giving thanks to the Father for sending His Son.

I shared with this lady that she can wake up every day and say, "Father, I thank You that You have qualified me to walk in victory, healing and prosperity." I told her that she should not be racking her brains wondering what she must DO to qualify for God's goodness. His goodness is **already** hers!

There are too many teachings today telling believers what they must do to qualify for this and that. God's way is for us to know that through Jesus, we are already qualified.

At the end of the dinner, I said, "Test whatever I have shared with you about the goodness of God, His grace and Jesus' work at the cross, against what you have heard in your church. Which produces peace in your heart?" She replied, "While I may not understand everything about Jesus because I am a baby Christian,

I know that all that you shared has produced great peace and joy in my heart."

Beloved, joy and peace are the trademarks of the kingdom of God. God is not the author of confusion. He is calling His people out of confusion. Ask yourself this: What produces more peace and joy in your heart — hearing about His judgment and indignation, or hearing about His goodness and grace? What brings abiding peace and joy — to know that God will never punish and condemn you again for your sins because Jesus has already been punished and condemned for you, or to hear that God is sometimes pleased but sometimes angry with you depending on how you perform? What produces true repentance — the fear of judgment or His unconditional goodness?

Your answer is found in His grace, not in your own doing.

My friend, if you are honest, you know that the answer is found in Jesus and His finished work. It is found in His grace, not in your own doing. By trying to qualify yourself today for God's blessings with all your Bible reading, praying and hard work, you are saying together with the children of Israel at the foot of Mount Sinai, "All that the Lord has spoken we will do." You are telling the Lord not to assess, judge and bless you according to His goodness and faithfulness. You are asking Him to assess and judge you according to **your** goodness and faithfulness. Is that what you really want? If not, then begin to put your trust in the finished work of Christ today and enjoy the blessings that flow from His unconditional goodness!

Chapter 18

One Thing You Lack

Are you struggling to live the Christian life today? Your rest is found at the cross of Jesus. If you want to experience effortless success, then realize that it is no longer about you doing this or that right. It is about depending on what Jesus has done for you. Look at what man's own doing has produced. Has any good come from his own efforts to keep the law of Moses? When man boasted in the law, the next thing we saw was a golden calf. This is not God's way. We are no longer under the law of Moses. Praise be to God, we are now under the covenant of His bountiful grace!

God's Goodness Leads Us To Repentance

"But Pastor Prince, we have to preach God's law and His judgment, or there will be no repentance from the people."

My friend, God's heart is never to condemn. We want judgment, but God wants mercy. The Bible says that "the goodness of God leads you to repentance"[1]. Do you know how Jesus transformed a foul-mouthed fisherman like Peter? Being a fisherman, Peter was probably also a big, burly guy. So how did

Jesus bring him to his knees? Was it fiery preaching on God's judgment or a hard sermon on the law of Moses that broke this fisherman? Neither! Jesus blessed Peter with a boat-sinking, net-breaking load of fish, and when Peter saw God's goodness, he bowed down at Jesus' feet and said, "Depart from me, for I am a sinful man, O Lord!"[2] Now, pay close attention here. Which came first — Peter's repentance or the goodness of God? Clearly, it was the goodness of God that came first. My friend, it is truly the goodness of God that leads us to repentance!

It is when we experience His love for us that we can respond with our love for Him.

Nevertheless, there are still people who insist that we have to preach on repentance. Well, I disagree! I think that we should do it God's way — preach the goodness of God and allow the goodness of God to lead people to repentance. Such repentance will be true repentance. It will not be a repentance that is motivated by the fear of judgment and indignation. It will be a genuine repentance that is motivated by His grace, unconditional love and compassion. After all, our ability to love God stems from our first tasting His love for us. It is when we experience His love for us that we can respond with our love for Him. The Bible says, "We love Him because He first loved us."[3]

Do you know how the Word of God defines love? Apostle John said, "In this is love, not that we loved God, but that He loved us and sent His Son to be the propitiation for our sins."[4] This is the Bible's definition of love. It is not about **our** love for Him, but rather **His** perfect love for us. As opposed to conventional belief, true repentance from the heart results from a revelation of God's immense and unyielding love. It is not found in laws, judgment and indignation. When Peter saw Jesus' goodness and love, he fell to his knees in total surrender to Jesus.

So let's be scriptural, my friend. It is not the preaching of wrath, fiery indignation and judgment that will cause people's hearts to turn back to God. It is His goodness, grace and mercy. When you catch a glimpse of that, you cannot help but be overwhelmed by all that He is, and this will lead to true repentance. Let people come to church to enjoy God's goodness because when they are impacted by His **grace**, repentance, holiness and godliness will surely follow. In the same way that you cannot be under the sun without getting a tan, you cannot be under grace without becoming holy.

Time To Change Your Mind

By the way, for all of you who feel that there should be more preaching on repentance, do you know what the word "repent" means in the first place? The word "repent" is the Greek word *metanoeo*, which according to Thayer's Greek Lexicon, simply means "to change one's mind"[5]. But because we have been influenced by our denominational background as well as our own religious upbringing, many of us have the impression that repentance is something that involves mourning and sorrow. However, that is not what the Word of God says. Repentance just means changing your mind.

When John the Baptist said, "Repent, for the kingdom of heaven is at hand!"[6] he was essentially saying, "Change your mind, for the kingdom of heaven is at hand!" This means that even if we do not use the word "repent" all the time on God's people, every time they sit under the anointed preaching of His Word, repentance is still occurring — their minds are being changed through the preaching of the gospel.

As they hear the gospel of Jesus preached, they are changing their minds about their old beliefs that held them in bondage, and receiving the truth that liberates them. Even as you are reading this book, repentance is going on. You are renewing your mind with the good news of Jesus. You are becoming more and more conscious of His finished work and your righteousness in Christ. When you begin to receive the revelation that you are no longer under the old covenant of law, but are now under the new covenant of grace, the Bible calls that repentance!

Repentance From Dead Works

Believers are often exhorted to repent from sin. However in the New Testament, we are actually exhorted to repent from dead works. You see, sin is simply the **fruit**, dead works are the **root**.

It says in the book of Hebrews that the first foundation stone of our faith is "repentance from dead works and of faith toward God"[7]. Now, "dead works" are not sins. They are the so-called good works that people do to gain righteousness with God. If you pray because you think that praying makes you right with God, that's a dead work. But if you pray because you **are** right with God and you know that He loves you, there is power there. Can you see the difference? It is the same activity — prayer — but the basis and motivation for doing it are completely different. One is a dead work while the other is a living work by grace.

Similarly, if you study the Bible because you think that doing so makes you right with God, you have missed it. There will be no flow. There will be no revelation because you are not flowing with the Spirit of truth, who bears witness with your spirit that you are already right with God. But if you study the Bible because you know that you are right with God and that the Bible is a love letter from the One who made you right, treasures from the Word of God will open up to you.

My friend, have you ever repented from dead works?

Jesus said, "Repent, and believe in the gospel."[8] In other words, He was saying to the Jews of His time, "Change your mind and believe the good news — I will shed My blood, and through My suffering and passion, all your sins will be forgiven!" If you are still living under the law and depending on your own efforts to qualify yourself and please God, it's time to repent (change your mind) from dead works and believe the gospel!

One Thing You Lack

I want to show you two Bible stories that effectively contrast law and grace. These stories are found in Luke chapters 18 and 19. In Luke 18:18–23, we have the story of the rich young ruler who came to Jesus and asked, "What must I do to inherit eternal life?" Now, think about this question for a moment. What should the right evangelical answer be?

The right evangelical answer should be, "Believe on Me and you will inherit eternal life." But that was not what Jesus said to him. Instead, Jesus gave him the law of Moses, saying, "You know the commandments: 'Do not commit adultery,' 'Do not murder,'

'Do not steal,' 'Do not bear false witness,' 'Honor your father and your mother.'" Jesus gave him the Ten Commandments. Why? Because the young ruler came with pride, believing that he could **do** something to earn and deserve eternal life. Whenever you come boasting in your efforts, Jesus will give you the law of Moses.

Now, listen to what the young man said in response to Jesus: "All these things I have kept from my youth." Amazing! This man actually claimed that he had kept all the Ten Commandments from his youth! Like the Pharisees, some people really think that they are able to keep all the laws of Moses, not knowing that they have lowered God's law to a place where they think they can keep it. Jesus came to bring the law back to its pristine standard — not only must there be an outward adherence to the law, there must also be an inward adherence. Jesus showed that God's law is beyond man's own efforts. The young man was probably expecting Jesus to compliment him on his law-keeping, and was feeling really confident of himself. But notice what Jesus said to him. Instead of complimenting him, He said, "**One thing you still lack**."

You see, every time you boast in your law-keeping, Jesus will find something that you lack. In this case, He told the young man to sell all that he had, give it to the poor and follow Him. The young man had boasted that he had kept all the commandments, but now, Jesus was giving him the very first commandment, "You shall have no other gods before Me,"[9] (not even money) and look at what happened. The young ruler walked away, sorrowful. He was not even able to give one dollar to the Lord!

Think about the amazing privilege to follow Jesus. Jesus gave the man an opportunity to follow Him, but the man could not because he could not bear to part with his wealth. In all his boasting, he could not even keep the first commandment.

My friend, if you come to the Lord full of self-righteousness, boasting in your ability to keep the law, He will show you that, according to the law, there is "one thing you still lack".

Grace Opens Your Heart

Now, let's go over to Luke 19:1–10. Jesus walked into Jericho and a crowd gathered to see Him. Then, as He passed by a sycamore tree, He looked up and saw Zacchaeus, short, little Zacchaeus who had climbed the tree hoping to catch a glimpse of Jesus as He walked by.

Zacchaeus was a corrupt tax collector, a sinner. But instead of giving him the Ten Commandments, Jesus showed him grace (undeserved favor) and invited Himself to Zacchaeus' house. Of course, the people in the crowd were displeased and they said, "He has gone to be a guest with a man who is a sinner."

Now, observe what happened at Zacchaeus' house. Before the dinner was over, Zacchaeus stood up and said to the Lord, "Look, Lord, I give half of my goods to the poor; and if I have taken anything from anyone by false accusation, I restore fourfold." Jesus smiled at Zacchaeus and said, "Today, salvation has come to this house."

I believe that it was the Holy Spirit who put these two stories side by side. I don't believe that they happened chronologically. I believe that the Holy Spirit placed them in this divine order to show us the contrasting effects of being under the covenant of law, and being under the covenant of grace.

When the rich young ruler came boasting in his law-keeping, Jesus **answered with the law**. And the young man could hardly give a dollar to Jesus and walked away sorrowful. But in the very next chapter, when Jesus **gave no law but showed His grace**, it not only opened Zacchaeus' heart, it also opened up his wallet! Can you imagine this? It opened up the wallet of a corrupt tax collector. That's truly the power of grace! It leads one to true repentance. When you experience His grace, you can't help but be generous.

The law condemns the self-righteous,
but grace will transform the sinner.

After Jesus lavished His unconditional love and grace on Zacchaeus, Zacchaeus' heart overflowed with the undeserved, unmerited and unearned favor of God. He knew deep in his heart that as a sinner and corrupt tax collector, he did not deserve to have Jesus come to his house. All he had hoped for was to catch a glimpse of Jesus from the sycamore tree, but God's goodness far exceeded his expectations. And just as Peter was brought to his knees when he saw Jesus' goodness, Zacchaeus was led to repentance when he experienced Jesus' goodness. You see, the law condemns the self-righteous, but grace will transform the sinner.

Unlike the young ruler, Zacchaeus did not come to Jesus boasting in his law-keeping. He knew that he was undeserving and that is why Jesus was able to shower grace on him. In the same way, many believers today won't allow themselves to receive grace from the Lord because like the young ruler, their trust is in their own righteousness and law-keeping. When you depend on the law, the law will be given back to you to expose the areas that you are lacking in. Once you think that you have perfectly kept the law, there will always be "one thing you still lack".

The role of the law is to bring you to the end of yourself, to bring you to a place where you know in no uncertain terms that you cannot do anything to deserve God's salvation, blessings and favor. Our heavenly Father is waiting for us to give up on our own efforts. The moment you begin to repent from all the dead works that you have been doing to try to qualify for and deserve God's acceptance and blessings, God will lavish on you His abundant grace — His undeserved, unearned and unmerited favor.

God Is After Inward Heart Transformation

"But Pastor Prince, if I give up on keeping the law of Moses, what is going to govern my behavior and ensure that it is acceptable to God?"

You don't have to worry about how your behavior will be governed without a consciousness of the law. The Word of God says that grace will teach you — "For the grace of God... has appeared to all men, teaching us that, denying ungodliness and worldly lusts..."[10]

Grace is a teacher and it taught Zacchaeus. Do you remember his response after he experienced the abundance of grace? He said, "I give half of my goods to the poor; and if I have taken anything from anyone by false accusation, I restore fourfold." It is grace that leads people to true repentance. Grace does not result in superficial behavior modification, but inward heart transformation.

It is not fiery preaching on God's judgment that leads us to repentance. It is the goodness of God that leads us to repentance.

Get hold of anointed teachings, and hear more and more about the grace of God, His finished work and His goodness. Start "changing your mind" — from putting yourself under the old covenant of law to seeing yourself enjoying the undeserved favor of God under the new covenant of grace!

It is grace that leads people to true repentance and inward heart transformation.

Chapter 19

The Key To Effortless Victorious Living

People are afraid to preach the gospel of grace because they think that if they preach grace, believers will go out and sin. They seem to have more confidence in man's flesh to keep the law than in the power of the cross. Yet, it is not grace that stirs up sin, it is the law[1].

Don't forget that after Israel boasted to God, "All that the Lord has spoken we will do,"[2] they broke the very first commandment and made a golden calf at the foot of Mount Sinai. Have you ever read, **"the strength of sin is the law"**[3]? The more you try to keep the law and not sin, the worse it becomes. For example, if I tell you **not** to think of a purple dinosaur right now, what is the first thing that pops into your head?

Come on, I told you **not** to think of a purple dinosaur. Get that picture of the purple dinosaur out of your head! (Say, are you thinking of Barney?)

The more you try not to see a purple dinosaur, the more your mind is occupied with that silly purple dinosaur. You see, you cannot help it. The harder you try, the more you will see that purple dinosaur. In the same way, the more you put yourself under the law — the more you try not to sin — the more conscious you will be of sin.

Self-Effort Results In Defeat

Imagine a man who knows that he has a problem with lust. When he gets up in the morning, he tells the Lord, "Lord, give me victory today. Help me not to lust after women. I do not want to lust, so help me not to lust today. I will not lust. I will not lust. I will not..."

But the moment he steps out of his apartment and sees someone walking by in a skirt, what do you think would be his first thought? It would be a lustful thought! The more he tries not to lust, the more his mind is occupied with lust. In fact, anything in a skirt would trigger his mind to lust, even if the person walking by in a "skirt" is a Scotsman in a kilt!

Imagine another scenario where a lady says to herself, "I really can't stand that colleague. She always seems to say things to me that make me so angry. But since I am a Christian, I will do my best to love her. I will obey the law. I will love her. I will love her as myself. I will..." Even as she drives to work, this lady thinks to herself, "I will not be angry with her when I see her. I will love her."

But guess what? The moment she steps into her office, the colleague that she is **trying** to love greets her with a bright and chirpy "Good morning!" Instantly, instead of love, she feels anger and irritation — "It's the way she says 'good morning'. It's so pretentious! She's such a hypocrite! I hate her!" And the more she tries to like her colleague, the worse it becomes. Have you been there before?

Effortless Victorious Living

Let's take another Christian who has a problem with lust and anger. But this Christian believes in grace, so when he wakes up, he tells the Lord, "Lord, I am not even going to try today. I know that I cannot overcome this on my own. Lord, I rest in You. You live the victorious life for me. I cannot overcome lust by my own strength. I cannot love that colleague by my own strength. My eyes are on You. Even though I cannot, I know that You can. Thank You for Your grace. I will just be cool."

Then, he leaves his home and goes to work. As he is driving to work, he sees a huge billboard showing a woman in a bikini. And when he feels tempted to lust, he says, "Thank You Father, I am the righteousness of God in Christ. I know that You are here with me. I have not lost Your presence. Even when I fail, You are with me. Thank You for Your grace." The temptation comes and the temptation goes. He is at rest. He does not pull over to the side of the road and lament, "Oh God, why is this happening again? Please forgive me, Lord!" because he knows that the more he confesses and focuses on his weakness, the worse it becomes.

People who are living under guilt and condemnation are doomed to repeat their sins.

By the way, do you know what people, who believe in confessing their sins in order to be forgiven, usually do? Many a time, they say to themselves, "I will save my confessions for tonight. In the meantime, since I am already guilty of lust, let me watch this raunchy movie and indulge in this men's magazine. I will compile these sins and confess them all at the end of the day."

You see, people who are living under guilt and condemnation are doomed to repeat their sins. They think that since fellowship with God has already been broken, they might as well go all the way and indulge their weaknesses before they reconcile themselves with God.

On the other hand, believers under grace know that they are always righteous and that fellowship with God is never broken. Even when they fail, they know that Jesus is still with them. They know that righteousness is a gift and that the Holy Spirit is present to convict them of their righteousness in Christ. The more they believe that they are righteous, the more they experience true victory over sin. My friend, we've established this before: **Right believing always produces right living**.

Let's come back to the Christian who believes in grace. Now, when he steps into the office, he is greeted by the colleague he dislikes. This colleague chirps a shrill "Good morning!" right into his ears. Even though he is irritated and feels anger rising within him, he is able to give thanks: "Lord, thank You for loving me even when I feel like this." Instead of saying, "God, forgive me for being such a failure," he is able to rise above his feelings of anger and irritation, and catch a fresh revelation of God's unconditional love for him.

Instead of feeling irritated and angry with himself for being irritated and angry with his colleague, he overflows with God's grace and is empowered with a supernatural ability to love even the most unlikable colleague. Can you see the difference between those who believe in God's grace and forgiveness, and those who try to overcome sin by their own efforts? Those who depend on God's grace see His power flowing in their lives!

My friend, every once in a while, you will be tempted to sin. But while the law only stirs up your flesh to be more aware of sin, grace gives you the power to be effortlessly victorious over sin. That is why Apostle Paul said, "For sin shall not have dominion over you, for you are not under law but under grace."[4] When you put yourself under the law, the moment you are tempted, you condemn yourself, and in that state of guilt and condemnation, you are more likely to follow through with that temptation and sin.

However, when you put yourself under the grace of God, the moment you are tempted, you receive a fresh dose of His grace and His forgiveness. You see yourself righteous and this gives you the power to rise above the temptation.

Awake to righteousness and sin not[5]. When you believe that you are righteous **even** when you sin, your thoughts and actions will come in alignment with your believing. In contrast, believers who do not know that they are righteous even when they sin will remain in their cycle of sin.

Right Believing Leads To Right Living

Charles Haddon Spurgeon, probably the first pastor ever to build a mega-church in London, the Metropolitan Tabernacle, was a famous and respected preacher in the early 1900s. He was known as the "prince of preachers", and regardless of which denomination they belonged to, many ministers and theologians respected and still respect Spurgeon. This is what Spurgeon had to say about grace:

No doctrine is so calculated to preserve a man from sin as the doctrine of the grace of God. Those who have called it "a licentious doctrine" did not know anything at all about it. Poor ignorant things, they little knew that their own vile stuff was the most licentious doctrine under heaven. If they knew the grace of God in truth, they would soon see that there was no preservative from lying like a knowledge that we are elect of God from the foundation of the world. There is nothing like a belief in my eternal perseverance, and the immutability of my Father's affection, which can keep me near to Him from a motive of simple gratitude.

Nothing makes a man so virtuous as belief of the truth. **A lying doctrine will soon beget a lying practice. A man cannot have an erroneous belief without by-and-by having an erroneous life.** I believe the one thing naturally begets the other. Of all men, those have the most disinterested piety, the sublimest reverence, the most ardent devotion, who believe that they are saved by grace, without works, through faith, and that not of themselves, it is the gift of God. Christians should take heed, and see that it always is so, lest by any means Christ should be crucified afresh, and put to an open shame[6].

Isn't that beautiful? Spurgeon was saying that if your behavior is wrong, it is because there is something wrong with your beliefs. The grace of God is the power to preserve you from sin.

Right believing leads to right living. Believe that you are righteous because of the blood of Jesus, and the result of believing this will be righteous thoughts and actions.

If your behavior is wrong, it is because there is something wrong with your beliefs.

Victory In Your Thought Life

In the Song of Solomon, Solomon said, "Your temples… are like a piece of pomegranate."[7] The temples are a reference to the head. The Bible actually compares your head to a pomegranate. When you cut a pomegranate in half, you will find that it is filled with white seeds in a beautiful red liquid. When I was in Israel, I was told that the red liquid is very strong — if you get it on your shirt, the stain will be very difficult to remove.

Now, this is a very powerful picture for you to have if you want victory over your thought life. You may be struggling with temptations, lustful and angry thoughts, or thoughts of guilt and condemnation, but the Lord wants you to have victory over these battles in your mind. He wants you to picture your head like a pomegranate. The rich red liquid is a picture of the blood of Jesus Christ and the many seeds, your thoughts. The blood of Jesus is constantly washing and cleansing your thoughts. The temptation that you had in your head just now has already been washed away. Your thoughts are under a constant waterfall of cleansing and forgiveness.

When the Bible declares in 1 John 1:7 that the blood of Jesus Christ cleanses us from all sin, the tense here in the Greek for the word "cleanses" denotes a present and continuous action. In other words, Jesus' blood "keeps continually cleansing"[8]. This means that the blood never ceases to cleanse your thoughts. Even right now, your thoughts of guilt and condemnation are being washed away. Angry and lustful thoughts are being washed away. All manner of temptation is being washed away! The moment you think a bad thought, it is being washed away. The problem with believers today is that they think to themselves, "I am a Christian, so how can I have such terrible thoughts?"

My friend, listen carefully to what I am about to say: You cannot stop birds from flying over your head, but you can certainly stop them from building a nest on your head! You cannot stop your flesh and the devil from putting negative thoughts and temptations in your mind. But you can have victory over your thought life by seeing that **all** your thoughts are continually being cleansed by the blood of Jesus. His redemptive work is your victory over your thought life.

Accusations Against Grace

In the book of Romans, Paul said, "What shall we say then? Shall we continue in sin that grace may abound?"[9] Obviously, Paul was misunderstood and accused of telling people to sin more so that grace may abound. This is the same accusation that has been leveled against me.

But Paul **never** said, "Let us sin more so that grace may abound," and neither have I. I want to make this explicitly clear again: I, Joseph Prince, am vehemently, aggressively and irrevocably against sin! Sin is evil and it leads to destructive consequences.

I am on the same side as everyone who is against sin, only with this difference: Some believe that victory over sin is found in preaching more of the law, but I find that in the Scriptures, victory over sin is found in the preaching of God's grace.

Let's read what Paul said in its context:

Romans 5:20
[20]Moreover the law entered that the offense might abound. But where sin abounded, grace abounded much more.

Have you noticed that the law entered so that sin might abound? It clearly means that the more you preach the law, the more sin will abound. After all, the strength of sin is the law. Therefore, when you see sin and you preach more of the law, you are literally adding wood to fire.

The Superabundance Of God's Grace

In saying that "where sin abounded, grace abounded much more", I am preaching the same message that Paul (it is good to be in Paul's company) preached. What Paul meant, which is also what I mean, is this: **Sin does not stop God's grace from flowing, but God's grace will stop sin.** Ask yourself which is greater, your sins or God's grace? The answer is obvious. God's grace is always greater! In fact, when you read "where sin abounded, grace abounded much more" in the original Greek, it actually says that where sin abounds, grace **"superabounds"**[10]. So where there is sin, God's grace is in superabundance!

We cannot be afraid to preach grace because it is the only power to stop sin in people's lives. When you fail, instead of feeling guilty and condemned, receive the superabounding grace of God that tells you that you are still the righteousness of God! It is His superabounding grace that will rescue you from that sin. Those who wallow in guilt and condemnation are the ones who have no ability to overcome their sins. Since they believe that God's grace has departed, what hope can they have? Victory over sin comes only when people encounter the superabundance of God's grace. It is His grace that has made sinners righteous!

Victory over sin comes only when people encounter the superabundance of God's grace.

God's Justice Is On Your Side Today

"Pastor Prince, how can I be righteous when I have done nothing right, and especially when I have just failed?"

I will answer your question if you can tell me this: How could Jesus be condemned as a sinner when He committed no sin?

Jesus took all your sins upon Himself on the cross. And once your sins have been punished, it would be "unrighteous" of God to demand payment for your sins again. He cannot punish your sins twice! Yes, it is holy, right and just for God to punish sin. But having punished sin on the body of your substitute Jesus Christ, God will not demand punishment for your sins again, precisely because He is holy and just.

So if you understand that God's justice has already been executed at the cross, you will see that today, as a new covenant believer under grace, God's holiness, God's righteousness and God's justice are ON YOUR SIDE demanding your acquittal, deliverance, healing, prosperity... God's justice today demands that you have and enjoy **all the benefits of the cross**.

Don't miss out on this powerful revelation. This is the gospel of Jesus! Because all your sins have been punished in the body of your substitute Jesus Christ, God's righteousness is on your side, demanding your justification and forgiveness. That is why, even when you fail, God's grace will superabound and swallow up your failure. It has been paid for at Calvary.

The Bible says that "if anyone sins, we have an Advocate with the Father, Jesus Christ the righteous. And He Himself is the propitiation for our sins"[11]. Jesus is your Advocate today and He demands your acquittal. His blood has been shed and He became the propitiation (mercy seat) for all your sins. When God looks at you, all He sees is the blood of Jesus that makes you completely righteous. Hallelujah!

Apostle Paul Preached Grace Radically

I am preaching the gospel that Paul preached, and I am preaching it radically like he did, so that God's people can enjoy true liberty and victory in His grace. But because I preach this good news, my name has been dragged through the mud in some circles. I find that the people who have heard my preaching either hate me or love me. Well, I believe that I am in good company. There is one thing you need to know about Jesus: You cannot sit on the fence when it comes to Him. There is no middle ground. Either you love Him, or like the Pharisees, you hate Him with a passion. For those who hate me, I don't take it personally because they are actually hating the gospel. They are defending the law, not realizing that it is the ministry of death and condemnation[12].

Now, whatever I have preached to you in this book, have I pointed you to the Bible? Have I exalted Jesus Christ and His finished work? Or am I one of those who exalts man and his efforts? One thing about the gospel of grace is that it makes nothing of man and points everything back to Jesus. Conversely, the law always points to man. It tells you that unless **you** do this, or unless **you** do that, you will not have this miracle or that breakthrough.

Years ago, there were some really nasty words spoken about me concerning the gospel of grace that I was preaching, and I felt discouraged. This was in the year 2000. During that period, I happened to be in New York with Wendy and as was my custom, I went hunting for a Christian bookstore. I found one, but before I walked into it, I said, "God, can You please encourage me? I know that this gospel is from You, but I just need a bit of encouragement from You."

When I was in the bookstore, I wandered to a corner where I found a series of books by Dr Martyn Lloyd-Jones. Dr Martyn Lloyd-Jones had been the pastor of the Westminster Chapel in London for some 30 years. He was well respected within both the charismatic and non-charismatic circles, and was considered by many as the Charles Spurgeon of the modern church. However, I wasn't familiar with his teachings at that time as I had never heard him preach nor read what he taught about grace. But this was about to change.

I remember wondering to myself why I was even drawn to that section, since Dr Martin Lloyd-Jones' books were also available back home. Nevertheless, I followed the leading of the Holy Spirit and picked up a book randomly. It fell open to Dr Lloyd-Jones' teaching on Romans 8:1, which says, "There is therefore now no condemnation to those who are in Christ Jesus." He said, "The apostle [Paul] is asserting that if we are Christians, your sins and mine — past sins, present sins and future sins — have already been dealt with once and forever!" Wow, I was excited because this sounded like what I had been preaching, and there had been a dearth of such teachings. You don't hear much preaching like this these days. And of all the books in the bookstore, I was drawn to this one. I knew that it was the answer to the prayer I had said before I entered the bookstore, so I read on:

> The apostle [Paul] is asserting that if we are Christians, your sins and mine — past sins, present sins and future sins — have already been dealt with once and forever! Had you realized that? Most of our troubles are due to our failure to realize the truth of this verse. 'There is therefore now no condemnation to them which are in Christ Jesus' is so often understood to mean nothing more than that past sins have been dealt with. Of course it means that; but it also means your present sins; even more, it means that any sin you may ever chance to commit has already been dealt with. You will never, you cannot ever, come under condemnation. This is what the apostle is saying — nothing can

ever bring the Christian again into a position of condemnation...

The Christian can never be lost, the Christian can never come under condemnation. 'No condemnation' is an absolute word, and we must not detract from it. To do so is to contradict and to deny the Scriptures...

But why does the apostle say this, and on what grounds does he say it? Is it not a dangerous thing to say? **Will it not incite people to sin? If we tell Christians that their past sins, their present and their future sins have already been put away by God, are we not more or less telling them that they are free to go out and sin? If you react in that way to my statements I am most happy, for I am obviously a good and true interpreter of the apostle Paul**[13].

As I read the passage, I felt really refreshed and nourished. It was so good to hear from a seasoned man of God who had preached this same gospel even before I was born. He was effectively saying that if ministers are not being accused of the same things that Paul was accused of, then it means that they are not being true interpreters of Paul's message. (Remember that Paul was accused of saying that we should sin more so that grace might abound.) So when I read his writing, I felt that I was in good company, first with Paul, and then with dear Dr Martyn Lloyd-Jones.

When you preach the true gospel, radical grace must be preached. When I was in Switzerland in 1997, the Lord told me,

"If you don't preach grace radically, people's lives will never be radically blessed and radically transformed." I have been doing that ever since and with the fresh encouragement from the Lord in that New York bookstore, I knew that I would not stop preaching grace radically because I want to see lives radically transformed and believers living with true victory over every destructive habit and sin. It is the gospel that Paul preached.

It is the gospel that will lead you to effortless victorious living in Christ Jesus!

When grace is preached radically, people's lives will be radically blessed and transformed.

Chapter 20

The Problem With Mixture

D o you know why many believers today have a confused perspective of God? What would cause believers to think that God is sometimes angry with them, but at other times pleased with them? Why would some believers think that their heavenly Father would actually punish them with sicknesses and diseases when it would be unthinkable for them to inflict such draconian measures on their own children? What accounts for this apparent schizophrenia that exists in the body of Christ today? I submit to you that this confusion stems from what is called "Galatianism".

Galatianism is essentially a mixture of covenants. It is the intermingling of teachings about God which contain a little bit of the law as well as a little bit of grace. The church in Galatia was struggling with this and from the severity of Apostle Paul's tone to the Galatians, it is obvious that Paul regarded this issue very seriously.

You will never find Paul saying to the believers in the church of Corinth, "O foolish Corinthians!" Yet, we know that the church in Corinth was in a mess. The people were involved in all kinds of outward sins. They were in strife, envy and jealousy, and some of them were even going to temple prostitutes. There were believers suing one another in court. The people were also misusing the gifts of the Spirit. All in all, there were all kinds of immoral activities going on in the church of Corinth. There was utter chaos! Yet, not once did Paul call them "foolish Corinthians", or in our modern vernacular, "STUPID Corinthians!" Search your Bible. You won't find even one instance.

On the contrary, Paul affirmed the Corinthians and told them, "God is faithful, by whom you were called into the fellowship of His Son, Jesus Christ our Lord."[1] He spoke positively to them, assuring them that they "come short in no gift" and that they would be confirmed to the end, and "be blameless in the day of our Lord Jesus Christ"[2]. Isn't that amazing?

Wrong Doctrine Is Worse Than Wrong Behavior

Now, notice the stark contrast between Paul's treatment of the Corinthian church and the Galatian church. To the church in Galatia, he said, "O foolish Galatians! Who has bewitched you…?"[3] Further on, he says again, "Are you so foolish?..."[4] Paul was angry! He was upset with what was happening in Galatia and he made it clear that he was not happy at all with the Galatians. Most people would expect Paul to be more upset with the believers in Corinth, but he was not. His intense reaction toward the church in Galatia reveals **what is of priority to God**. It is clear that in God's eyes, **believing the wrong doctrine is worse than exhibiting wrong behavior!**

In case you didn't get it the first time, let me say it again: To God, **wrong doctrine is far worse than wrong behavior!** When it came to wrong behavior in Corinth, Paul was cool and collected toward the believers. He was able to handle their wrong behavior because he knew that the grace of God was able to take care of their spree of wrong behavior. That is why he was able to speak positively to them, even telling them, "I thank my God always concerning you for the **grace of God** which was given to you by Christ Jesus…"[5] But when it came to wrong doctrine in Galatia, he rebuked the believers there because they nullified God's grace by mixing it with the law.

In the very first chapter of Galatians, Paul says, "I marvel…" or as you and I would say today, "I am appalled…" What appalled him? Paul continues: "I marvel that you are **turning away** so soon from Him who called you in the **grace of Christ**, to a different gospel, which is not another; but there are some who trouble you and want to pervert the gospel of Christ."[6]

Paul was angry because the Galatians were turning away from the "**grace of Christ**" to "a different gospel", and because there were some people who wanted to "pervert the gospel of Christ". Paul had preached the gospel of grace to the Galatians, but he found that there were Judaizers who introduced elements of the law to them, mixing God's grace with the law. Do not belittle this problem. It was a serious problem and it made Paul very angry. Since Paul was full of the Holy Spirit and his anger was Spirit-inspired, it would benefit us to really understand why the mixture of law and grace angered him.

Grace Is The Solution To Wrong Behavior

Imagine that you have a pile of dirty laundry in your living room and every day, the pile grows bigger. The stench from the pile gets stronger and more unbearable as each day passes. Is this a big problem? Well, it depends. As long as your washing machine is working, it will not be a problem for long. No matter how much dirty laundry you have, as long as your washing machine is working, there is still hope. The dirty laundry only becomes a problem if you destroy or get rid of the washing machine. Without a washing machine, the dirty laundry that is piling up certainly becomes a big problem. What are you going to do with all that dirty laundry if you don't have a fully functioning washing machine?

You see, the dirty laundry is "wrong behavior" and the washing machine is "grace". Now, don't get me wrong, we certainly don't want our homes to stink. But if you have wrong behavior, as long as there is grace in the church, grace will teach and give you the power to overcome your wrong behavior. But if there is no grace in the church, or if grace is mixed with the law and nullified, then what hope is there for overcoming your wrong behavior?

Allowing Mixture Perverts The Gospel Of Christ

That is why Paul had to be firm with the Galatians. By allowing grace to be mixed with the law, the Galatians had perverted the gospel of Christ. Paul had preached the gospel of grace to them, but after he left, some Judaizers came and told them lies like, "Yes, it is good that you are saved by grace, but it is not enough for you to just have Jesus. You must also know and abide by the law of Moses to be pleasing to God." In essence, they were saying, "Grace is good, but grace must be balanced with the law." So they taught the Galatians things like the Ten Commandments and told them that they had to be circumcised. Paul's response was to pronounce a double curse on those who preached the false gospel to the Galatians! His tough stance toward those who preached mixture represents the heart of God today.

You Cannot Balance Grace With Law

"Pastor Prince, you believe in grace while I believe that you must keep the law to be justified. Does it really matter if I believe differently from you?"

Well, it mattered enough to Paul for him to pronounce the double curse. Many believers do not think that it is a serious matter to have mixture. But our response to the mixture of law and grace should be in alignment with Paul's — He was appalled that the Galatians were mixing law and grace.

In most places today, the problem is not pure law. You will not find pure law in Christian churches. What you will find in many places today is a mixture of law and grace. You will hear teachings that combine the old and new covenants. You will hear things like, "Yes, you are saved by grace, but now that you are saved, you had better not take it for granted. You have to start living a holy life by keeping the Ten Commandments." This is called mixture — you have a little bit of grace and a little bit of law. Many believers think that this — balancing law and grace — is all right. However, the Lord has shown me that **what man calls balance, God calls mixture**.

My friend, you cannot balance law and grace. Your justification is either entirely a work of His grace or it is by your own works. His grace will be nullified when you add even a little mixture of man's own efforts to be justified. This is serious. God hates mixture.

While most people have no problem with agreeing that they have been saved by grace, they are nevertheless still subjecting themselves to the law. They are depending on the "works of the law" or their obedience to the law to earn, merit and deserve God's blessings. When they do well in their own estimation, they expect to be blessed. But when they fall short and fail, they heap on themselves guilt and condemnation, and expect to be punished.

Grace is the undeserved, unmerited and unearned
favor of God — the moment you try to merit
the free favors of God, His grace is nullified.

In the new covenant, God doesn't want us to be blessed when we obey the law and cursed when we fail. Doesn't such a system sound awfully similar to the old covenant? Grace is the undeserved, unmerited and unearned favor of God — the moment you try to merit the free favors of God, His grace is nullified.

In the new covenant, God wants us to be blessed on account of His Son and what He did on the cross. It has nothing to do with our performance or ability to keep the law. Those trying to be justified by their law-keeping still have an old covenant mentality, even if they profess that they are in the new covenant. They have reverted to the old system that was based on works and obedience, rather than trusting in the new system that is based on faith and believing. When there is mixture between the old and new covenants, between the covenant of law and the covenant of grace, you lose both and the benefits of the two covenants are nullified! How do we know this? What is the scriptural basis for this? Let's look at what Jesus said:

> Mark 2:22
> ²²"And no one puts **new** wine into **old** wineskins; or else the new wine bursts the wineskins, the **wine is spilled**, and the **wineskins are ruined**. But new wine must be put into new wineskins."

What was Jesus referring to when He shared on the new wine and old wineskins? He was referring to the mixture of the two covenants. The new wine represents the new covenant of grace, while the old wineskin represents the old covenant of law. Have you seen old wineskins before? They are brittle, hard and inflexible. That's the law. It is inflexible. And when you pour the new wine of grace into the old wineskin of the law, you will lose both because the wineskin will be ruined and the wine will be spilled. The virtues of both the old and the new covenants will be cancelled out and lost.

I can't understand why many believers are still trying to balance law and grace. If you are for the law, be for the law completely. If you are for grace, then be for grace completely. It is impossible to balance the two of them! That is why Jesus also said:

> Revelation 3:15–16, KJV
> ¹⁵I know thy works, that thou art neither cold nor hot: **I would thou wert cold or hot**. ¹⁶So then because thou art lukewarm, and neither cold nor hot, I will spew thee out of My mouth.

For years, I have heard preachers preaching that in Revelation 3:15–16, Jesus was referring to people who are not "red-hot for Jesus". Have you heard that expression before? And what does being "red-hot for Jesus" mean? Traditionally, we have been taught that it means that you are reading 10 chapters of the Bible a day, witnessing to your colleagues and attending every prayer meeting you can find! To be cold means just the opposite — you stop doing these things entirely.

The verse has always been preached as though it were about our actions and behavior. But Jesus said that He would rather we be cold or hot, and not lukewarm. This wouldn't make sense if He was referring to actions and behavior, because wouldn't being lukewarm for Jesus still be better than being completely cold? So why would He want the church of Laodicea to be cold (if they weren't hot)? Come on! I always tell my church this: When you come on Sunday, don't forget to bring your brains along! Don't just take in everything you hear. You have to test the message and make sure that it is consistent with the gospel of Jesus. The gospel simply means "good news". So if what you are hearing is not good news, but instead deposits fear, doubt, judgment and condemnation in your heart, throw it out, my friend, because it's not the gospel of Jesus.

Be Hot Or Cold, Not Lukewarm

Now, would you like to know what Revelation 3:15–16 really means? The two verses would only make sense when they are interpreted in the light of the mixture of the covenants of law and grace in the church of Laodicea. The Lord was saying that He would the church be cold — entirely under law, or hot — entirely under grace. You see, if you were at least completely under law, it would lead you to despair and into the saving arms of Jesus. The law would unveil to you your sinfulness and inability to keep the full measure of it, and this would cause you to see your need for His grace.

But when you have mixture, where you believe in grace, but still hold on to the law, you neutralize the convicting power of the law to bring you to the end of yourself so that you will cry out for the grace of the Savior. That is why you cannot be cold and hot at the same time, or be for both law and grace at the same time. The moment you attempt to balance grace with the law, you neutralize both and each covenant is robbed of its full effect in your life. You become lukewarm because of the mixture, and God hates mixture because it robs you of the power to reign in life through the abundance of His grace! You cannot put new wine into old wineskins. You will lose both!

Trying to balance grace with the law robs you of the power to reign in life through the abundance of His grace.

This is exactly what Paul was saying to the Galatians when he explained to them the purpose of the law:

Galatians 3:24–25
[24]Therefore the law was our tutor to bring us to Christ, that we might be justified by faith. [25]But after faith has come, we are no longer under a tutor.

The law was our "tutor", or according to the King James Version, our "schoolmaster", to bring us to the end of our own efforts and to Christ. The law is an impossible standard for man to keep. The Pharisees brought the law down to a level where they could keep it. They really thought that their works, their reading the Scriptures and their loud prayers could justify them. But when Jesus stepped onto the scene, His harshest words — He called them a "brood of vipers"[7] — were reserved for these very legalists. He brought the law back to its pristine standard. According to Jesus, once you fantasize about a woman, you are guilty of adultery. Once you are angry with a brother without cause, you are guilty of murder.

"Pastor Prince this is an impossible standard. We will all fail!"

Exactly! Finally, you are getting it. Jesus was showing us the true standard of God's law and holiness. It is impossible for man to keep His law! If you are **not** for grace, then make sure that you are entirely "cold" — completely under law. Don't mix law and grace. When you put yourself completely under law, you will find that the law will be your tutor to bring you to the end of yourself. When you finally acknowledge that you cannot save yourself, you will turn to the Savior and His grace will fill your heart. You see, when you think that **you can**, His hands are tied and He cannot. But when you know that **you cannot**, that's when HE CAN! Get it?

Can You Save Yourself?

Before a lifeguard attempts to rescue someone who is drowning, he will wait for the person to give up on his efforts to save himself. If the person is still struggling, with his hands flailing and legs kicking everywhere, a well-trained lifeguard will not come close to him just yet because he knows that he will be pulled down and both will drown. So even though the lifeguard wants to save the drowning person, he cannot until the person has exhausted his strength and gives up trying to save himself. Then, the lifeguard immediately grabs hold of him and brings him to safety.

Similarly, when you think that you can still save yourself, God's grace cannot flow. If you mix law and grace, both will "drown" and you will lose BOTH. In other words, the person who is "drowning" must **know** that he is drowning and that he cannot save himself. (Now, isn't that a deep revelation!) Only when he gives up on his efforts can grace come and rescue him. Jesus had no effect on the Pharisees precisely because they thought that they were self-sufficient in their law-keeping and saw no need for the Savior. They had no revelation that they were drowning!

Falling From Grace

Paul told the Galatians, "Christ is become of no effect unto you, whosoever of you are justified by the law; ye are **fallen from grace**."[8] This is the true definition of "falling from grace". Today, when someone sins, ministers say that the person has "fallen from grace". But Paul **never** told the Corinthians that they had fallen from grace despite all their sins. To fall from grace then is to fall into the law. Notice that grace is the high ground. When you are under the law, you have fallen from your high ground of grace. In the ark of the covenant, the mercy seat is positioned

above the Ten Commandments. You fall from grace when you go back to the Ten Commandments.

The law makes everything of man's efforts, while grace gives all the glory to God. That is why Paul told the Galatians that the gospel is not a man-pleasing gospel[9]. He was essentially saying, "If I want to please man, I would be preaching the law." Legalistic people react when they hear that they can no longer boast in their self-efforts to keep the law. The only people who appreciate grace are those who have come to the end of themselves, to the end of their own efforts to save themselves. They have tried over and over again until they have finally given up and admitted that they cannot meet the law's unyielding standard. That's the time when they are ready to receive God's undeserved favor — His saving grace.

We are all against sin, but grace is the
power to get out of sin.

My friend, we are all against sin, but grace is the power to get out of sin. The more entangled you get with the law, the more the law will stir up sin in you. The law was designed to expose sin. It is sad that many preachers refuse to accept the gospel of grace until they themselves are caught in sin. Only when they find themselves ensnared by sin do they realize that only grace can give them true power over sin. This is what Paul asserted when he said, "For sin shall not have dominion over you, for you are not under law but under grace."[10]

The good news is, you can embrace the grace of our Lord TODAY and have dominion over sin TODAY!

My Journey Toward Understanding Grace

By the way, in case you are wondering, **I was not introduced to the gospel of grace because of any moral sin**.

The Lord revealed His grace to me through my own struggles against all the erroneous teachings I had received in my youth. I heard so much legalistic preaching that I really believed that I had lost my salvation. I believed that I had committed the unpardonable sin of blaspheming the Holy Spirit. I would walk down the streets evangelizing to people, all the while thinking that I had lost my salvation. I did this because I had hoped that one day, those whom I had witnessed to would go to heaven and God would ask them, "How did you get saved?" and they would say, "By someone called Joseph Prince." Then, God would realize that I was in hell and He would remember me. I really believed that!

I tried with all my might, all my strength and all my vigor to keep the law. I was confessing all my sins almost every waking minute, until my mind nearly snapped. It was only until I came to the end of myself that I saw the need for my beautiful Savior Jesus Christ, and it was He who opened my eyes to the new covenant of grace. Well, that was my journey toward discovering the gospel of grace. So my friend, I know what it means to be under the law. I have first-hand experience of the impossibility of keeping the law and it has led me to Christ, just as Paul said that it would.

It Is Time To Leave Babylon

Beloved, mixing law and grace is dangerous. It will cause you to live in confusion. It will cause you to think that God is sometimes pleased with you, but at other times angry with you. Confusion makes you believe that the same God who can heal you today may also punish you with a disease the next day. Mixture leads to confusion and God is not the author of confusion. But praise be to God, the Gospel Revolution is setting God's people free all around the world.

I see the body of Christ coming out of Babylon. The word "Babylon" means "confusion by mixing"[11], and I see the church coming out of the bondage of mixture and confusion. Hallelujah! The church has been in Babylon for too long, but it is coming out.

My friend, it is time for you to come out of mixture and confusion. Choose either the covenant of grace or the covenant of law. Either you enjoy the blessings of the Lord through His undeserved, unearned and unmerited favor, or you trust in your own efforts and your own behavior to deserve, earn and merit favors from the Lord. You cannot hold on to both. I pray that you will choose the first. Come out of Babylon and enjoy the abundance of His grace today!

Chapter 21

The Secret To Great Faith

Have you ever felt like you needed more faith? Have you ever looked at yourself and told yourself that if you just had more faith, you would see your financial breakthrough or healing?

My friend, I have good news for you today: Faith is not a struggle. The **hearing of faith** and the **works of the law** are total opposites. And since the law is about our self-efforts, **there is no self-effort in faith**.

I give thanks to God for my roots in the Word of Faith teachings. It is truly on the shoulders of great men of God like Brother Kenneth E Hagin that we are able to see further into the Word of God today. Growing up, I learned a lot about faith from Brother Hagin who truly had a special revelation of faith from the Lord. I deeply honor and respect him for all that he has taught me.

However, after many generations of faith teachings, there are people who have turned faith into a work. Have you heard people saying, "Oh, this thing happened to you because you don't have enough faith" or "Oh, you have to have great faith to see that breakthrough"? I don't know how you feel when you hear things like that, but I always felt condemned for not having more faith.

The Ministry Of Disqualification

For years, my ministry was a ministry that disqualified people. I would preach, "The reason you are sick is that there is something wrong with you." I would teach on "the seven reasons" why people were not getting healed, and the more I preached along those lines, the more I saw our people not getting healed. I would tell my congregation, "There's nothing wrong with God, nothing wrong with His Word, so there must be something wrong with you!" I thought that this was good preaching because it was what I heard other preachers preaching as well. But one day, as I was preaching like this, I heard the Lord speaking to me on the inside. He said, "Stop disqualifying My people! My blood has already qualified them. Stop disqualifying them!"

There's nothing wrong with God, nothing wrong with the Word and through the blood of Jesus, nothing wrong with you! Receive your miracle!

Now, I know that faith is the opposite of the law, and that the more people become self-conscious, and the more they look at their self-efforts to receive from the Lord, the more faith is depleted from them. So when the Lord opened my eyes to grace, I changed what I was preaching entirely and I began to declare to my people, "There's nothing wrong with God, nothing wrong with the Word and guess what? Through the blood of Jesus, there's **nothing wrong with you!** Receive your miracle!"

Hallelujah! Once I stopped pointing the people to what was wrong with them and pointed instead to **what was right with them because of Jesus**, faith was imparted and we began to experience an explosion of healing miracles like never before. Cancers were healed, tumors were supernaturally removed and lives were transformed. That is what happens when believers know that they have been made righteous by the blood of Jesus. They begin to understand that they have the blood-bought right to be healed, to experience financial breakthroughs and to enjoy restoration in their marriages!

Faith no longer becomes a barrier to receiving God's promises. People stop thinking that they are unable to receive breakthroughs because they do not have enough faith. No way! When believers catch the revelation that there is nothing wrong with God, nothing wrong with His Word and by His grace, nothing wrong with them, guess what? Something happens to their faith. They begin to see more of Jesus. They begin to become more and more conscious of Jesus having been crucified on their behalf. And the more they see what Jesus has done for them, the more they see what Jesus has QUALIFIED them for, the more faith springs up within them and miracles break forth. Hallelujah!

Beloved, you don't have to wish that you had more faith for whatever miracle you are asking God for right now. See Jesus on the cross for you, and the faith you need to face any situation or challenge will come into your life. Just look to Jesus! He is the author and finisher of faith[1]. Faith comes by hearing and hearing by the Word of Christ. The more of Jesus you hear, the more faith rises in your heart. Get hold of teachings that preach all about Jesus and His finished work. There is no power in human philosophy or the traditions of man, but there is power in the gospel of Jesus Christ!

I received a powerful testimony of a lady in our church who just sat in one of my services, hearing Jesus being preached. There was no laying on of hands or any specific prayer for the sick that day. But when she went home that evening, she passed out a cyst that had been in her body for months. All praise and glory to Jesus! God confirms His Word through signs and wonders. When people hear the gospel of Jesus, faith is imparted and healing flows.

The Secret To Receiving Your Miracle

I attended a conference years ago and I remember hearing about all kinds of things that we had to do to work the miracles of God. For instance, we were told that we had to pray long prayers. Please don't misunderstand me. I am not saying that I don't believe in praying. I love going to my Abba in prayer. I have also taught our church about the importance of praying, especially praying in tongues. But is the secret to having miracles take place in your life found in praying?

I have also heard people saying that the key to miracles is found in fasting 40 days and 40 nights.

"Pastor Prince, I would have you know that Jesus fasted 40 days and 40 nights!"

Well, that was Jesus. The question we should be asking is, "Did Jesus tell us to fast?" Now, I know that when Jesus' disciples were unable to cast out a certain spirit from a boy, the NKJV (as well as the KJV) Bible does record that Jesus, in reference to the spirit, said, "This kind can come out by nothing but prayer and fasting."[2] So people have read this one verse and concluded that the secret to spiritual power is fasting. But do you know that in the original Greek text, the word "fasting" does not appear in that verse[3]? It was added by the translators! And if you look at the NASB and NIV translations, you won't find the word "fasting" in that verse.

In 1 Corinthians, when Apostle Paul said that husbands and wives should not deprive each other of sexual relations "except with consent for a time, that you may give yourselves to fasting and prayer"[4]. Again, after reading this one verse from Paul, people have run off saying that the secret to spiritual power is to abstain from intimate relations with your spouse! Now, if you check the original Greek text (or the NASB and NIV translations), the word "fasting" does not appear here either[5]!

If you are curious about what Paul was really talking about, then let me tell you that he was actually encouraging husbands and wives to have a healthy sex life, and not to deprive each other of sexual pleasure. God wants you to enjoy your marriage, and when you do, the Word of God declares that the devil will have no room to tempt you. In the same verse, Paul tells husbands and wives to "come together again so that Satan does not tempt you because of your lack of self-control". Think of it this way: After a man has eaten at home, he wouldn't be hungry anymore when he goes out with his friends. (He who has ears, let him hear!)

Throughout the New Testament, Paul hardly spoke about fasting. Yet, the body of Christ has somehow managed to make man's own works (like fasting) the main emphasis. Paul's emphasis was the new covenant of grace, but instead of focusing on understanding the new covenant, people are obsessed with doing! They are saying, "Forget about grace. Just tell me what to do."

And have you seen how some people fast? When they fast, they make sure that the whole world knows. They smell bad, their hair is unkempt, they are grumpy, they get angry with their wives and children, and they even kick the dog! I can just imagine one of these guys saying to his wife, "Woman, don't you know that I am fasting today? Why did you cook such a wonderful meal for the kids? I can smell it from my study! Don't you know that you are causing me to stumble?" And when his child runs to him and wants to play, he curtly brushes the child away: "Go away, boy! Daddy is busy in the Word today. Go and play by yourself. Stop disturbing me." If that's what happens when you fast, well, I think it is better that you break the fast. Go eat something and enjoy your family!

If you are fasting, the whole world doesn't need to know about it. Please wash your face, shampoo your hair, put on some cologne and brush your teeth! That's advice from the Bible[6], by the way. It says that you should not declare your fasting to man so that they will be impressed by your efforts. Instead, you should anoint your head with oil!

Now, do I fast? Yes, I do, in the sense that many a time, I am so preoccupied with the Lord in prayer or with studying His Word that I forget to eat. He opens up my eyes to certain truths, one verse leads to another, and in my eagerness to read more of His Word, I unconsciously miss my regular meals, and I even find myself forgoing sleep to be in His presence. But I don't consciously go on a fast, believing that fasting would get me my miracle.

Are You Twisting God's Arm?

When you do not understand what it means to come under the law or to come under grace, you can end up trying to twist God's arm with your efforts to convince Him that you deserve a breakthrough or miracle from Him. Do you really think that because you have fasted 40 days and 40 nights, or prayed for 12 hours straight, that God has to answer your prayers? Are you trying to twist God's arm with your works? Come on, my friend, the only reason that God answers our prayers today is the finished work of Jesus. Don't be deceived any longer. God is a debtor to no man. Our efforts to pray long, hard prayers and our fasting don't impress Him. No man can deserve God's blessings by his self-efforts. It is not about our sacrifices. It is about **His** sacrifice!

By virtue of Jesus, all God's blessings and His miracle-working power are already yours when you believe in His Son.

All God sees is the work of His Son on the cross, and by virtue of Jesus, all His blessings and His miracle-working power are already yours when you believe in His Son. Listen carefully to what Paul said to the Galatians who were depending on their self-efforts:

Galatians 3:5

[5]... He who supplies the Spirit to you and works miracles among you, does He do it by the works of the law, or by the hearing of faith?

Look at all the people who received miracles from Jesus during His ministry on earth. Not a single one of them deserved it. They did nothing to earn their miracles. They simply received their miracles because of His grace. On the other hand, we don't find any record of those who were trying to deserve blessings from God — the Pharisees — receiving anything from Jesus!

When You See Jesus In His Grace, He Sees You In Your Faith

A few years ago, the Lord spoke to me and said, "**When My people see My grace, I see their faith**." Do you remember the woman with the issue of blood who had been bleeding for 12 years? She did not only see Jesus as being full of healing power, but she also saw Him as being full of grace. How do we know that? It's because she would have known full well that according to the law of Moses, she was considered unclean because of her condition, and was not supposed to touch anyone, let alone be found squeezing her way through a crowd. Yet, she believed that if she could just touch the hem of Jesus' garment, she would be healed.

Instead of expecting punishment for breaking the law of Moses, she was expecting to be healed! She did not see Jesus as hard and condemning. She saw Him as a gracious Savior overflowing with mercy and compassion. The moment she touched the hem of His garment, immediately, the fountain of her blood was dried up, and she felt in her body that she was healed of her affliction. Was she ever conscious of her faith? No, she was conscious only of Jesus and His grace. When she **saw His grace**, He turned around and **saw her faith**. With great tenderness, He said to her, "Daughter, your faith has made you well."[7]

Faith for any breakthrough or miracle in your life springs forth when you see His grace.

You do not have to try to conjure up faith for healing or finances. Faith for any breakthrough or miracle in your life springs forth when you see His grace. He died so that you might live! You did not deserve it, but He still did it for you. See Jesus on the cross for you. That is the demonstration of His grace. And when you see His grace, your faith becomes unconscious and miracles will break forth!

The Secret To Great Faith

Do you know that there were only two people in the Bible whom Jesus said had "great faith"?

The first was the Roman centurion[8]. He came to Jesus and said, "Lord, my servant lies at home paralyzed and he's suffering," and the Lord said, "I will come and heal him." The centurion replied, "No, Lord, I am not worthy to have You come under my roof. Just speak the word and my servant will be healed. I am also a man under authority, having soldiers under me. When I tell a soldier to come, he comes. When I tell a soldier to go, he goes.

And when I tell my servant to do something, he does it." Now, listen to Jesus' reply. He said, "I have not found such great faith, no, not in Israel."

As I was reading these scriptures one night, the Lord asked me, "Why did that man have great faith?" I immediately replied that it was because he, being a Roman centurion, was a man of authority and thus understood the authority of the Lord Jesus. I was confident of my reply, having been taught that to have great faith, we need to understand the Lord's authority and the authority that He has given to the believer.

The Lord said to me, "Good, and what about the other person whom I said had great faith?" He was referring to the Syro-Phoenician woman who had a demon-possessed daughter[9]. She had gone to Jesus and beseeched Him to cast the devil out of her daughter. But Jesus replied, "It is not good to take the children's bread and throw it to the little dogs." Jesus was saying that it was not good for Him to cast the bread meant for the Jews to a Gentile. But the woman replied, "Yes, Lord, yet even the little dogs eat the crumbs which fall from their masters' table." And Jesus said, "O woman, great is your faith! Let it be to you as you desire." That very hour, her daughter was healed.

The Lord continued, "Well, if the centurion had great faith because he understood authority, what about this woman? She was not a soldier. She was a homemaker." Now, the Lord got me there and I thought, "Well, there goes the theory that I had learned in my earlier years, for what authority could this homemaker have understood, not being a soldier?" Then, the Lord said to me, "Son, look for the common denominator between these two people and you will discover the secret to great faith."

Boy, was I excited. I was about to discover the secret to having great faith! But after more than half an hour, I was still sitting in my study, searching for the common denominator. I was searching and searching to no avail. I simply could not find the answer. Finally, my "lightning-fast" mind told me that I should ask the Lord for the answer. So I said, "Lord, You have to show me because I cannot see it." One was a man and the other was a woman. One was a solider and the other, a homemaker. I couldn't figure out what they had in common.

Then, the Lord said this to me, "Both were Gentiles. They were not Jews." And He said, "One was a Roman and the other a Canaanite. Both of them were not under the law of Moses and therefore they did not disqualify themselves. They were not under condemnation and so they could have great faith to receive from Me." Wow, what a powerful revelation! The law is indeed the opposite of faith!

Do you know that there is a verse in Galatians that says that **"the law is not of faith"**[10]? In Romans, it also says, "For if those who are of the law are heirs, **faith is made void** and the promise made of no effect"[11]. So clearly, there is no way that we can give people the law and yet expect them to have faith. The law will disqualify them from receiving any blessing from the Lord. It is only faith in His grace that will qualify God's people and cause them to have great faith to receive what they need from the Lord. This is the secret to having great faith for any situation in your life!

Don't just take my word for it. Search the Bible for yourself and see if the revelation that I received from the Lord is scriptural. It is right there in the Bible. I did not learn it from man. Neither did I read it in any book. It was a revelation from Him. And notice that when the Lord speaks, He always goes back to the Bible and He is always consistent with His written Word.

Unconscious Faith

I believe with all my heart that as you come under grace and are delivered from the works of the law, faith will no longer be a struggle or barrier because you will walk with unconscious faith. You will not be wondering, "Do I have enough faith?" all the time, but you will see Jesus in His grace, and faith will just spring forth from the inside. It is that simple. Everything that you receive from God, you receive by faith in His grace. We walk by faith. We fight the good fight of faith. We are saved by faith, healed by faith and made righteous by faith! The Christian life is a life of faith in His grace. The more of His grace you receive, the more faith springs forth. Our problem in the past was that we put our faith in our own faith, and it didn't work. We should put our faith in God's grace and love, for the Bible says that faith works by love[12]. This is not in reference to our own love, but to His love for us.

Faith is bringing out of the spirit realm what is already there, what is already true of you.

Faith is not trying to make something that is not already there happen. Faith is bringing out of the spirit realm what is **already** there, what is already true of you. I am not telling you to confess something that you are not. Whether you confess that you are the righteousness of God in Christ or not, you are still the righteousness of God in Christ. But when you confess it, you become conscious of it. You sense it, and it becomes powerful and real in your life.

You do not confess that you are righteous **in order to become** righteous. You confess that you are righteous because you **are already** righteous! Similarly, you confess that you are rich not to become rich. You confess that you are rich because you are already rich through Jesus. At the cross, He became poor so that you through His poverty might become rich[13]! You confess this to be conscious that through Jesus, you are already rich. That's not having faith in faith. It is faith in His goodness, in His grace.

Faith In The Blood Of Jesus

Many believers are so caught up in looking to their own faith to save them and bring about blessings in their lives. What they don't realize is that it is not their faith that saves them. It is His grace, His blood alone that saves them. When you believe that it is the blood that saves you, God sees that as faith in the blood. Yet, it is not your faith in the blood that protects, delivers or saves you. It is simply the blood alone that saves you. Let me illustrate this truth with an enactment of what might have happened on the night before the Israelites were delivered out of Egypt.

On the night of the Passover, God said, "When I see the blood, I will pass over you."[14] Remember, there were nine plagues, but it wasn't the plagues that delivered the Israelites out of Egypt. It was the blood of the lamb. After the nine plagues, Pharaoh's heart was still hardened, so God finally used His trump card and only then did Pharaoh release the Israelites.

God's trump card was the blood of the lamb. The devil has no defense against the blood. You see, the Israelites' firstborns were protected not because they were good. They were protected because of the blood of the lamb. If the children of Israel had failed to apply the blood of the lamb to their doorposts, their firstborns would not have been spared — they would have died along with the firstborns of the Egyptians. They were protected not because they were Jews either, but because of the blood of the lamb. God did not say, "When I see your good family name, all your wonderful titles or that you are of a particular nationality, I will pass over you." No, it was based entirely on the blood of the lamb! **"When I see the blood..."**

What does the blood of the lamb speak of? It speaks of the blood of our sacrifice, Jesus Christ. He is the true Lamb who takes away the sin of the world[15]. In the same way, today, God does not look at your good behavior, law-keeping, Christian heritage or titles to bless you and keep you from all evil. No, He looks at the blood of Jesus. From the moment you received Jesus Christ, His blood covers you perfectly!

Now, let's look at how two Jewish families might have spent the Passover night.

In the first family, where both father and son are firstborns, the son asks his father, "Daddy, did you put the blood on the doorposts?"

His daddy says, "Yes, son, I have done as Moses instructed. But I really hope that I have enough faith in the blood."

"Daddy, Daddy, do you have enough faith?"

"I don't know," the father shrugs helplessly. "I really don't know if I have enough faith in the blood!"

As they hear the screams and cries coming from the Egyptian houses, they hold each other tightly, trembling in fear throughout the night.

In the second family, another firstborn father and son are waiting to pass this significant night. But in this household, both father and son are singing praises and worshipping God.

The father smiles at his son and says, "Son, we have done what God told us to do. We have put the blood on the doorposts and lintel. Now, we leave the rest to Him. He will protect us. We don't have to fear."

They too hear the heartrending screams and cries coming from the Egyptian houses, but they continue singing praises and worshipping God.

Now, let me ask you this: Which family was delivered? Which family was saved? The answer is BOTH! Both families were delivered because the angel of death saw the blood on their doorposts and passed over both households. The first family therefore feared and suffered needlessly. For the second family, it was neither their faith in the blood, nor their praising and worshipping God, that saved them. The blood alone saved them! However, because they believed that the blood would save them, they did not worry and tremble in fear needlessly, but spent the night in rest, joy and shalom peace.

When you believe that it is the blood that saves you, God sees that as faith in the blood. Yet, it is not having faith in the blood that saves you. It is the blood alone that saves you. Stop wondering if you have enough faith and just believe that it is His blood that saves, delivers and blesses you. Believe that it is His blood **alone**, and not His blood **plus** your own works (your own faith), or His blood **plus** your keeping the commandments, that saves you.

Stop wondering if you have enough faith and just believe that it is His blood alone that saves, delivers and blesses you.

So don't be caught up in or dependent on your ability to have faith, or on your works to keep your faith up. Have a fresh revelation of Jesus and His sacrifice on the cross, and you will see His grace for you. You will have no doubt that God, who did not withhold His Son, will freely give you all things[16]!

My friend, **when you see His grace, God will see you in your faith**. Faith is no longer a struggle when you see Jesus! It will spring forth unconsciously and you will walk in true victory over every area of defeat in your life today!

Chapter 22

Good Things Happen

Some years ago, I had the opportunity to fellowship with a Word of Faith preacher who pastors a church in Bergen, Norway. He shared a testimony from one of his church members with me. This particular church member was a businessman, who had developed the habit of viewing pornography in his hotel room during his many and frequent business trips. He tried his best to break the habit, employing all kinds of spiritual discipline, but he just could not stop, and was consumed with shame and condemnation.

Each time he had to leave his family for another business trip, his heart would be filled with dread because he knew that he could not overcome the temptation no matter how disciplined he tried to be. Then, on one of his business trips which brought him to Singapore, he visited our church and got hold of some of my sermon CDs on the grace of God. After listening to the messages for about three weeks, he found himself completely set free from this unclean habit! Hallelujah!

Today, when this precious brother travels, he does not depend on his own willpower to overcome the temptation to indulge in pornography in his hotel room. He will just completely rest in the revelation that he is as righteous as Jesus by God's grace. And the more he is conscious that he is righteous, the more the temptation to sin secretly in his hotel room dissipates. Awake to righteousness and sin not! It is the grace of God that gives us true victory!

That is the power of the gospel. It is the power of God unto your wholeness! You can rely on your self-efforts and willpower all you want, but they can only bring you so far. My friend, put your dependence completely on His grace. It is the only power that can set you free from all bondages!

I was told another exciting testimony when I was in Norway for a conference at my dear friend Pastor Åge Åleskjær's church. Pastor Åge shared with me about a miracle which had happened to someone from another church in Norway. This church member was completely healed of deafness in one ear after listening to recordings of messages that I had preached at the conference. As he was listening to one of my messages, his ear just popped open and he was HEALED! No hands were laid on him. Neither did anyone pray for him. He was healed just by hearing the gospel of Christ preached. All glory to Jesus! That's the power of the gospel, my friend.

The more we hear the good news, the more miracles and breakthroughs we will see.

When people hear the good news that all their sins have been forgiven because of the cross of Jesus, something supernatural happens. This is what happened in the book of Acts. When Apostle Paul preached on forgiveness, healing miracles occurred as the people listened. The man who was lame from his mother's womb leapt up and walked for the first time in his life. People in the church are looking for great power, but where is it found? The book of Acts declares that where there is great grace, there is great power[1]!

The Gospel Revolution is breaking out all over the world. Mark my words: When more and more people hear the true gospel that is unadulterated by man's efforts, you will hear of more and more of these miracles and supernatural breakthroughs in the church. It has pleased God to heal, rescue, prosper and deliver those who simply believe the gospel through the foolishness of preaching. So as His Word goes forth, when you believe that you are forgiven and righteous, you will be made whole! Right now, even as you are reading this book which is all about Jesus, you are being healed, being prospered and being blessed!

Good Things Happen To Those Who Believe That God Loves Them

"But Pastor Prince, what does forgiveness have to do with healing?"

Let's read what the Word of God says in Psalm 103:

> Psalm 103:1–5
> [1]Bless the Lord, O my soul; and all that is within me, bless His holy name! [2]Bless the Lord, O my soul, and forget not all His benefits: [3]Who forgives all your iniquities, who heals all your diseases, [4]who redeems your life from destruction, who crowns you with lovingkindness and tender mercies, [5]who satisfies your mouth with good things, so that your youth is renewed like the eagle's.

Observe the way the Holy Spirit has ordered His benefits: Forgiveness of your iniquities comes before the healing of your diseases. In other words, once you know that you have been forgiven of **all** your sins, past, present and future, the healing of all your diseases follows.

There are many believers who are suffering from sicknesses and diseases because of guilt. Whether or not there is any real basis for their guilt and condemnation, the guilt and condemnation are still destructive. That is why the gospel is so powerful. It is the good news of God's grace and forgiveness that frees the believer from every sense of feeling dirty or condemned, and gives him the power to break free from the vicious circle of condemnation and sin.

Guilt and condemnation perpetuate the cycle of sin, whereas His grace, His blood and His righteousness liberate and provide freedom from sin. Jesus said to the woman caught in adultery, "Neither do I condemn you; go and sin no more."[2] The power to overcome sin is found in the gift of no condemnation. My friend, God has forgiven you of all your iniquities. Don't ever forget this benefit as well as all the other benefits that Jesus' finished work has bought for you. Bless the Lord for all His benefits and blessings toward you every day!

Once, when I was preparing to preach, the Lord shared this with me: "Good things happen to people who believe that God loves them." I used this as the title for my sermon. It is probably one of the longest sermon titles that I have ever received from Him, but it is so powerful. Good things happening to you does not depend on who you are, what academic qualifications you hold or what your profession is. Good things simply happen to you when you believe that God loves you! He loves you all the time. Even when you fail, He loves you! His love is not like our love. Our love is conditional, but His love is not contingent on our behavior. It is contingent entirely on His grace and the work of His Son Jesus Christ.

Good things simply happen to you when you believe that God loves you!

Do you know what Paul prayed for the church of Ephesus? This was one of the most spiritual churches in his time, and he prayed that they may be able to comprehend "what is the width and length and depth and height" of "the love of Christ"[3]. Can you see the picture of the cross of Jesus here? The width, length, depth and height point to the four corners of the cross.

Notice Paul's emphasis on the love **of** Christ. In other words, it is not our love **for** Christ. Paul was praying for them to have a revelation of Jesus' love for them and not their love for Jesus. Now, observe closely the result of them knowing His love for them: They would be "filled with all the **fullness of God**". I have heard many sermons saying that if you do this and do that, you will be filled with the fullness of God. But that's not what the Bible says. It says that when you **know the love of Christ**, you will be filled with the fullness of God!

Paul doesn't stop there. He goes on to say, "Now to Him who is able to do exceedingly abundantly above all that we ask or think…"[4] God becomes big in your life when you know His love. He will give you not just exceedingly, not just abundantly, but exceedingly abundantly above ALL you can ask or think. So when you know His love for you, you can ASK BIG and THINK BIG, and God will still exceed all that you ask or think!

Yet, there are people today who continue to boast in their love for God, believing that He would bless them in tandem with their good works. That's wrong!

A Fresh Revelation Of His Love

In my own life, there have been some things that I had been believing God for, but for years, nothing happened, until I realized just how much God loves me. When I realized how much He loves me, it was like all of a sudden, the floodgate of His blessings opened wide, and all kinds of good things started happening to me, in me and around me. Good things happen to those who know that God loves them.

I remember one incident in which God revealed His love for me so clearly. My daughter Jessica was about two years old and she was suffering from a viral attack. Wendy and I had brought her to the doctors. They stuck all kinds of needles into her for blood tests, but they could not find any reason or remedy for her illness.

My heart ached to hear my Jessica crying all day and night. I tried everything I knew. I was binding and loosing, I was confessing the Word of God, I was shouting, I was laying hands… all to no avail. For days, my little darling just kept crying in pain. When I finally couldn't take it any longer, I went to the Lord and started to weep in His presence, the sound of my baby's cries still audible even though I had shut myself in my study. I cried, "Lord, You have to speak to me. What is happening? I have tried doing everything that I know."

The Lord then brought me to Genesis 22, where God told Abraham to offer his son Isaac as a burnt offering to Him. God said to Abraham, "Take now your son, your only son Isaac, whom you love…"⁵ Even though Abraham had two sons, Isaac and Ishmael, God only recognized Isaac, who was born of the Spirit (a picture of a result by grace). He did not recognize Ishmael who was born of the flesh (a picture of a result by self-effort). Anyway, as I read what God said to Abraham about Isaac being his son and his only son, I thought to myself, God is really pushing it here. It must have been very difficult for Abraham to sacrifice his son and God had to "rub it in" by emphasizing that Isaac was his only son, whom he loved — "Take now your son, your **only** son Isaac, **whom you love**".

Then, I came to the part where Abraham was about to kill his son and God stopped him. Abraham then looked behind him and found a ram caught in the thicket by its horns. God had provided a ram for the sacrifice! As they were going up on one side of the mountain, the ram was going up on the other side. (My friend, when you don't seem to see your provision coming toward you, don't worry. Every time you move toward God's purpose, He will provide for you. Your provision is on its way on the other side of the mountain!) So God stopped Abraham from plunging his knife into his son. He said, "Do not lay your hand on the lad, or do anything to him; for now I know that you fear God, **since you have not withheld your son, your only son, from Me**."⁶

When I read the last portion of that verse, the Holy Spirit opened my eyes in a flash. He showed me that God had actually been talking about Himself. He was the Father who would give up His Son. The whole story of the boy carrying the wood on his back and going to the place of sacrifice was a picture of Jesus carrying the cross on His back and going to the place of sacrifice at Calvary! God was telling us that He would give us His Son — **His only Son, the Son whom He loved** — as a ransom for us. Until you know how much God loves Jesus, you will never know how much God loves you, because God gave Jesus up to save you.

He loved you so much He did not withhold His Son,
His only Son, the Son whom He loved, for you.

As I read the passage, I realized just how much God loved me. He loved me so much He did not withhold His Son, His only Son, the Son whom He loved, for me. By this time, I had begun to cry afresh in my study, but these were no longer tears for my daughter. They were tears that came from a deep and intimate sense of God's overwhelming love for me. At that moment, I felt His love all over me. And right there and then, my daughter stopped crying in the other room. From that point onwards, she was completely healed! As I was experiencing a fresh revelation of His love for me, the miracle for my daughter happened! Beloved, good things happen to those who know that God loves them.

The Law Is A Heavy Burden

The reason people are full of bitterness, anger and resentment is not that God does not love them. It is that they think that they must earn God's love by their conduct and doing good works. When Jesus said, "Come to Me, all you who labor and are heavy laden, and I will give you rest"[7], He was not talking to people who were tired from working in their secular jobs. He was talking to people who were under the burden of the law. He was talking to those who were laboring under the law to please God, those who were heavy laden with the law. He was telling them to cease from their self-efforts and to let Him give them rest. You see, the law demands, whereas grace imparts rest. The law says, "Do good get good. Do bad get beat!" Doesn't every other belief system say that?

Sometimes, when I hear the way some preachers preach, I really wonder, has the cross changed anything? The system of being blessed when you do good and being cursed when you fail was already in place before Jesus came. Why are they still teaching that we are under that system today? Come on, my friend, don't negate the cross of Jesus. The cross of Jesus changed everything. Jesus received all our "bad" and we took on all His "good"! That's the gospel of Jesus Christ. It is based entirely on His grace!

You Are God's Beloved

When Jesus was baptized in the river Jordan, a voice from heaven said, "This is My beloved Son, in whom I am well pleased."[8] This is recorded in the Bible for your benefit. Today, God has accepted you in the Beloved. Right now, He is well pleased with you because you are in Christ. Today, the way in which Jesus is God's beloved Son is the same way in which you are God's beloved child. In fact, Jesus prayed to the Father that His disciples (that covers us also) would know that the way in which His Father loves Him is the same way in which His Father loves them[9].

Immediately after Jesus was baptized, He was led by the Spirit into the wilderness to be tempted by the devil. What did the devil say to Jesus? He said, "If You are the Son of God, command that these stones become bread."[10] Notice that the devil craftily dropped one vital word when he taunted Jesus to prove that He was the Son of God. God had audibly announced that Jesus was His "beloved Son", but the devil made no mention of the word "beloved". He deliberately dropped the word "beloved" when he came to tempt Jesus. He does the same thing with you today because he knows that if he reminds you that you are God's beloved, all his plans, plots and evil strategies to tempt you will be foiled. **Once you know that you are God's beloved, whatever the devil wants to bring against you will fail**.

People give their lives to sin when they feel rejected and unwanted. But when they know that they are God's beloved, no temptation can succeed against them. Let's look at Jesus' reply to the devil's first temptation. The first temptation was for Him to turn stones into bread. Is there any law in the Old Testament that says that you cannot turn stones into bread? No. So what was the devil saying?

When the devil said, "Command these STONES to become bread," he was, in fact, telling Jesus to get His nourishment from the law that was written on STONES. Now, look at Jesus' reply: "Man shall not live by bread alone, but by every **word** that proceeds from the mouth of God."[11] When Jesus referred to the "word that proceeds from the mouth of God", He was referring to the *rhema*[12] word or "now word". What did God just say to Jesus before He entered the wilderness? He had said, "This is

My **beloved** Son, in whom I am well pleased." This is the word that we are to live by today as well!

You are God's beloved through Jesus Christ. We are not to live by the Ten Commandments written and engraved on stones. There is no nourishment in the ministry of death and condemnation. Jesus died on the cross so that we can be in Him, and so that we can live by the same word that proceeded from the mouth of God when He called Jesus His beloved. Today, God sees you in Christ. Hear Him say to you, "You are My beloved, in whom I am well pleased"!

Roll Away The Stone

The Lord told me many years ago, "Son, your ministry is to roll away the stone." Let me explain to you what this means. In the story of Lazarus[13], Jesus commanded the people to roll away the stone from Lazarus' tomb. Even though the people protested that Lazarus had already been dead for four days and that the stench would be terrible, Jesus persisted because He knew that Lazarus had been resurrected.

You see, even though Lazarus was alive, the resurrection life could not flow as long as he was bound behind the stone. The stone had to be removed for resurrection life to come forth. That is what my ministry is about — rolling away the stone. There are many believers who **have** resurrection life because they have been saved, but they are not experiencing breakthroughs in their bodies, finances, family lives and careers because they are bound hand and foot, and trapped behind the stone. Before resurrection life can flow, the stone must be rolled away!

My friend, the stone is a picture of the law. The law was written and engraved on stones, and as long as believers are under the law, the ministry of death and condemnation binds them. My commission from the Lord is to roll away the stone from believers who are saved and born again. You need to remove the law that binds. When you roll away the stone, that's when Lazarus comes forth, that's when you see the glory of God!

People are afraid that if you roll away the stone of the law, you will give people a license to sin. But have you noticed that people are already sinning without a license and that being under the law has not stopped sin? The answer to sin is found in grace. It is grace that will stop sin. We are not rolling away the stone from dead, stinking flesh (the lost) but from resurrected people (believers). Just like Lazarus, who had already been made alive, the stone proves to be a hindrance to their coming forth.

My friend, knowing that you are made God's beloved by His grace will give you dominion in life to overcome sinful habits and temptations. Temptations cannot succeed when you have a revelation that you are God's beloved. When you know how precious and valuable you are to God, and the depths of your Abba's love for you, why would you want to waste your life engaging in sins that only bring destruction and death?

> *Temptations cannot succeed when you have*
> *a revelation that you are God's beloved.*

When the devil tries to throw temptations against you, he will never remind you that you are God's beloved. He wants you to question your identity and position as a beloved child of God because he knows that once you doubt that you are God's beloved, he can make you feel alienated from God. He can heap guilt and condemnation on you and tempt you further. He will say things like, "How can you think those thoughts? You call yourself a Christian?" So even when you fail, continue to see yourself as God's beloved. You are still the righteousness of God in Christ Jesus!

Be Occupied With His Love

"But Pastor Prince, how can I say that I am still the beloved of God when I have failed?"

You can because His love for you is constant and unconditional! Are you loved by God because of what you have done? No, it is because of what Jesus has done on the cross! So God will not stop loving you because of what **you** have done. In fact, He loved you when you were still in your mother's womb and will continue to love you when you see Him face to face.

Let me share with you my experience with God's love when I have failed and blown it. You know, Wendy is a wonderful wife. Not only is she really beautiful, she's very wise as well. Sometimes, she makes a certain suggestion to me and when I implement exactly what she suggested, people tell me, "Pastor Prince, this is a brilliant idea!" She really makes me look good. So obviously, she is really smart. But no matter how wonderful or smart she is, there are times we have "intense discussions" because she does not see "my wisdom". (You know, we pastors don't quarrel. We just have "intense discussions" with our spouses. Also, we never worry. We just have "concerns and apprehensions".)

The worst time to have these "intense discussions" is when we are on our way to church and I have to preach! In the past, these heated discussions would sometimes last for more than a day. But ever since I discovered how much the Lord loves me, right in the midst of the icy silence that usually follows these intense discussions, I would hear Jesus saying to me, "Son, do you know that in the midst of your anger, I still love you?"

Previously, I would not entertain that word from the Lord because I was taught that the moment you get angry or fail, you are out of fellowship with God. I was taught that the moment I failed, the blessings would disappear and His favor would stop! And because I believed that, it influenced the way I lived my daily life as well as my relationship with my wife. As a result, I used to get even angrier with her because I would blame her for causing me to be out of fellowship with God. So the anger just kept festering and growing.

But I know the truth today. I know that even when I fail, God and I are still "tight" (we are still "cool", you know what I mean?) because of the blood of Jesus. God still sees me as His beloved. I have the gift of righteousness apart from my performance. I know that God still loves me, that our fellowship is not broken and that His favor still flows in me.

Beloved, there is nothing you can do today to make God love you more, and there is nothing you can do to make Him love you any less. When you fail, that is the time you need to feed on His love for you. Begin to see yourself as the disciple whom Jesus loves. Personalize His love for you the way John did it. He referred to himself as "the disciple whom Jesus loved" five times in his own gospel! (Get my sermon CD *Becoming A Disciple That*

Jesus Loves — The Secret Of John. It will definitely bless you!)

The sun shines on every blade of grass in a field. But when you personalize God's love for you, it is like you are taking a magnifying glass and putting it over one blade of grass. Doing so intensifies the light and heat over that one blade and before long, it will burn. Beloved, it is not enough to know that God loves **everyone**. You need to know and believe that He loves **you**, and let that revelation burn in your heart, especially when you fail. And as you keep on feeding on His love for you, His love will start overflowing in you. That's what I do.

When you are full of His love for you, all anger dissipates. Once I had the revelation of His love for me even in the midst of my failures, I found that the "intense discussions" with Wendy became shorter and less frequent, and the love of Christ became more and more real. Instead of stewing in anger, I found that it became easy for me to turn to Wendy in the midst of our "discussions", smile at her and quickly reconcile with her. That's what happens when you are occupied with His love and not your own failures! By the way, today, my wife and I have one of the most exciting marriages on God's green earth, totally by the grace of God.

Be A David Who Takes Down Goliath

Beloved, start practicing God's love for you and it will translate into victory in your daily life. There was an ugly giant by the name of Goliath. I am sure you are familiar with the story of how a young shepherd boy named David came against Goliath and defeated him. There are no insignificant details in the Bible. Even the names in the Bible carry secrets for our benefit.

The name "Goliath" comes from the Hebrew root word *galah*, which means "to exile"[14]. To be exiled is to be stripped of everything you are and everything you own. So Goliath's name essentially means that he had been stripped of everything — an exile. What a name! Goliath is a picture of the devil — Jesus has stripped him of all his weapons against us[15]. The name "David" on the other hand means "beloved"[16]. The battle in the valley of Elah was thus a battle between a beloved of God and a stripped exile. Now catch this revelation! It takes someone who knows that he is the beloved of God to bring down a giant! This is the secret of becoming a giant slayer! It doesn't matter what your giant is today. It could be a marital problem or a financial situation. Begin to see that you are God's beloved and your giants will come tumbling down.

Begin to see that you are God's beloved and
your giants will come tumbling down.

My friend, God loves you. You are His beloved child regardless of what you have done. He loves you as you are because you have been washed whiter than snow with the blood of Jesus. Live every day by these words from your loving Father in heaven: "You are My beloved, in whom I am well pleased." His favor is all over you, in your family, in your place of work and in everything that you do. You are a blessing everywhere you go.

If God did not withhold His Son from you, why would He withhold healing, financial provision, protection, peace of mind and all the other blessings from you? When the Almighty God is your loving Father and you are His beloved, what fears can you have? Fear of the past, the present and the future? Fear of not having enough? Fear of sickness? Fear of death? Fear of punishment? Beloved, when you have a revelation of how much God loves you and that He sees you completely righteous by the blood of Jesus Christ, all your fears will dissipate, for if God is for you, who can be against you?

Beloved, look away from your circumstances and call out without fear to your Father. He loves you and will never judge or condemn you! He loves you with an everlasting love. Feed on His love for you and receive from Him exceedingly abundantly above all that you can ask or think!

Closing Words

Throughout this book, I have endeavored to show you the gospel of Jesus Christ through the Scriptures as well as through my own struggles with the erroneous teachings that I had received as I was growing in the Lord. I have shown you that under the dispensation of grace, God is not judging you and does not punish His own children with sicknesses, diseases or accidents. Because of Jesus' finished work at the cross, He will never be angry with you nor rebuke you even when you fail. So don't ever forget the main clause of the new covenant, which says that your sins and your lawless deeds, He remembers no more!

Many believers are defeated today because they do not know the God of the new covenant of grace. I believe with all of my heart that because you took this wonderful journey with me down the road of Emmaus and saw for yourself, beginning from Moses to the Prophets, all the things concerning Jesus Christ and His finished work, your heart would now burn with His extravagant love for you. Jesus truly puts the "amazing" back into grace!

Today, God is all about blessing you with His grace — His undeserved, unearned and unmerited favor — in every area of your life. Stop trying to deserve and earn your own acceptance before God with your own works and efforts. It will only frustrate the grace of God and nullify the effects of the cross in your life. My friend, Jesus already finished the work. Believe with all your heart that it is not about what you need to do today, but about what has already been done and accomplished on your behalf.

Beloved, I have preached to you the gospel of Jesus Christ and am fulfilling the commission He gave me in 1997 to preach grace radically so that lives can be radically transformed. I know that if you have believed this good news of His grace, your life has begun to be radically transformed, together with the countless believers around the world who have already been impacted by the Gospel Revolution.

I pray that this book has torn down the fences of controversy that the enemy has erected around the teaching of God's grace and gift of righteousness, so that you may indeed receive not just grace, but the **"abundance of grace"**, and receive not just righteousness, but the **"gift of righteousness"**, and **start reigning in life**. Start reigning over sin, over sickness, over condemnation, over financial lack and over the curse of the law through the ONE, Jesus Christ.

All that I have shared works most powerfully and effectively within the environment of the local church. These truths are for the greater good of the body of Christ and should never result in you becoming a law unto yourself. Beloved, I want to see you enjoying the safety of the covering of a local church where there is accountability and submission. This is where our blessings are tremendously multiplied.

I thank you for taking this journey with me and for giving me the opportunity to unveil more and more of Jesus to you. You have been a wonderful traveling companion. We should do this again sometime soon! In the meantime, I look forward to hearing from you about how our Lord Jesus has touched and impacted your life with His amazing grace.

It is all about Jesus and His finished work!

You are destined to reign through Him.

**This is the secret to effortless success,
wholeness and victorious living!**

Notes

Chapter 1
Destined To Reign

1. NT:936, Biblesoft's New Exhaustive Strong's Numbers and Concordance with Expanded Greek-Hebrew Dictionary. Copyright (c) 1994, Biblesoft and International Bible Translators, Inc.
2. Crowther, J., Kavanagh, K., Ashby, M. (eds). *Oxford Advanced Learner's Dictionary Of Current English, Fifth Edition*. Great Clarendon Street, Oxford: Oxford University Press, 1995. p.85.
3. John 19:30
4. R Badham, Magnificent, *Blessed*, CD album by Hillsong Australia, 2002.
5. Colossians 2:13
6. Hebrews 10:11
7. 1 Corinthians 15:10

Chapter 2
The Law Has Been Fulfilled

1. Galatians 2:21
2. Colossians 2:14
3. Matthew 5:17, NIV
4. Ephesians 6:12
5. Romans 3:20
6. Romans 4:15
7. Revelation 12:10

Chapter 3
Controversies Surrounding The Gospel Of Grace

1. John 10:10
2. Luke 6:19

3. 2 Corinthians 8:9
4. Matthew 7:11
5. Hebrews 8:7–8
6. 1 Corinthians 15:56
7. Romans 10:3
8. 2 Corinthians 5:21
9. 1 Corinthians 15:34, KJV
10. Matthew 10:16
11. Matthew 11:28–30, NIV
12. John 14:6

Chapter 4
We Have Been Robbed!

1. 2 Corinthians 5:21
2. Colossians 2:13
3. Revelation 1:8
4. Romans 6:14

Chapter 5
Is God Judging America?

1. 2 Peter 3:9
2. 1 Kings 22:52
3. 2 Kings 1:1–15
4. Genesis 19:25
5. 2 Timothy 2:15
6. Luke 9:54–56
7. John 3:17
8. John 10:10
9. Genesis 18:32
10. Genesis 19:22–24
11. Romans 4:8
12. 1 John 2:1
13. 1 John 4:17
14. Matthew 5:21–22, 27–28
15. James 2:10
16. Romans 3:23

Chapter 6
The Evil Conspiracy

1. Leviticus 26:28
2. Isaiah 53:2
3. Psalm 103:4
4. Thayer's Greek Lexicon, Electronic Database. Copyright (c) 2000 by Biblesoft
5. 2 Corinthians 12:7
6. Numbers 33:55
7. 2 Corinthians 12:9
8. Matthew 10:16

Chapter 7
The Gospel That Paul Preached

1. Romans 10:17, NASB
2. NT:5547, Biblesoft's New Exhaustive Strong's Numbers and Concordance with Expanded Greek-Hebrew Dictionary. Copyright (c) 1994, Biblesoft and International Bible Translators, Inc.
3. Acts 14:7
4. Acts 13:44
5. Acts 13:45
6. Matthew 27:51
7. John 10:10
8. Acts 14:3–4
9. Acts 14:5
10. Acts 14:3
11. Galatians 1:8
12. Galations 1:9

Chapter 8
The Main Clause Of The New Covenant

1. Matthew 12:31
2. John 15:26
3. Mark 3:22
4. Mark 3:28–30
5. Matthew 5:29–30
6. Matthew 12:34, 23:33
7. Colossians 2:13
8. NT: 3956, Biblesoft's New Exhaustive Strong's Numbers and Concordance with Expanded Greek-Hebrew Dictionary. Copyright (c) 1994, Biblesoft and International Bible Translators, Inc.
9. Matthew 26:28
10. John 19:30

Chapter 9
The Waterfall Of Forgiveness

1. Luke 7:44–47
2. Matthew 5:21–22, 27–28
3. Romans 14:23, KJV
4. 1 Corinthians 6:19
5. Wuest, Kenneth S. (1954). 'In These Last Days: The Exegesis Of First John', *Wuest's Word Studies From The Greek New Testament Volume II*. Grand Rapids, Michigan: Wm. B. Eerdmans Publishing Company. p.103.
6. Hebrews 9:12, Ephesians 1:7
7. Hebrews 10:1–14
8. Mark 2:3–12

Chapter 10
The Ministry Of Death

1. 2 Corinthians 3:6
2. 2 Corinthians 3:13
3. Exodus 32:28
4. Acts 2:41
5. 1 Corinthians 15:56
6. Romans 6:14
7. Hebrews 8:7
8. Hebrews 8:6
9. Hebrews 8:13
10. Romans 1:16
11. James 2:10
12. Romans 5:20
13. Romans 3:20
14. Galatians 3:24, KJV
15. Genesis 3:22
16. Genesis 3:24
17. John 10:10

Chapter 11
Unearthing The Deepest Root

1. © 1998–2007 Mayo Foundation for Medical Education and Research (MFMER). *Stress: Unhealthy Response To The Pressures Of Life*. Retrieved 24 April 2007 from www.mayoclinic.com/health/stress/SR00001
2. Goleman, Daniel. (15 December 1992). New Light On How Stress Erodes Health. *The New York Times*. Retrieved 24 April 2007 from query.nytimes.com/gst/fullpage.html?sec=health&res=9E0CEF DB103FF936A25751C1A964958260

3. Colbert, Don, M.D. (2005). *Stress Less.* Lake Mary, Florida: Siloam, A Strang Company. p.14–15.
4. Hebrews 10:22
5. Hebrews 10:2
6. OT:7853, Biblesoft's New Exhaustive Strong's Numbers and Concordance with Expanded Greek-Hebrew Dictionary. Copyright (c) 1994, Biblesoft and International Bible Translators, Inc.
7. Revelation 12:10
8. Hebrews 8:12
9. John 14:16
10. 1 Corinthians 15:34, KJV
11. Matthew 12:35
12. John 3:17
13. John 14:26, KJV
14. Proverbs 10:6

Chapter 12
Condemnation Kills

1. 2 Corinthians 3:7, 9
2. Romans 7:10–11
3. Romans 7:7–8
4. Romans 5:20
5. Romans 7:15
6. Romans 7:19, 24
7. Wuest, Kenneth S. (1955). 'Romans In The Greek New Testament', *Wuest's Word Studies From The Greek New Testament Volume I*. Grand Rapids, Michigan: Wm. B. Eerdmans Publishing Company. p.127.
8. Romans 7:25
9. Deuteronomy 21:18–21

Chapter 13
The Gift Of No Condemnation

1. Matthew 26:28
2. John 9:1–7
3. OT: 7853, Biblesoft's New Exhaustive Strong's Numbers and Concordance with Expanded Greek-Hebrew Dictionary. Copyright (c) 1994, Biblesoft and International Bible Translators, Inc.
4. Romans 8:1, NIV
5. Isaiah 54:17
6. Hebrews 9:22
7. John 8:4
8. Romans 6:14
9. Romans 7:15
10. Romans 7:24
11. Romans 8:3

Chapter 14
No More Consciousness Of Sin

1. Luke 7:37–39, 48
2. Titus 2:11–12
3. Strong, James, LL.D., S.T.D. (2001). *The New Strong's Expanded Exhaustive Concordance of the Bible, Red-Letter Edition.* Nashville, Tennessee: Thomson Nelson Publishers. NT:38
4. Psalm 139:23
5. Hebrews 8:12
6. 1 John 4:17
7. John 10:15, 17
8. John 1:29
9. 2 Corinthians 5:21
10. Hebrews 10:14
11. Hebrews 10:10
12. Leviticus 1:9, 13, 17
13. Hebrews 10:1–4
14. Hebrews 10:19
15. Hebrews 10:22
16. Matthew 9:2–7

Chapter 15
The Road To Emmaus

1. Luke 4:18
2. Luke 24:17
3. Luke 24:32
4. NT:1695, Biblesoft's New Exhaustive Strong's Numbers and Concordance with Expanded Greek-Hebrew Dictionary. Copyright (c) 1994, Biblesoft and International Bible Translators, Inc.
5. NT:1695, Thayer's Greek Lexicon, Electronic Database. Copyright (c) 2000 by Biblesoft
6. Proverbs 4:22
7. Luke 24:13
8. Luke 24:33
9. Psalm 119:25, KJV
10. Acts 14:8–10
11. 1 Kings 17:18
12. Romans 8:17
13. John 3:14–15
14. Proverbs 25:2
15. Numbers 21:4–5
16. Psalm 78:24–25
17. John 6:48–50
18. 1 Corinthians 1:23–24
19. Numbers 21:6
20. Numbers 21:8
21. Numbers 21:9
22. Romans 8:3
23. Exodus 27:1–4

Chapter 16
The Secret Of David

1. Acts 13:22
2. OT:7521, Biblesoft's New Exhaustive Strong's Numbers and Concordance with Expanded Greek-Hebrew Dictionary. Copyright (c) 1994, Biblesoft and International Bible Translators, Inc.
3. Psalm 132:4–5
4. Psalm 132:8
5. 1 Samuel 4:4
6. Exodus 25:22
7. Exodus 25:10–22, Exodus 37:1–9
8. Isaiah 55:12, Mark 8:24
9. Isaiah 2:20; Song of Solomon 5:11, 14–15
10. OT:3727, Biblesoft's New Exhaustive Strong's Numbers and Concordance with Expanded Greek-Hebrew Dictionary. Copyright (c) 1994, Biblesoft and International Bible Translators, Inc.
11. Numbers 17:1–10
12. Psalm 78:24–25
13. Numbers 21:5
14. 1 John 2:2
15. NT:2435, Biblesoft's New Exhaustive Strong's Numbers and Concordance with Expanded Greek-Hebrew Dictionary. Copyright (c) 1994, Biblesoft and International Bible Translators, Inc.
16. 1 Samuel 6:19
17. James 2:13
18. Psalm 30:5, 106:1
19. OT:7157, Biblesoft's New Exhaustive Strong's Numbers and Concordance with Expanded Greek-Hebrew Dictionary. Copyright (c) 1994, Biblesoft and International Bible Translators, Inc.
20. Psalm 132:6
21. Psalm 132:14
22. Exodus 32:16–28
23. Acts 2:1–41
24. Revelation 3:20
25. Revelation 3:14
26. John 1:17
27. Matthew 18:20

Chapter 17
Picture Of Pure Grace

1. Genesis 3:21
2. John 1:29
3. Revelation 5:5–6
4. Exodus 7:14–18
5. John 2:1–11
6. Exodus 14:11

7. Exodus 15:23–25
8. Exodus 16:2–4
9. Exodus 17:3
10. Exodus 19:12
11. James 2:10
12. Exodus 20:3
13. Exodus 32:1–8
14. Exodus 34:7
15. Hebrews 8:12, 10:17
16. Romans 7:7
17. Hebrews 8:13
18. Acts 13:39
19. Colossians 1:12

Chapter 18
One Thing You Lack

1. Romans 2:4
2. Luke 5:8
3. 1 John 4:19
4. 1 John 4:10
5. NT:3340, Thayer's Greek Lexicon, Electronic Database. Copyright (c) 2000 by Biblesoft.
6. Matthew 3:2
7. Hebrews 6:1
8. Mark 1:15
9. Exodus 20:3
10. Titus 2:11–12

Chapter 19
The Key To Effortless Victorious Living

1. Romans 7:7–8
2. Exodus 19:8
3. 1 Corinthians 15:56
4. Romans 6:14
5. 1 Corinthians 15:34, KJV
6. Charles Haddon Spurgeon. A Defense Of Calvinism. The Spurgeon Archive. Retrieved 15 April 2007, from www.spurgeon.org/calvinis.htm
7. Song of Solomon 4:3
8. Wuest, Kenneth S. (1954). 'In These Last Days: The Exegesis Of First John'. Wuest's Word Studies From The Greek New Testament Volume II. Grand Rapids, Michigan: Wm. B. Eerdmans Publishing Company. p.103.
9. Romans 6:1–2
10. NT:5248, Biblesoft's New Exhaustive Strong's Numbers and Concordance with Expanded Greek-Hebrew Dictionary. Copyright (c) 1994, Biblesoft and International Bible Translators, Inc.

11. 1 John 2:1–2
12. 2 Corinthians 3:7–9
13. Lloyd-Jones, D Martyn. (1973). *Romans — The Law: Its Functions & Limits: Exposition Of Chapters 7:1–8:4*. Grand Rapids, Michigan: Zondervan Publishing House. p.272–273.

Chapter 20
The Problem With Mixture

1. 1 Corinthians 1:9
2. 1 Corinthians 1:7–8
3. Galatians 3:1
4. Galatians 3:3
5. 1 Corinthians 1:4
6. Galatians 1:6–7
7. Matthew 12:34, 23:33
8. Galatians 5:4, KJV
9. Galatians 1:10
10. Romans 6:14
11. OT:894, The Online Bible Thayer's Greek Lexicon and Brown Driver & Briggs Hebrew Lexicon. Copyright (c)1993, Woodside Bible Fellowship, Ontario, Canada. Licensed from the Institute for Creation Research.

Chapter 21
The Secret To Great Faith

1. Hebrews 12:2
2. Mark 9:29
3. Wuest, Kenneth S. (1950). 'Mark In The Greek New Testament'. *Wuest's Word Studies From The Greek New Testament Volume I*. Grand Rapids, Michigan: Wm. B. Eerdmans Publishing Company. p.187.
4. 1 Corinthians 7:5
5. Wuest, Kenneth S. (1961). 'The Epistles: 1 Corinthians'. *The New Testament: An Expanded Translation*. Grand Rapids, Michigan: Wm. B. Eerdmans Publishing Company. p.393.
6. Matthew 6:16–18
7. Mark 5:34
8. Matthew 8:5–13
9. Matthew 15:21–28
10. Galatians 3:12
11. Romans 4:14
12. Galatians 5:6, KJV
13. 2 Corinthians 8:9
14. Exodus 12:13
15. John 1:29
16. Romans 8:32

Chapter 22
Good Things Happen

1. Acts 4:33
2. John 8:11
3. Ephesians 3:18–19
4. Ephesians 3:20
5. Genesis 22:2
6. Genesis 22:12
7. Matthew 11:28
8. Matthew 3:17
9. John 17:23
10. Matthew 4:3
11. Matthew 4:4
12. NT:4487, Thayer's Greek Lexicon, Electronic Database. Copyright (c) 2000 by Biblesoft
13. John 11:1–44
14. OT:1540, Biblesoft's New Exhaustive Strong's Numbers and Concordance with Expanded Greek-Hebrew Dictionary. Copyright (c) 1994, Biblesoft and International Bible Translators, Inc.
15. Colossians 2:15
16. OT:1732, The Online Bible Thayer's Greek Lexicon and Brown Driver & Briggs Hebrew Lexicon. Copyright (c)1993, Woodside Bible Fellowship, Ontario, Canada. Licensed from the Institute for Creation Research.

Salvation Prayer

If you would like to receive all that Jesus has done for you and make Him your Lord and Savior, please pray this prayer:

Lord Jesus, thank You for loving me and dying for me on the cross. Your precious blood washes me clean of every sin. You are my Lord and my Savior, now and forever. I believe that You rose from the dead and that You are alive today. Because of Your finished work, I am now a beloved child of God and heaven is my home. Thank You for giving me eternal life, and filling my heart with Your peace and joy. Amen.

We Would Like To Hear From You

If you have prayed the salvation prayer, or if you have a testimony to share after reading this book, please send us an email at info@josephprinceonline.com

About Joseph Prince Ministries, Inc.

For more information on how you can partner and support this ministry, do visit our website at **www.josephprince.org** where you can also subscribe to our free online devotional. Be part of the Gospel Revolution that is liberating God's precious people to reign in life through the abundance of grace and the gift of righteousness.

Additional copies of this book available at
www.harrisonhouse.com.

Destined to Reign Devotional

Daily Reflections for Effortless Success, Wholeness and Victorious Living

In this fast-paced world where many things scream for our attention, Jesus tells us that only one thing is needful- sitting at His feet and allowing Him to minister to us through His Word. Destined to Reign Devotional helps you do just that, with daily devotionals that will establish you firmly in the grace of God and new covenant truths. Come to know the tender heart of the Father toward you as well as the perfection of Jesus' finished work. Each devotional inspires faith while dealing with practical issues such as wisdom, healing, provision and protection.

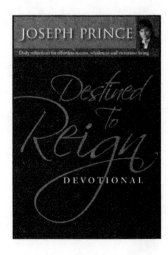

Destined to Reign Devotional
978-157794-943-5

Available in stores everywhere or from
www.harrisonhouse.com

Fast. Easy. Convenient.

For the latest Harrison House product information
and author news, look no further than your com-
puter. All the details on our powerful, life-changing
products are just a click away. New releases, E-mail
subscriptions, Podcasts, testimonies, monthly spe-
cials—find it all in one place. Visit
harrisonhouse.com today!

harrisonhouse

The Harrison House Vision

Proclaiming the truth and the power

Of the Gospel of Jesus Christ

With excellence;

Challenging Christians to

Live victoriously,

Grow spiritually,

Know God intimately.